GOLD experience
2ND EDITION

Student's Book

B2+ Pre-Advanced

CONTENTS

Unit	Reading	Grammar	Vocabulary
1 Passions page 7	**topic:** passions **skill:** identifying attitude **task:** multiple choice	present tenses and time expressions (p10) phrasal verbs (p13)	achievements (p11) idioms (p11) adverb collocations (p14)
2 Perceptions page 21	**topic:** language and thought **skill:** recognising opinion **task:** cross-text multiple matching	cleft sentences for emphasis (p24) relative clauses (p27)	the senses (p25) adjective + noun collocations (p25) noun suffixes (p28)
3 Influence page 35	**topic:** teen stereotypes **skill:** understanding cohesion **task:** gapped text	the passive (p38) reporting verbs and the passive (p41)	the media (p39) collocations (p39) words with similar meanings (p42)
4 Going places page 49	**topic:** online travel photos **skill:** recognising points of view **task:** multiple matching	participle clauses (p52) prepositions with *-ed* forms (p55)	tourism (p53) verb + noun collocations (p53) prefixes (p56)
5 Citizenship page 63	**topic:** reviews of a self-help book **skills:** locating opinions on the same topic in a text; recognising points of view **task:** cross-text multiple matching	modal verbs in the past (p66) emphasising comparatives and superlatives (p69)	working with phrases (p67) dependent prepositions (p70)

Listening	Use of English	Speaking	Writing	Switch on
topic: adversity in sports **skill:** understanding context **task:** multiple choice: short texts	key word transformation (p13) multiple-choice cloze (p14)	**topic:** friends and shared interests **skill:** using appropriate tone and register **task:** introductions; social interaction	**topic:** teens and screens **skill:** developing an argument **task:** essay	**video:** drone trouble **project:** odd hobbies
topic: the smells of childhood **skill:** inferring attitude and mood **task:** multiple matching	open cloze (p27) word formation (p28)	**topic:** communication **skill:** speculating **task:** long turn	**topic:** holding a music festival **skill:** building ideas towards a conclusion **task:** report	**video:** as I see it **project:** colour idioms
topic: false beliefs **skill:** understanding idiomatic language **task:** multiple-choice: longer text	key word transformation (p41) multiple-choice cloze (p42)	**topic:** influences on children **skill:** conversational strategies **task:** collaborative task	**topic:** young people and science **skill:** organising paragraphs **task:** essay	**video:** fashion followers **project:** blogging campaign
topic: virtual reality travel **skill:** listening for clarification **task:** sentence completion	key word transformation (p55) word formation (p56)	**topic:** journeys to school **skills:** putting forward a clear argument; using formal English **task:** discussion	**topic:** dream study trip **skill:** adding ideas **task:** formal letter	**video:** alone at sea **project:** young adventurers
topic: good and bad gifts **skill:** listening for ideas expressed in different ways **task:** multiple matching	key word transformation (p69) multiple-choice cloze (p70)	**topic:** community work **skill:** using a variety of phrases **task:** long turn	**topic:** family and friends **skill:** writing effective introductions and conclusions **task:** essay	**video:** sweet treats **project:** animal communities

CONTENTS

Unit	Reading	Grammar	Vocabulary
6 Urban tales page 77	**topic:** modern ruins **skill:** understanding connected ideas **task:** gapped text	past and present narrative tenses (p80) phrasal verbs (p83)	describing city life (p81) compound words (p81) adjective suffixes (p84)
7 Mind and body page 91	**topic:** a girl's view on tidiness **skill:** understanding writer purpose **task:** multiple choice	subject-verb agreement (p94) quantifiers (p97)	health and diet (p95) phrasal verbs of food and drink (p95) similar words (p98)
8 Entertain me page 105	**topic:** storytelling in games **skill:** dealing with unknown vocabulary **task:** multiple matching	the future (p108) conditional sentences (p111)	entertainment (p109) prepositional phrases (p109) negative prefixes (p112)
9 It's a wild world page 119	**topic:** why humans are interested in wild animals **skill:** understanding inferred meaning **task:** cross-text multiple matching	verb + *-ing* form or infinitive (p122) reported speech (p125)	compound nouns on the environment (p123) adjective + noun collocations (p126)
10 Speak to me page 133	**topic:** communicating in different cultures **task:** multiple matching		

Grammar file	page 142	**Activity file**	page 171
Extend vocabulary	page 160	**Speaking tasks**	page 176
Exam file	page 162	**Audioscripts**	page 178

Listening	Use of English	Speaking	Writing	Switch on
topic: street fashion **skill:** understanding agreement and disagreement **task:** multiple choice: longer text	open cloze (p83) word formation (p84)	**topic:** important features of a city **skill:** coming to a conclusion in a minute **task:** collaborative task and discussion	**topic:** a film with an important location **skill:** using higher level vocabulary **task:** review	**video:** Banksy's school visit **project:** art planning
topic: becoming more competitive **skill:** predicting words you might hear **task:** sentence completion	open cloze (p97) multiple-choice cloze (p98)	**topic:** exercise and relaxation **skill:** linking ideas **task:** long turn	**topic:** changes to a canteen **skill:** expressing ideas in a neutral way **task:** proposal	**video:** Pepper the robot **project:** robot analysis
topic: attracting attention **skill:** following an argument **task:** multiple choice: short texts	key word transformations (p111) word formation (p112)	**topic:** a world without music **skill:** talking about potential consequences **task:** collaborative task and discussion	**topic:** documentaries for teens **skill:** paraphrasing and cohesion **task:** essay	**video:** do you think it's funny? **project:** the greatest prank
topic: funny things pets do **skill:** following contrasting ideas and corrections to opinions **task:** multiple matching	key word transformation (p125) multiple-choice cloze (p126)	**topic:** working at night **skill:** using a variety of phrases **task:** long turn	**topic:** outdoor activities **skill:** effective introductions and conclusions **task:** informal email	**video:** turtle survival **project:** environmental protection
topic: attracting attention **task:** multiple choice: short extracts	multiple-choice cloze open cloze word formation key word transformation	**topic:** how we communicate **tasks:** interview; long turn; collaborative task; discussion	**topics:** work experience; a talent show; a summer festival **task:** Part 2 choices	

The only
source of
knowledge
is **experience**.
Everything else
is just information.

Albert Einstein

> "I try to do **something I love** every day."

Look at the photo and discuss the questions.
1 Do you do something you love each day? If so, what?
2 What passions did you have when you were younger?
3 Are there any disadvantages to being passionate about something?

Passions

READING
topic: passions
skill: identifying attitude
task: multiple choice

GRAMMAR
present tenses and time expressions
phrasal verbs

VOCABULARY
achievements; idioms; adverb collocations

LISTENING
topic: adversity in sports
skill: understanding context
task: multiple choice: short texts

USE OF ENGLISH
key word transformation
multiple-choice cloze

SPEAKING
topic: friends and shared interests
skill: using appropriate tone and register
task: introductions; social interaction

WRITING
topic: teens and screens
skill: developing an argument
task: essay

SWITCH ON ▶
video: drone trouble
project: odd hobbies

1 Passions

READING

Power up

1 Which three of these activities are definitely hobbies? Which three are definitely not? Work in pairs and discuss your ideas.

blogging   cooking   eating   gaming   hanging out with friends
listening to music   shopping   supporting a sports team
surfing   watching box sets

Read on

2 Read the title and introduction to the article (paragraph A). Which of the below do you expect to find in the article? Why?

- reasons why we choose a passion
- the effects of our hobbies on our brains
- how science helps us feel motivated
- ways in which our interests help us learn

3 Read the exam tip about paragraphs B and C. Answer the questions.

exam tip: multiple choice

Writers don't always express their attitudes or feelings openly but you can identify them by looking at the language they use. Ask these questions to help you:
1 Does the writer use any adjectives which express emotions (e.g. *terrible*, *incredible*, etc.)?
2 Does the writer use any comment adverbs (e.g. *luckily*, *disappointingly*, etc.)?
3 What do these adjectives/adverbs tell us about the writer's attitude? Do they express anger, pessimism, surprise, etc.?

4 e Read the article and choose the answer (A, B, C or D) which you think fits best according to the text.

1 In paragraph B, the writer suggests that the *nucleus accumbens* directly contributes to people
- A feeling emotional.
- B developing strengths.
- C overcoming difficulties.
- D attempting a range of tasks.

2 According to Dr Holmes in paragraph C, chemicals in our body stop us
- A participating in sport.
- B feeling discomfort.
- C experiencing pleasure.
- D getting injured.

3 The writer mentions Leonardo da Vinci to make the point that
- A good things come to brilliant people.
- B creative people do many activities.
- C clever people are passionate people.
- D successful people pursue their interests.

4 What does Dr Holmes suggest people do to make life positive?
- A set a goal and work towards it
- B copy other people's hobbies
- C discover what interests them
- D identify what prevents achievement

5 Evidence connecting interests and happiness has been weak in research studies because
- A too few people were asked to complete the questionnaire.
- B participants assessed their own feelings of satisfaction.
- C the questionnaires were too complicated to complete.
- D they represented people who were already motivated.

6 The author is optimistic that future research will prove a link between passions and
- A a reduction in poor health.
- B an improvement in productivity.
- C a greater desire to be successful.
- D a better performance in a variety of tasks.

5 Find words or phrases in the article that mean the following.
1 determination and energy to succeed (para A)
2 great and unusual intelligence, ability or skill (para D)
3 find by searching for a long time (para E)
4 full of enthusiasm (para G)

Sum up

6 Work in pairs and discuss the questions.
1 According to the article, what benefits can people gain from having a passion? Do you agree?
2 How would you describe the writer's overall attitude towards having a passion? Why?

Speak up

7 Work in groups and discuss the questions.
1 How do your hobbies make you feel? Why?
2 Do you think your hobbies help you to achieve more in other areas? Why/Why not?
3 If you could only follow one passion in your life, what would it be?

'Happy is the man who can make a living by his hobby.'   (George Bernard Shaw)

The science of having PASSION

A We all know someone who has a passion in life – something they seem to live and breathe every day. Having a passion like this can give a person energy and drive, but why is this? What is the science behind people's passions, and how can having a passion benefit us in our daily lives?

B Doing something we are passionate about has a surprising effect both on our brains and our body chemistry. The nucleus accumbens, an area of the brain which plays a central role in the human body's reward system, lights up and then releases feel-good hormones into the bloodstream when we do something we love. This, in turn, gives us drive; it helps us to push through when things get hard because we're so committed to the activity. It helps us to get extraordinary things done.

C One such astonishing thing is the ability to cope with physical problems that would normally prevent us from carrying on. According to clinical psychologist Dr David Holmes, passion, and the chemical response of our bodies when we feel it, can help us deal with enormous pain. This is undoubtedly the reason why, every now and then, sportspeople finish a match on top of the world only to later discover they've actually broken a bone halfway through. It's only when their chemical responses to the joy of playing disappears that they realise what's happened.

D One man who recognised the importance of passion was Leonardo da Vinci. Renowned for his many achievements, he wrote 500 years ago that: 'It had long since come to my attention that people of accomplishment rarely sat back and let things happen to them. They went out and "happened to things".' Da Vinci 'happened' to plenty of things. He painted the *Mona Lisa*; in his journals were the ideas for inventions such as steam cannons and even helicopters. He was an anatomist, a sculptor and a musician. Although we think of someone like da Vinci as being driven by a force of genius, what he said was that truly successful and ambitious people like him make it their life's work to follow their passions.

E According to Dr Holmes, we should all be attempting to make our passions an important part of our lives. He adds: 'Passion is what can make a good day really great. To be happy, we need plenty of those.' But it isn't always easy. Passion is incredibly personal. You have to do something that has meaning to you as an individual – you can't get it from following someone else's passions or dreams, or by merely going through the motions. 'For one person, that sense of satisfaction might come from completing a marathon; for another, it could be finally tracking down a first-edition book they have spent years searching for.'

F In recent years, researchers have been trying to prove whether a passion can lead to greater happiness but they have so far been unable to do so. This is down to the fact that participants in studies are usually asked to self-report their own emotions in questionnaires. Such self-assessment is a cheap and simple way to collect data, especially if you want to get information from a very large number of people. However, it relies on participants being honest, as well as interpreting levels of happiness and passion in the same way. So, although we might feel that having things we enjoy is beneficial, unfortunately, science hasn't confirmed this yet.

> **Passion is what can make a good day really great.**

G However, scientific techniques are improving as we speak, so hopefully one day researchers will be able to show that our passions affect not just our happiness but also our ability to do well in all aspects of our lives. We will hopefully discover that our passions allow us to feel more energised and able to cope with the stresses of everyday life. We may find out that our passions help us to cope with activities we typically don't enjoy, allowing us to achieve more in a wider range of areas. Wouldn't it be great if we could prove that spending your weekends on the football pitch could actually improve your maths grades? In the meantime, we'll have to make do with knowing that our passions can provide the drive we need to get up and enjoy life.

1 Passions

GRAMMAR

1 Read the grammar box. Complete it with time expressions from these sentences.

In recent years, researchers have been trying to prove whether a passion can lead to greater happiness, but they have so far been unable to do so.

Scientific techniques are improving as we speak.

Every now and then, sportspeople finish a match and discover they've broken a bone.

explore grammar → p142

present tenses and time expressions

Learning which time expressions are typically used with which tenses can help you to understand and use tenses appropriately.

present simple
regularly, typically, several times a year, once in a while, from time to time, every so often, ¹..............................

present continuous
at the moment, right now, for the time being, currently, this (year), these days, ²..............................

present perfect simple/continuous
for, since, this (week), in/over the last/past (two days), all year, recently, my whole life, ³.............................. ⁴..............................

2 ▶ 🔊 1.1 Watch or listen to eight people in London talking about their interests. What is each person's hobby? What has their hobby helped them achieve?

3 ▶ 🔊 1.2 Choose the correct verb form in each sentence. Watch or listen again to check your answers.
1 As we speak, I **wear / am wearing** a scarf that I knitted myself.
2 For several years now, I'**m doing / 've been doing** pottery.
3 Since I was twelve, I'**m / 've been** doing acting.
4 I'**ve been / am being** into football for quite a long time.
5 I'**m actually / 've actually been** a cheerleading coach at the moment.
6 Over the past few years I've **put / been putting** it a bit on the back burner.
7 I've **written / been writing** my whole life so it's my main hobby.
8 Recently, I've started **doing / to do** a lot more baking.

game on

Work in groups. Complete the sentences with true information.
1 Three of us have .... over the past week.
2 Two of us .... from time to time.
3 One of us is .... these days.

Choose one of your answers to tell the class. Can your classmates guess who it's about?

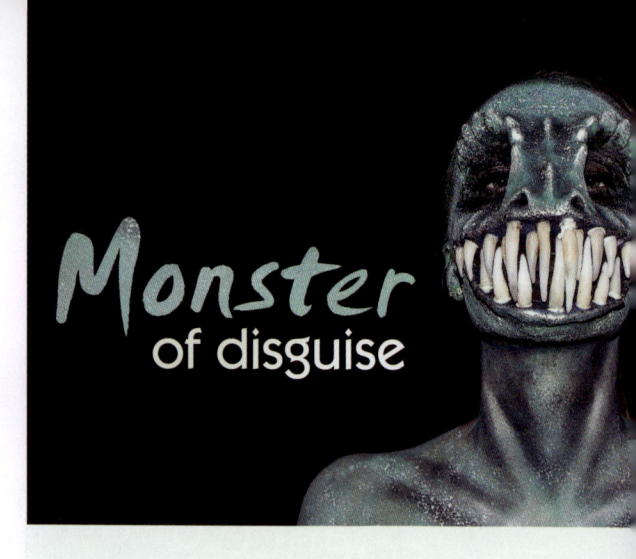

Monster of disguise

Right now, most sixteen-year-old girls ¹.............................. schoolwork, friends and going to concerts but Lara Wirth from Melbourne has quite a different hobby. Several times a week, the self-taught special effects make-up and body artist ².............................. herself into monsters, reptiles and creative characters. She ³.............................. hundreds of face and body paintings over the last two years and believes that her blue, giant-teethed 'Monster' creation is the best thing that she ⁴.............................. so far. Her designs ⁵.............................. bigger and better all year, something you can see from her Instagram page, where she regularly ⁶.............................. her creations. Lara ⁷.............................. up many fans since the Instagram homepage featured one of her photos. In fact, this year alone she ⁸.............................. an extra 50,000 followers.

Typically, Lara ⁹.............................. much of her week on her hobby but as her exams are coming up, she's got less time. So, for the time being, she ¹⁰.............................. just one design a week but hopes to pursue her passion as a career one day soon.

4 Read about Lara Wirth's interest. Complete the text with the correct present form of these verbs. Look at the time expressions to help you. More than one verb might be possible.

create   do   gain   get   juggle   make   pick   share   spend   transform

Speak up

5 Work in pairs and discuss the questions.
1 What skills has Lara learnt from working with special effects make-up?
2 What skills have you learnt from your hobby?

Teen Benjamin Kapelushnik turned his passion into profit by selling designer trainers.

VOCABULARY

achievements

1 🔊 1.3 Listen to Max and Katy presenting a podcast. What does each one argue? Who do you mostly agree with?

2 🔊 1.4 Match the first half of each sentence (1–8) with the second half (A–H). Listen and check your answers.

1 School isn't always the best thing for helping you to **accomplish**
2 You can learn more from **pursuing**
3 It's not only knowledge that helps you **flourish**;
4 Hobbies present new **challenges**
5 There are always other people to help you overcome
6 Schools can't cater for everyone's interests
7 Lots of students have to do out of school activities to **fulfil**
8 The key thing is not to let homework **occupy**

A which push us to achieve.
B or **talents**.
C your interests outside of school.
D those **setbacks**.
E all your time.
F their potential.
G your goals.
H you need skills too.

3 Match the words in bold in Ex 2 with these synonyms. Some words may match more than one synonym.

abilities   achieve   difficult tasks   following   problems   reach   succeed   take up

4 Complete the comments about the podcast with six of the words in bold in Ex 2.

Candy4 Add message | Report
I agree it's important to ¹............................ interests outside of school as we all have a different set of ²............................ , but school is important. Work hard at both and you can **have the best of both worlds**.

ZakBe Add message | Report
School has helped me to ³............................ a lot of things. I recently passed the highest violin exam **with flying colours** thanks to my music teacher there.

Bluecaramel Add message | Report
I've taught myself quite a few skills **from scratch** using online videos so that was my support. My latest ⁴............................ is to learn how to do card tricks, but that's not going to get me into college. I think school and free time pursuits **go hand in hand**.

Jonny2000 Add message | Report
School gets you **on track** in life, but exams ⁵............................ too much of our time. Focussing purely on academic stuff doesn't teach you the skills to deal with ⁶............................ later in life.

5 Work in pairs. Talk about your achievements so far. Try to use as many words from Ex 2 as you can.

idioms

6 Read the language box. Choose the correct word in the example.

> ### explore **language** ⇒ p160
>
> **idioms**
>
> An idiom is a group of words with a special meaning different to the meaning of each separate word. As an idiom is a fixed or semi-fixed expression, it's important to remember the exact words to avoid it sounding strange.
>
> Mountain biking taught me to **have / keep** my cool.

7 Work out the meaning of the idioms in bold in Ex 4. Check your ideas in a dictionary.

8 Write three questions, each one with a different idiom from Ex 4. Ask and answer your questions in pairs.

Speak up

9 Work in pairs. Whose responsibility is it to teach you life skills such as managing money, cooking or changing a tyre? One of you argue for 'school', the other argue for 'parents'.

1 Passions

LISTENING

Power up

1 Work in pairs and discuss the questions.
1. What's your biggest dream for the future?
2. What challenges might you face when trying to pursue that dream? How will you overcome them?

2 Read the news story. What do you think the words in bold mean? Check your ideas in a dictionary.

> Many ¹**gifted** sportspeople have had to overcome problems to ²**ultimately** achieve their dreams and gain ³**respect** in their field. One common ⁴**obstacle** is a lack of access to good facilities and coaching ⁵**expertise** for children. Parents sometimes ⁶**campaign** through online ⁷**petitions** or even ⁸**demonstrations**, to get the ⁹**funding** they want for their children or force the local authority to ¹⁰**compromise**.

Listen up

3 Read the exam tip. Then look at the task in Ex 5 and answer the questions in the exam tip.

> **exam tip: multiple choice: short texts**
>
> To follow a conversation, it is important to understand the relationship between the speakers and the context so that you are prepared for what they might say.
>
> Read the introductory sentence for each pair of questions and the question or stem of each one. Who are the speakers? What topic are they talking about? What do you expect them to say?

4 🔊 1.5 Listen to the three short conversations about sport. Check your ideas from Ex 3.

5 e 🔊 1.6 Listen again. Choose the answer (A, B or C) which fits best according to what you hear.

Extract 1

You hear two teammates talking about playing American football.

1. Why did the girl fight to be allowed to play football with the boys?
   A She was convinced she was stronger than some other team members.
   B She felt confident that she could contribute to the success of the team.
   C She resented the way decisions about the team were taken.
2. What is the boy's opinion about how the girl should continue her campaign?
   A It would be worth appealing to the media.
   B She ought to attempt to increase her support online.
   C Holding protests on the streets might be particularly effective.

Extract 2

You hear two friends discussing opportunities for Olympic athletes.

3. They agree that sportspeople
   A can win without access to good facilities.
   B should be praised for working hard.
   C only achieve success when they face adversity.
4. How does the woman feel about big sporting events?
   A She is annoyed by the way athletes are exploited.
   B She is concerned about how fair some events are.
   C She is annoyed by the approach of some countries.

Extract 3

You hear two friends talking about some research into sports and child development.

5. What is the woman's attitude to the research?
   A She is surprised by the overall results.
   B She is concerned about the methods used.
   C She is doubtful it will have an impact on school sports.
6. What are the man's feelings towards his own past experience at school?
   A He is annoyed at having been held back academically.
   B He is irritated at having been forced to do sports.
   C He is happy with his choices.

Speak up

6 Work in groups and discuss the questions.
1. How much do you think people are affected by their gender and background in terms of being successful?
2. What personal qualities do you think a person needs to be successful?
3. Should girls and boys be allowed to play sports together at school? Why/Why not?

When the first female entrant of the Boston Marathon was running in 1967, an official tried to stop her!

USE OF ENGLISH 1

1 Read the summary. What do the phrasal verbs in bold mean?

> Development plays a hand in a child's sporting success. A child too small to **knock** an opponent **down** in a football game won't get picked for the team and may **end up** believing they're no good and **give in**. Conversely, an early developer flourishes at first but may later fail to **live up to** expectations.

2 Read the language box. Complete it with the phrasal verbs from Ex 1. Can you think of more phrasal verbs for each category?

explore language → p142

phrasal verbs

There are four types of phrasal verb:
1. An object is not needed, e.g. ....
2. The verb and particle can be separated. An object is needed, e.g. .... Pronouns must go between the verb and particle.
3. The verb and the particle cannot be separated. An object is needed, e.g. ....
4. There are three words which cannot be separated, e.g. ....

3 Read the article. What fear did each sportsperson suffer from?

OVERCOMING FEAR on the way to SPORTS SUCCESS

To become a swimmer, Adam Peaty had to [1]............................. his biggest fear: water. He was so terrified of it that, at a young age, he refused to shower and even [2]............................. standing up in the bath rather than sitting. Despite screaming whenever he was taken for swimming lessons, he [3]............................. them .... and eventually went to the Olympic Games in Rio, where he [4]............................. winning two gold medals aged twenty-one.

Cliff diver Gary Hunt [5]............................. his fear of heights every time he competes. It's hardly surprising as he must enter the water feet first from a twenty-seven-metre high platform or risk serious injury. Despite this, he hasn't let his fear [6]............................. him .... in his career. He's managed to [7]............................. stiff competition to win several championships.

Tennis player Rafael Nadal's childhood coach knew he was afraid of storms, so he [8]............................. the idea of telling him the thunder gods would punish him if he didn't play his best. It obviously worked.

4 Complete the article in Ex 3 with the correct form of these phrasal verbs. You may need to put the particle after the object.

beat off   come up against   come up with   end up
get over   hold back   see through   take to

5 [e] Complete the second sentence so that it has a similar meaning to the first sentence using the word given. Do not change the word given. Use between three and six words.

1. Taking part in the tournaments was fun at first but soon became very stressful.
   OUT
   Taking part in the tournaments .... fun but soon became very stressful.

2. Ignoring the opportunity to enter the competition means you won't win.
   PASS
   If you .... compete, you won't win.

3. Withdrawing from the competition meant that Marnie could now relax.
   PULLED
   Because Marnie .... , she could now relax.

4. If competitors make a mistake, they will be given a second chance.
   MESS
   Competitors .... will be given a second chance.

5. There were more sponsorship opportunities for Ben once he started winning.
   OPENED
   Sponsorship opportunities .... once he started winning.

6. Lily won the tournament after surviving a challenging match.
   CAME
   Lily .... win the tournament.

Speak up

6 Work in groups and discuss the questions.

1. What fear might hold you back in future? How can you get over it?
2. If something becomes really difficult, do you see it through or give in?
3. Are you a good loser? How easily do you bounce back from defeat?

1 Passions

USE OF ENGLISH 2

1 Work in pairs. What is the typical stereotype of a gamer? Do you think these ideas are accurate or are they misconceptions?

2 🔊 1.7 Listen to four gamers. What misconception does each one talk about?

3 🔊 1.8 Read the language box. Listen again and complete each example sentence with an adverb.

explore language → p160

adverb collocations

Using adverb + adjective collocations and adverb + verb collocations will make your language sound natural.

It's [1]............ unknown.

Games are [2]............ considered to be a waste of time.

Games have [3]............ increased my intelligence.

It's a misconception that [4]............ annoys me.

4 Choose the correct adverbs to complete the collocations in the quotes. Which syllable in each collocation has the main stress?

> I think gaming is [1]**generally / newly** accepted to be a mainstream activity these days. It's [2]**highly / virtually** impossible to ignore its popularity. The fact that games appear in mainstream media [3]**clearly / fully** shows they're not just for nerds!

> I don't think games are a good way for kids to spend time. Some are so [4]**easily / well** designed they're almost too real. When games are that [5]**closely / widely** modelled on the real world, they might confuse young kids. That's why I don't think they should be [6]**immediately / readily** available.

5 Read the exam tip and the article below. How does the writer of the article answer the question in the title?

exam tip: multiple-choice cloze

Read the text quickly before you fill in the gaps. Understanding the gist will help you make better choices.

16 SEP

Are hobby stereotypes dangerous?

💬 6 COMMENTS

Stereotypes exist everywhere and pastimes are no [1]........ . If you're a surfer, people [2]........ assume the same thing – you're relaxed but lazy. They think people who like cosplay – dressing up as a fictional character – should go out and find more friends; people who go to the gym love themselves and book lovers are boring, librarian types. But are these [3]........ stereotypes just a bit of harmless fun or are they [4]........ dangerous?

One way of answering this question is to consider whether such stereotypes [5]........ influence a person's decision to be friends with us or not. The truth is that it is [6]........ unlikely as people mostly decide if they like us long before they find out what our interests are. However, our hobbies themselves may be influential. This is because our interests help to [7]........ our character, and a person's decision to be friends with us is [8]........ based on that character. So, a hobby could indirectly prevent a friendship from forming but a stereotype is unlikely to.

	A	B	C	D
1	occasion	novelty	contrast	exception
2	intentionally	automatically	reliably	impulsively
3	interpreted	perceived	understood	believed
4	potentially	likely	certainly	possibly
5	happily	negatively	considerably	closely
6	easily	fully	highly	significantly
7	impact	bend	shape	invent
8	largely	relatively	greatly	extremely

6 🇪 Read the article in Ex 5 again. Decide which answer (A, B, C or D) best fits each gap.

Speak up

7 Work in pairs and discuss the questions.
1 What misconceptions do people have about your interests?
2 Are some interests simply cooler than others? Why/Why not?

SPEAKING

Power up

1 Read the questions (1–6) and match them with the answer prompts (A–F).

1 How do you usually spend free time with your friends?
2 How important is it for you to spend time with your family?
3 Are you the kind of person who works hard to accomplish your goals?
4 What would you say is a perfect day for you?
5 If you could visit any city in the world, where would you go?
6 How good are you at doing more than one thing at the same time?

A One where I …
B We tend to …
C I'm not that great because …
D I'd probably …
E I think so because …
F It's crucial because …

2 Match these words and phrases with a possible answer to each question in Ex 1. Can you think of more words or phrases you might use to answer each question and demonstrate a high level of English?

> backpack   be on the same wavelength   chill out
> determined   hang out with   immediate family
> I'm rubbish at   not really my thing

3 Work in pairs. Take turns to ask and answer question 1 in Ex 1. Use phrases from Ex 2 to help you, and include two or three pieces of information.

4 🔊 1.9 Listen to four speakers, each answering a different question from Ex 1. Which question does each speaker answer?

5 🔊 1.10 Listen again and choose the correct words.
1 Ela sounds **interested / uninterested**.
2 Ben sounds **friendly / too formal**.
3 Rei sounds **interesting / uninteresting**.
4 Martin sounds **friendly and interested / too formal and uninterested**.

6 Read the exam tip. Complete it with adjectives from Ex 5.

> **exam tip: interview**
> When speaking to people we don't know well, like an examiner, we use a polite but ¹............ tone with a mix of neutral and less ²............ language, like phrasal verbs and idioms. We use stress and intonation to sound ³............ and engage the listener.

7 Look at the audioscript and follow these steps.
1 Expand Ela's answer by adding three more pieces of information.
2 Make Ben's tone sound friendlier and less formal. Use language from Ex 2 to help you.
3 Find the words that Rei should stress and decide where she should pause.

Speak up

8 🇪 Work in pairs. Ask and answer the questions in Ex 1. Listen to your partner's answers. Does he/she:
1 sound friendly and have an appropriate tone?
2 sound interested
3 expand answers sufficiently?

Speaking extra

9 Work with another pair. Read the opinion below. Two of you argue for this view; two of you argue against it.

> "Friends are the most positive thing in a person's life."

1 Passions

WRITING

Power up

1 Work in pairs. Read the quote and discuss the questions below.

> "Young people spend so much time looking at a screen; they're just not active anymore."

1. Do you agree or disagree with the view in the quote? Why?
2. Is it important for young people to be active? Why/Why not?
3. If yes, whose responsibility is it to ensure this? Why?

Plan on

2 Read the task. In pairs, add two more opinions related to each idea in the notes.

> In your class you have listened to a radio debate about how to encourage young people to be more active. You have made the notes below:
>
> Ideas for encouraging young people to be more active:
> - school sports
> - youth clubs
> - parental leadership
>
> Some opinions expressed in the debate:
>
> 'Only a few sports are offered at school so if teens don't like these, they're put off doing anything.'
>
> 'There just aren't enough local facilities for young people, so they end up staying at home.'
>
> 'Parents don't limit the time their children spend looking at a screen.'

Write an essay for your teacher discussing **two** of the ideas in your notes. You should **explain which idea for encouraging young people to be more active is more effective, giving reasons** in support of your answer.
You may, if you wish, make use of the opinions expressed in the debate, but you should use your own words as far as possible. Write your essay in **220–260** words.

3 Read the essay. Which two ideas from the notes has the writer used? Does she include the opinions from the notes or her own ideas? Do you agree with what she says? Why/Why not?

> Many young people do regular activities that keep them fit, but with the growing popularity of online activities, some teenagers are becoming less active. Two potential ways of addressing this issue are to increase the variety of sports offered at school and to fund more youth clubs.
>
> Offering a wider variety of sports at school is likely to be the best method of encouraging young people to be more active. This is because currently, there are just a small number of sports offered, which do not engage everyone. The majority of the sports are team sports such as hockey. However, not everyone enjoys these so they stop playing. Offering activities such as yoga or T'ai Chi may tempt more people to do sport.
>
> A second option is to provide more youth facilities locally. As young people often stay home, the purpose is to allow more opportunities for young people to leave home and participate in arts and crafts and drama, as well as the kinds of sports mentioned above. These youth clubs encourage young people to be active while pursuing their interests and socialising with others. However, funding is required by local government to facilitate these ideas.
>
> In conclusion, both schools and local government can encourage young people to be more active through more sports being offered at school and more youth club activities. The former will probably have greater success as all school students are required to do school sports, whereas youth clubs often attract younger teens. Older teens tend to feel they are uncool and stop attending.

4 Decide if each statement about the essay in Ex 3 is true or false. Give reasons or examples.

1 The content of the essay is appropriate.
2 Each paragraph has a clear purpose.
3 The writer gives reasons for her opinions.
4 The writer has used simple grammar and vocabulary.
5 The writer has used contractions and abbreviations.
6 The writer connects ideas with linkers and other phrases.

5 Answer the questions.

1 What phrases are used in paragraphs 2 and 3 to introduce reasons?
2 Which of these phrases could be used to do the same thing?

> A second option is to   One reason for this is that
> This is due to   Two potential methods are

6 Look at the highlighted words and phrases in the essay. What is their purpose? What kind of words/phrases are they?

7 Complete the examples in the language box with the highlighted words and phrases in the essay.

explore language

Academic writers often don't want to sound too sure of their opinions, so they use adverbs of frequency (e.g.¹ ....), adverbs of certainty (e.g.² ....), modal verbs (e.g.³ ....) and phrases like 'be likely to' or ⁴ .... to make them sound less definite.

8 Look at the task in Ex 2 again. Make the three opinions in the quotes sound less definite.

Write on

9 Work in pairs. Read the task on page 171 and brainstorm as many additional opinions for each idea as possible. Make notes.

10 Work with another two pairs. Each pair should argue for one different idea in the notes. Debate your opinions and reasons. Which pair presents the best arguments?

> The best idea is … for the reason that …

11 Prepare to write your essay.

1 Use your notes from Ex 9 and choose the best two ideas to write about.
2 Select the best one or two opinions and reasons for each idea to explain in more detail.
3 Outline what information will go in each paragraph in the plan below. Write key words/phrases.

Paragraph 1: introduction	
Paragraph 2: first idea and reasons	
Paragraph 3: second idea and reasons	
Conclusion: which idea is best and why	

12 e Write your essay in 220–260 words.

Improve it

13 It's a good idea to read your essay twice, once for content and again for accuracy. Read your essay. Have you:

- answered the question effectively?
- organised your ideas clearly into paragraphs?
- given reasons for your opinions using appropriate phrases?
- used language to make opinions sound less definite?
- used formal language (e.g. no contractions)?

14 Use your answers to Ex 13 to improve your essay. Make changes where appropriate.

15 Read your essay again and correct any grammar or vocabulary errors.

What do you get when you cross a computer and a life guard?   → p172

SWITCH ON

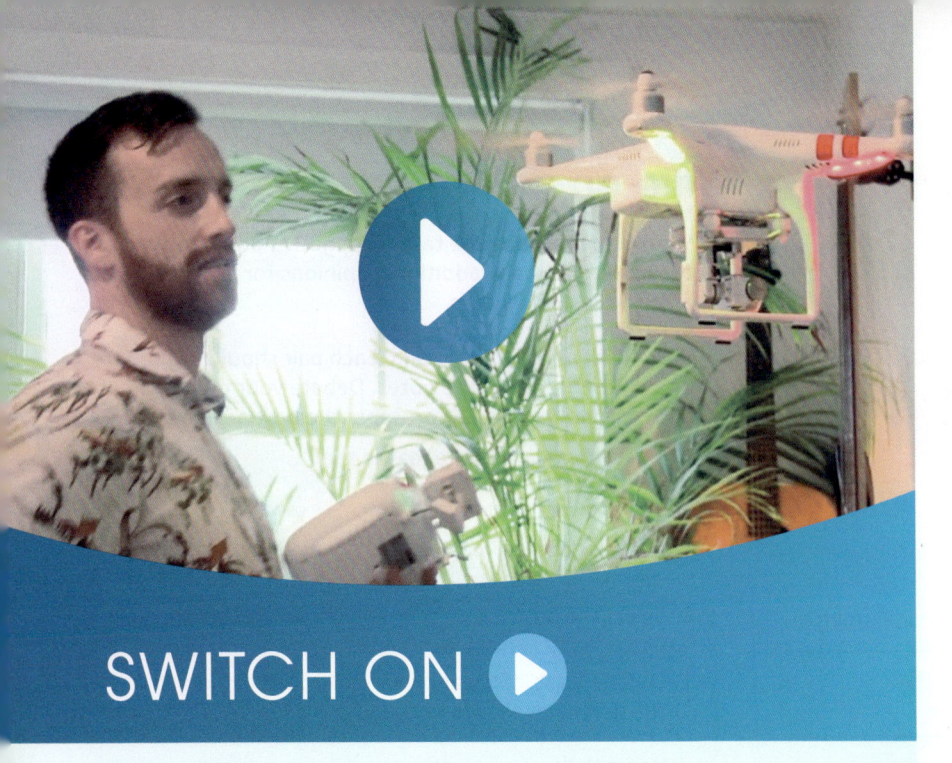

Drone trouble

1 Work in pairs.
1. Imagine that you have your own weekly vlog with a large following. Discuss the name of your channel, the theme and the content.
2. If you already have your own vlog, tell your partner all about it.

2 ▶ Watch the clip. Why does Stefan want to film the Natural History Museum with a drone?

3 ▶ Watch again. Explain why Stefan resents having to take a test in order to use his drone camera.

4 Work in pairs and discuss the questions.
1. What would you film if you had the licence to fly a drone? Why?
2. What rules do you think drone pilots should follow? Why?

5 Work in small groups and discuss. Stefan breaks the rules trying to get footage that he really wants. Would you bend the rules to achieve something you are passionate about?

Project

6 Work in pairs to write a blog.
1. Search for new hobbies that you haven't heard of before or don't know much about.
2. Choose one that intrigues both of you and learn more about it.
3. Write a blog post about the hobby. Explain:
   - what you love about it
   - when and how it is done
   - the benefits and challenges
   - who you would recommend it to.

INDEPENDENT LEARNING

Self-assessment

1 Complete the sentences about self-assessment with these words. Which do you agree with the most strongly?

improve   mistakes   plan   regularly   review

1. Self-assessment is important because it can help you .... your work.
2. It is important to .... your work to learn about what you do well and where you can do better.
3. You should look back at your work .... and check for .... that you can correct.
4. Making a .... for how you will improve your skills is very important.

2 Work in pairs and match these skills with self-assessment strategies A–F below. Some may match more than one skill. Can you think of any more ideas?

Reading   Writing   Speaking   Listening
Vocabulary   Grammar

A Compare pieces of work you have done and pick out good points as well as things that could be better.

B Look back at the unit goals and rate the skills with numbers 1–5 (1 = need to work on, 5 = mastered).

C Reread your work, paying attention to how accurate your use of language is.

D Go back and look at exam tips. See which ones you could use more to improve your language skills.

E Think about how easily you can give opinions or share your ideas clearly with others.

F Record yourself speaking and assess your range of language.

3 Write down ways you would find helpful to assess your own work and progress.

UNIT CHECK

Wordlist

Achievements
accomplish (your goals) (v)
flourish (v)
fulfil (your potential) (v)
occupy (your time) (v)
(overcome) a setback (n)
(present) a challenge (n)
pursue (your interest) (v)
talent (n)

Idioms
(be) a pain (phr)
(do smth) from scratch (phr)
go hand in hand (phr)
keep your cool (phr)
(be) on track (phr)
(have) the best of both worlds (phr)
(pass) with flying colours (phr)

Phrasal verbs
beat off (competitors)
come up against (a problem)
come through (a difficult time)
come up with (an idea)
end up (doing smth)
get over (a problem)
give in
hold back
knock out (an opponent)
live up to (expectations)
mess up (an exercise)
open up (opportunities)
pass up (an opportunity)
pull out (of smth)
see (smth) through
start out
take to (swimming)

Adverb collocations
automatically assume (adv + v)
clearly show (adv + v)
closely modelled (adv + v)
consistently annoy (adv + v)
generally accepted (adv + v)
generally considered (adj + adj)
greatly increase (adv + v)
highly (un)likely (adv + adj)
largely based (on) (adv + v)
negatively influence (adv + v)
potentially dangerous (adv + adj)
readily available (adv + adj)
relatively unknown (adv + adj)
virtually impossible (adv + adj)
well designed (adv + adj)

Other
campaign (v/n)
compromise (v/n)
demonstration (n)
drive (n)
energised (adj)
engage (v)
expertise (n)
funding (n)
genius (n)
gifted (adj)
obstacle (n)
petition (v/n)
related to (adj)
respect (v/n)
track down (phr v)
ultimately (adv)

Vocabulary

1 🔊 1.11 Listen to six people. What word from the *Achievements* and *Idioms* sections of the wordlist does the beep represent?

1 ....
2 ....
3 ....
4 ....
5 ....
6 ....

2 🔊 1.12 Listen and check your answers.

3 Replace the highlighted word(s) in each sentence with a verb from the *Phrasal verbs* section of the wordlist.

1 Films that people love rarely meet my expectations.
2 The tennis player defeated a tough opponent.
3 Our team had to withdraw from the competition due to illness.
4 If you think of a good plan, let me know.
5 I never decline the opportunity to meet new people.
6 It was a horrible task but we decided to continue to the end.

4 Complete each sentence with an adverb collocation or a word from the *Other* section of the wordlist.

1 You can't get your own way in life all the time. Sometimes you have to ....
2 I'd love to be an actor but it's .... to make a living from it.
3 Einstein was very clever. He was obviously a(n) ....
4 Because I'm shy, people .... I'm boring but I'm not.
5 Fast food advertisements aimed at children are .... and could harm their health.
6 It's .... that the storm will hit us tonight, according to the weather report.
7 Problems .... running include painful muscles and joints.
8 This novel is .... on the life of a real-life female adventurer from the 1950s.

UNIT CHECK

Review

1 Match the first half of each sentence (1–6) with the second half (A–F).

1 I've entered several teen dance competitions
2 She doesn't take photos every day but she does it
3 School drama competitions are increasing in number
4 We've already performed our song
5 He's been practising his piano piece
6 They've been top of the league

A all day.
B every so often.
C today.
D over the past few years.
E since 2016.
F these days.

2 🔊 1.13 Complete the sentences with these verbs in the correct form. Listen and check your answers.

| check | concentrate | create | improve |
| look | sell | take | try |

1 This year I .... to turn my hobby into a job.
2 I .... over ten new paintings in recent weeks to sell.
3 Every now and then I .... them to a market to sell them.
4 I .... around ten so far, which is positive.
5 For the time being, I .... on producing more items to sell.
6 My productivity .... over the last few weeks.
7 Several times a week, I .... how many people visit my website.
8 Three people .... at my site as we speak.

3 Complete the blog post with these phrasal verbs in the correct form and one of these objects where necessary.

come up with   end up   get through
knock out   mess up

a business idea   it   our presentation   winning

Challenges, challenges

What have you done to challenge yourself in recent years? Last year I entered a competition with some classmates where we had to ¹............... to present to some of the top business leaders in the area. The whole thing was pretty daunting but we worked hard on it. We ²............... a bit at first but managed to ³............... all the way to the end. We got ⁴............... but we didn't mind because we had some really nice feedback from the judges and it gave me lots of confidence. There were a lot of really good teams and actually, someone I know from my neighbourhood ⁵............... first prize.

So, over to you. What have you done to push yourself?

4 Complete the second sentence so that it has a similar meaning to the first sentence using the word given. Do not change the word given. Use between three and six words.

1 A seventeen-year-old cellist won BBC Young Musician of the Year after overcoming stiff competition.
   BEAT
   A seventeen-year-old cellist .... win BBC Young Musician of the Year.

2 Sheku began by competing in the strings competition before getting to the overall final.
   OUT
   Sheku .... a competitor in the strings competition before getting to the overall final.

3 A broken string didn't stop him doing well in the first round.
   HOLD
   He didn't let .... in the first round.

4 Sheku's sister got to a previous final but didn't win the competition.
   ENDED
   Sheku's sister reached the final in a previous year but .... the competition.

5 Sheku's new-found fame will no doubt create new opportunities for him.
   OPEN
   Sheku's new-found fame is likely .... new opportunities for him.

6 Despite performing brilliantly on a TV talent show in 2015, a dancing dog beat Sheku's family to the main prize.
   LOST
   Sheku's family performed brilliantly in a 2015 TV talent show .... on the main prize to a dancing dog.

5 Write a reply to the blog post in Ex 3. Use at least four different phrasal verbs from the wordlist on page 19.

> "I find it easy to **switch off**."

Look at the photo and discuss the questions.
1. Do you think that people pay enough attention to their surroundings? Why/Why not?
2. Do you think you are a perceptive person? In what situations?
3. Do you think people sometimes have feelings that can't be expressed in words? Give examples.

Perceptions

2

READING
topic: language and thought
skill: recognising opinion
task: cross-text multiple matching

GRAMMAR
cleft sentences and inversion for emphasis
relative clauses

VOCABULARY
the senses; adjective + noun collocations
noun suffixes

LISTENING
topic: the smells of childhood
skill: inferring attitude and mood
task: multiple matching

USE OF ENGLISH
open cloze
word formation

SPEAKING
topic: communication
skill: speculating
task: long turn

WRITING
topic: holding a music festival
skill: building ideas towards a conclusion
task: report

SWITCH ON ▶
video: as I see it
project: colour idioms

2 Perceptions

READING

Power up

1 Work in pairs and discuss the questions.
1 Which abilities do you think you use most each day?
2 If you had to lose one of your senses for a month, which would it be?
3 What if you lost the ability to speak? How would your life be affected?
4 The boy in the photo is 'face palming'. How would you express that in your language? Do you think there are other expressions that you can't easily translate?

Read on

2 Read the blurb from an online book store. Who wrote the book? What is its title? What is the book about? Who might want to read this book?

> Guy Deutscher is a rare talent – an academic who can write in an entertaining way. In his book *Through the Language Glass* he explains that your mother tongue really can influence the way you think and see the world.

3 Read the exam tip and the highlighted part in Section A of the article. What is the topic?
1 the effect of grammar on how people think
2 the ease or difficulty of learning a language

> **exam tip: cross-text multiple matching**
> First, identify the part of each section that talks about a topic. Then read each section carefully to identify each opinion on that topic.

4 Highlight the parts of Sections B, C and D which talk about the topic you identified in Ex 3. One section does not mention it at all.

5 Decide if each section of the article says that learning a language is easy or difficult. What words tell you this?

6 e Read the article. For questions 1–4, choose from the reviewers (A–D).
Which reviewer:
1 agrees with reviewer C about the ease of learning a second language?
2 has a different opinion to reviewer A on who would enjoy Deutscher's book?
3 expresses similar views to reviewer B on the effect of grammar on how people think?
4 has a different opinion from the others on what academics think about language and thought?

7 Look at the opinion phrases in bold in the article and match them with these functions.
1 disagreeing with an idea
2 finding an idea surprising
3 giving evidence or providing an example
4 emphasising a point
5 supporting the opinion of others

Sum up

8 What arguments does the article give to support the idea that the language you speak influences the way you think? What arguments does it give against this idea?

Speak up

9 Work in pairs and discuss the questions.
1 What's your favourite word in your language? Why? Do you think it would be easy to explain to a speaker of another language?
2 Look at three difficult words to translate from English to other languages. How would you express these ideas in your language?

> **bumf** (*n*) – boring written information that you have to read

> **serendipity** (*n*) – when interesting or valuable discoveries are made by luck

> **Wow!** (*interjection*) – used when you think something is very interesting or surprising

22   Did you know that one researcher identified over fifty words for 'rain' in English?

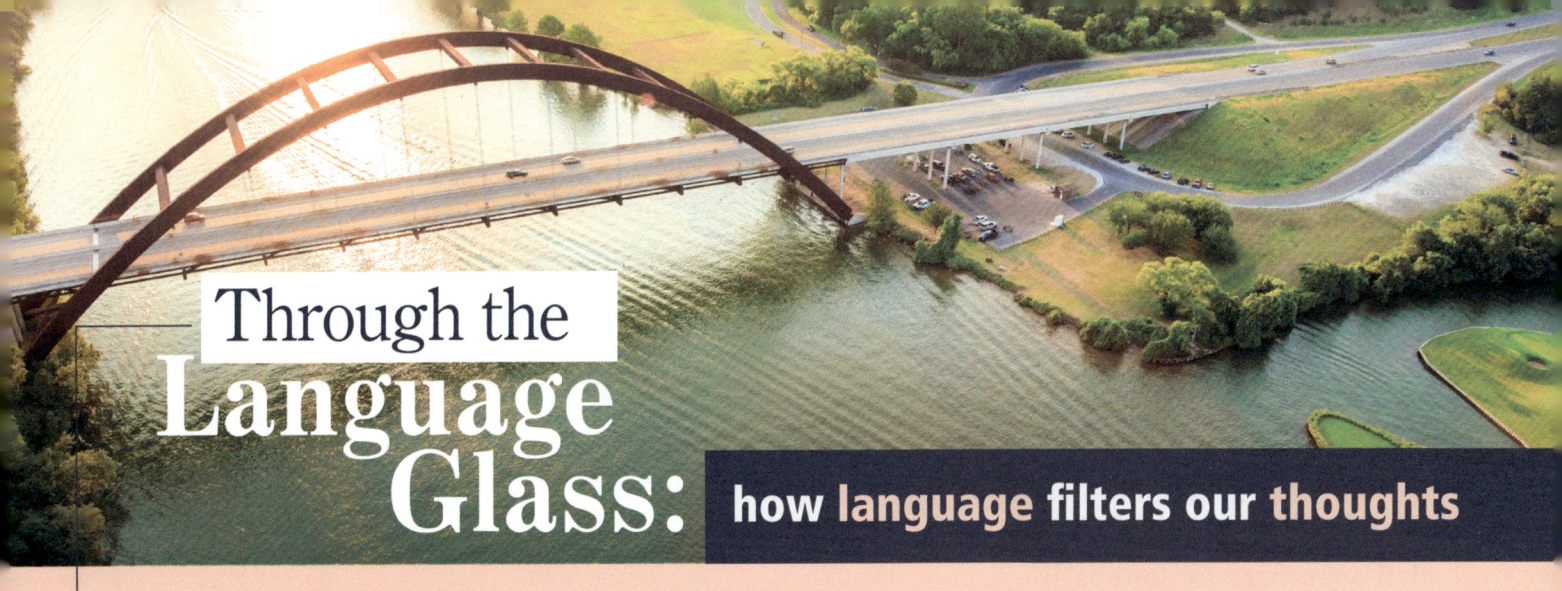

Through the Language Glass: how language filters our thoughts

Four reviewers comment on Guy Deutscher's book.

A **What Deutscher stresses** throughout his book is that little things matter and his views reflect those in a growing academic community who believe that language does impact our thoughts. Even the small differences between languages make them unique and difficult to translate. It's true that if every language were completely translatable, then picking up a new language would be more straightforward than it is. But unfortunately, all language learners end up having to battle with new concepts and new ways of looking at the world. Even simple things like grammar can change how we think about objects. For example, the word *bridge* is masculine in Spanish, and Spanish speakers tend to describe bridges as strong, long or towering. However, in German, bridges are feminine and are more likely to be described as elegant, curvy and generally more feminine. Deutscher's book is interesting to flick through, and some may find the ideas convincing. However, anyone looking for something more serious should avoid it.

B There has been a lot of debate over the years about language and thought, and Deutscher's book introduces some fascinating examples of language difference around the world. For that reason alone, it will appeal to newcomers to the topic and experts alike. However, in general, the idea that the language you speak limits the way you think has fallen out of favour in the academic community over the years, and **I would certainly challenge** Deutscher's view that language differences have a serious impact on the way we see the world. The Turkish language **is a good case in point**. You use different tenses for things you have observed yourself and things you have heard about second-hand. Deutscher argues that English and Turkish speakers are therefore thinking and seeing the world in a different way when they speak. However, it could equally be argued that the grammar is simply reflecting their choice to talk about experiences in a different way, and nowhere does he address such criticism.

C The majority of academics, myself included, now agree that the differences between languages are relatively minor, and that most ideas and concepts can be expressed in any language. However, **Deutscher puts forward a convincing case** that language has some influence on thought, and less demanding readers will find it enjoyable. Deutscher provides some interesting examples to support his point. Take grammatical gender, for example. In English there are three genders: male, female and a neutral 'it' for objects. In Australian Aboriginal, there are up to sixteen genders, which divide the world into some unlikely groups. **The one that constantly challenges our ideas** is 'women, fire and dangerous things'. These grammatical groupings bring together things that we would not necessarily associate with each other, and that can teach us to see the world in different ways. It also shows how much we can gain by investing the little amount of effort needed to learn another language.

D The connection between language and thought has been debated for decades. Language, of course, is closely related to understanding. In English, for example, you can only use the present perfect tense to talk about people who are alive. But does this small grammatical point actually mean that English speakers perceive the living and the dead differently? It's really just a matter of how we discuss events around us. Most academics now agree that human thought is shaped by a range of factors – and language is only one of those – but it can direct your attention in specific ways. For example, if you speak a language that has one form of *you* for friends and family, and another for people above your social status, you are forced to categorise every person you meet. But to say language controls how you think is going too far. If it did, studying a second language would be much harder than it really is. Deutscher's book is full of fascinating nuggets of information like these, which will appeal to the broader public, even if experts might challenge the conclusions.

2 Perceptions

GRAMMAR

1 Read the sentences. What do you notice about the verbs?

What Deutscher stresses is that little things matter. Nowhere does he address this criticism.

2 Read the grammar box and write the sentences from Ex 1 under the correct rule.

explore grammar → p144

cleft sentences for emphasis

We can start a sentence with a *what* clause to stress the information that follows.

What he doesn't appreciate **is** how hard new concepts can be.

1 ....

inversion for emphasis

We can use negative words and phrases such as *nowhere*, *at no time* or *never* followed by an inversion to stress the information that follows. The verb is always positive. This structure is formal.

At no time did he say that anything was wrong.

2 ....

3 🔊 2.1 You are going to hear the start of a talk. Look at the photo. What do you think the speaker will talk about? Listen to check your ideas.

4 🔊 2.2 Listen again and complete the sentences.

1 Never before .... such rich information available.
2 Nowhere .... illustrated than in characters from popular culture.
3 What .... that information is filtered through our senses.
4 What .... that gorillas can be hidden almost anywhere.

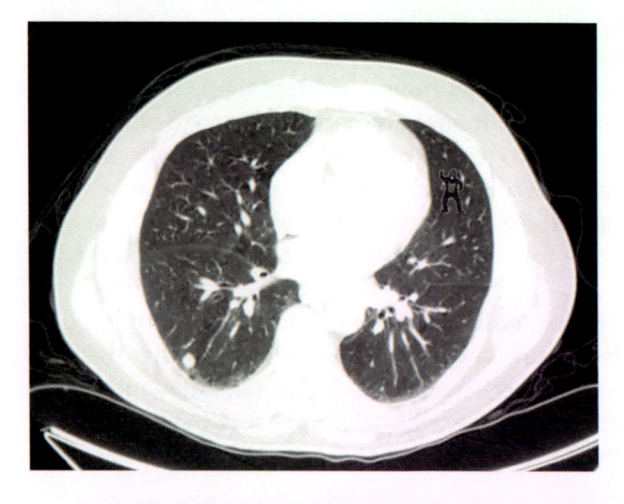

5 Read the text. Which experiment do you find the most surprising? Why?

The missing gorilla!

Experts have been studying perception for many years now, and they have found some surprising results. Check out these great research projects!

Missing gorilla

Researchers from Harvard asked a group of radiologists to examine some X-rays for signs of cancer. What [1].. (they / not mention) that they had hidden an image of a gorilla in the photo. At no time [2].. (experts / suspect) that anything was wrong. In fact, eighty-three percent failed to spot the gorilla.

Sound perception

Another group of researchers had been playing around with the idea of sound perception. They asked people to take notes on a lecture delivered by a machine. The volume was low and it was hard to hear, but by the end all of them had produced a fairly reasonable set of notes. What [3].. (participants / not realise) that the voice on the machine was, in fact, just delivering nonsense but the people made sense of it.

Challenging touch

More recently, even the sense of touch and our idea of physical objects has been challenged. Scientists have been passing some energy forms through solid objects like human bodies since the discovery of X-rays. What [4].. (shock / scientific world) what happened after physicists succeeded in shooting neutrinos through 1,000 kilometres of solid rock and mountain. At no time [5].. (they / record / such speeds) before that moment.

6 Complete the text in Ex 5 with the correct form of the words in brackets.

Speak up

7 Work in pairs. Write three sentences beginning with 'What …'. Then take turns to share your sentences with your partner and say two more things about the topic.

What surprised me most about the article was …

What starts with 'P', ends with 'E' and has more than 1,000 letters? → page 173

VOCABULARY
the senses

1 🔊 2.3 Listen to a woman talking about how different senses affect each other. Which two senses is she comparing?

2 🔊 2.4 Complete the sentences with these words. Listen again to check your answers.

concept   illustration   impression   insight   perception   sensations

1 Those .... we get from the world around us aren't always translated into neutral thoughts.
2 A very good .... of this is an experiment with cherry-flavoured drinks.
3 Testers had the .... that it was orange flavoured.
4 Our .... of food and our expectations are so strong.
5 They had no .... of what the real colour was.
6 It gives us a clear .... into how much our brain filters information.

adjective + noun collocations

3 Read the text. What is unusual about the Fat Duck Restaurant?

One of the most famous restaurants in the UK is the Fat Duck. They like to experiment with different ways of presenting food. It's evident from ¹media / newspaper coverage that the ²large / main attraction is an orange that's actually made of meat. The details of the textured skin are deceptive and help to give the ³false / dishonest impression that the fruit is real. Most guests look on in ⁴absolute / utter disbelief as they slice into it. However, far from being disgusting, the dish contains a mouthwatering meat paté inside. Dining there puts a ⁵differing / different perspective on how we experience food. Sight, smells and even sound are all part of the meal and it offers a ⁶valuable / expensive insight into how we enjoy food. Nothing is as transparent as it seems.

4 Read the language box. Write one more adjective that commonly collocates with 'impression'. Then choose the correct words in the text in Ex 3 to complete the collocations.

explore language

adjective + noun collocations

A lot of adjectives and nouns naturally collocate with each other. Unless we want to emphasise the adjective, the stress is usually on the noun.

a good/first/lasting/ .... impression

5 Would you like to eat food that looked or smelt like something else?

6 Match the definitions (1–5) with the highlighted adjectives in the text in Ex 3.
1 giving you a feeling of dislike or disapproval
2 seeming to be one thing, but actually very different
3 delicious
4 easy to see
5 clear and easy to understand

7 Complete the questions with words from Exercises 1–5.
1 What food from your country would leave a positive .... on visitors?
2 Do you think people's .... of food changes as they get older?
3 Do you think people's taste in food gives you some .... into their personality?
4 Do you think food adverts express facts accurately or can they be .... ?

8 Work in pairs and discuss the questions in Ex 7. Use at least one different word/expression from this page in each answer.

Speak up

9 Work in pairs and discuss the questions.
1 What's the most unusual thing you've ever eaten? Did you like it?
2 Do you prefer to eat familiar food or try new foods? Why?
3 Do you think that the food you ate when you were young affects your tastes now?

Whoever snuck the 's' into 'fast food' was one clever dude!

2 Perceptions

LISTENING

Power up

1 What do you think are the top four scents that smell good to almost anyone? They're all food-related. Turn to page 171 for the answer.

2 Work in pairs and discuss the questions.
  1 What do you think the objects in the photos smell like?
  2 What scents can you remember from your childhood?
  3 What one smell always takes you back to when you were younger? What does it remind you of?

Listen up

3 🔊 2.5 Listen to a woman answering question 3 in Ex 2. What smell is she talking about? What does it remind her of?

4 Read the exam tip. Then read the options below and think about these questions.
  1 How could someone say they feel safe and cared for?
  2 How might someone express being proud of doing well?

> **exam tip: multiple matching**
> The speakers don't usually use the same words in the options when they speak. Listen for synonyms and paraphrases.

  1 Does the smell remind the woman of
   A a regular welcome?
   B a memory of a place to study?
   C an exciting experience?

  2 Does that scent make the woman feel
   A better about the past?
   B safe and cared for?
   C proud of doing well?

5 🔊 2.6 Listen to the woman again and choose the correct options in Ex 4. What phrases helped you?

6 e 🔊 2.7 You are going to hear five speakers talking about the scents that remind them of childhood. Listen and complete both tasks.

7 Read these phrases from the recording and check the meaning of any words you don't understand. Which phrases in options A–H in Task 2 have a similar meaning to these phrases?
  1 comfort and security
  2 ignore the pressing matters of my life
  3 stop showing off for others or worrying about their opinion
  4 I remember just how far I've come in life
  5 helps me to feel able to deal with things

Speak up

8 Work in pairs. What are your strongest memories from childhood? Do they involve any special sounds or smells? What smells and sounds from today do you think you will remember in the future?

Task 1

For questions 1–5, choose from the list (A–H) what the scent reminds each speaker of.

A a regular welcome
B a memory of a place to study
C an exciting experience
D an unpleasant day
E an attractive sight
F a difficult job
G a special holiday
H a natural environment

Speaker 1 1 ☐
Speaker 2 2 ☐
Speaker 3 3 ☐
Speaker 4 4 ☐
Speaker 5 5 ☐

Task 2

For questions 6–10, choose from the list (A–H) how the scent makes each speaker feel now.

A better about the past
B safe and cared for
C proud of doing well
D ready to meet challenges
E less anxious about problems
F full of energy
G unsure of the future
H less concerned what people think

Speaker 1 6 ☐
Speaker 2 7 ☐
Speaker 3 8 ☐
Speaker 4 9 ☐
Speaker 5 10 ☐

USE OF ENGLISH 1

1 Complete the sentences from the listening in your own words.
1. Whenever I notice the smell of bread or baking, I …
2. Whatever you may think of the smell of …, it takes me back to …

2 Read the language box and complete the examples with words from Ex 1.

explore language → p144

relative clauses – *whatever, whenever*, etc.

We can use *whatever* to introduce a contrast.
We can use *whenever, wherever*, etc. to show emphasis.

¹……………… you may think, I really love that smell.
Even now, ²……………… I notice that scent, it smells like comfort and home.

special uses of *which* or *whom*

We can use *which* or *whom* in certain expressions to refer to a number, quantity, thing or person.

some of which
as a result of which
many of whom

3 🔊 2.8 Listen to a boy talking about an animal. What is unusual about it?

4 🔊 2.9 Choose the correct words to complete the sentences. Then listen again and check.
1. **However / Whenever / Whatever** the elephants saw someone from the Kamba tribe, they were relaxed.
2. The Massai sometimes attack elephants, **many of which / as a result of which / which results in** their relation with them has suffered.
3. The Massai and Kamba have quite distinct diets, **that / which / what** would give them a different odour.
4. **Why ever / Whatever** the reason, it is the first time that animals appear to be able to classify another species.

5 e Read the exam tip. Then read the article below and complete the gaps with one word only.

exam tip: open cloze

Read the whole sentence. Sometimes the clue is before or after the gap.

Look before and after gap 6. What is the relationship between the skill of detecting gone-off food and the act of poisoning yourself? What word would express the idea that NOT having this skill is dangerous?

Why scents from childhood are **so strong**

For some it's the smell of food being heated on a camp fire; for others it's cleaning fluids. Whatever it ¹……………… that reminds you of your childhood, nothing transports you to the past faster than a scent, and technology ²……………… just begun to put a new perspective on this. Early studies into the link between smells and memory looked at volunteers, many of ³……………… were in their eighties, and found that memories could be more rapidly recalled through smell than any other sense. Now brain scans have revealed just ⁴……………… firmly lodged in our brains some smells can become, and this is true for both good and bad smells. Scientists believe it ⁵……………… sense for us to remember bad smells because they often give an early warning sign of gone-off food, ⁶……………… which early humans might have poisoned themselves. So our brains are designed to remember smells and at ⁷……………… time does a smell have quite as much impact as in childhood. Childhood scents leave a very particular signature on the brain. ⁸……………… we subsequently come into contact with that same smell, we are instantly reminded of that early moment.

6 Complete the sentences in your own words. Then work in pairs and compare your ideas.
1. Whatever I do, I just can't …
2. Whenever I smell coffee, I …
3. I have a lot of friends outside of school, many of whom …

Speak up

7 People in some cultures believe they can smell if someone is a good person or not. Would you want this ability? Work in pairs to think of three reasons for and three reasons against.

Did you know that while you sleep, your sense of smell shuts off completely?

2 Perceptions

USE OF ENGLISH 2

1 Look at the sign. If you saw that in a café, how would you feel? Do you think you live life through your mobile phone?

2 🔊 2.10 Listen to four people talking about mobile phone use. Which speaker says:

A they prefer a combination of recording events and being present?
B they think leaving their phone at home isn't always an annoyance?
C they don't need approval from others to use their phone?
D they feel under pressure to take photos?

3 What part of speech are the highlighted words in Ex 2? What other words (verbs, adjectives, adverbs, etc.) do you know which are formed from these words?

4 Read the language box. Form nouns from these words and write them under the correct endings in the table. Can you think of any other nouns with these endings?

brilliant   declare   depart   deny   disclose
distract   dominant   refuse

explore language ⟶ p160

noun suffixes

Here are some common noun suffixes.

-al	-ance	-ure	-tion
approv**al**	annoy**ance**	press**ure**	combina**tion**
....	....	....	....
....	....	....	....

5 e Read the text. Use the word given at the end of some of the lines to form a word that fits in the gap in the same line.

I was recently at a Taylor Swift concert, when a woman pushed through to get to the front. To the ¹.................... of the people she was standing in front of, she stayed there filming the whole concert through her phone. It seemed ².................... actually going to live music!   **ANNOY**

                                                                POINT

Of course, the ³.................... to snap a photo and share it with your friends is always there, but the ⁴.................... to show off shouldn't be more important than enjoyment. Taking a video camera out at the opera would receive instant ⁵.................... from angry members of the audience, but is phone usage at a rock concert in the same category? Of course, another problem is that phones and cameras can be an ⁶.................... and so it's no surprise that these days a number of artists consider them a huge ⁷.................... and provide special locked bags for audience members to place their phones in. The lock can only be ⁸.................... when the concert comes to an end.   **TEMPT**

                                                                PRESS

                                                                APPROVE

                                                                INTRUDE

                                                                DISTRACT

                                                                FASTEN

Speak up

6 Do you think people spend too much time experiencing real-life events through the screen or their mobile? Why/Why not?

game on

Play in two teams. Look at the list of noun suffixes. Can you think of an example for each? Which team has the most words at the end?

-al   -ance/-ence   -dom   -ee   -er/-or   -hood   -ism   -ist
-ity/-ty   -ment   -ness   -ry   -ship   -sion/-tion/-xion

Did you know that the average mobile phone has eighteen times more germs than a public toilet?

SPEAKING

Power up

1 Work in pairs and discuss the questions.
1. When was the last time you went out without your mobile phone? What was it like?
2. How would putting your mobile away change the way you experience the world around you?

2 Work in pairs. Look at photo A and discuss the questions.
1. What are the people in the photo doing?
2. Who is doing something different? How?
3. What problem do you think it shows?
4. What might be the reasons for the problem? What might be the effects?

3 Work in new pairs. Take turns to answer questions 1, 3 and 4 from Ex 2 with photos B and C. What do all three photos have in common?

4 🔊 2.11 Listen to a student comparing two of the photos. Which photos did she choose? Use the audioscript to help you.

5 🔊 2.12 Listen to another student comparing two of the photos. Which photos does he talk about? What similarities and differences does he note?

6 🔊 2.13 Read the exam tip. Then listen again. How does the student speculate on what is happening? Complete the sentences.
1. I .... at a big public event, it's .... that people would want to use their phones.
2. There's an old lady in the crowd and she .... she's enjoying it because she .... to be giving it her full attention.
3. It .... that she's just from a different generation.
4. There's another young guy, and .... he's out on a date, but .... he doesn't like the girl .... he's ignoring her, ... it .... that he's not very smart.

exam tip: long turn

Avoid giving descriptions of the photos. Instead, speculate on what is happening. Try to use a range of phrases.

It could be   I guess   I suppose   They seem   It's understandable that

Speak up

7 e Work in pairs. Turn to page 176 and follow the instructions. Then swap roles. Talk about a different pair of photos.

Speaking extra

8 Work in pairs. Describe and compare your two favourite photos on your phone but don't say why you like them. Let your partner speculate on why they are important to you. Did your partner guess correctly?

2 Perceptions

WRITING

Power up

1 Work in groups and discuss the questions.
1. Imagine you are at a summer music festival. What can you hear around you? What sights and smells are around you? How does that make you feel? Use these words to help you or choose your own.

| beat (*n*) catering tent (*n*) crowd (*n*) deafening (*adj*) |
| facilities (*n*) headline act (*n*) sing along (*phr v*) |

2. Do you think it's better to see a band play live or enjoy listening to their music at home? Why?
3. Which summer festivals would you like to go to? Why?
4. What would be the benefits and problems of holding a summer festival in your hometown?

Plan on

2 Read the task. How many parts are there to the question? What are they?

> You are part of a local committee that has been asked to assess the impact of hosting a music festival in your town. You have been asked to write a report to share with the local community.
>
> Your report should include:
> - information about the practical challenges of hosting the event
> - ways of raising money to fund the event
> - suggestions about the possible social impact of the event.
>
> Write your report in **220–260** words.

3 Read the task in Ex 2 again. Answer the questions about the report.
1. Who are you? Who are you writing to?
2. Why are you writing?
3. What kind of writing (formal/informal) do you need to produce?
4. How many paragraphs do you need to write? What should be the focus of each paragraph?
5. What does the layout for a report look like?
6. What information do you think you need to include in your conclusion?

4 Read the report and answer the questions on page 31.

Proposed music festival in Hoopers Hill

The aims of this report are to give an overview of the practical considerations, suggest ways to finance the event and consider the impact this event might have on our town. As preparation for this report, I interviewed a cross-section of local residents and business owners here in Hoopers Hill.

Music festival crowds create certain practical issues. We would need to provide parking and public transport facilities, all of which will require careful planning. We would also need to consider bringing in catering companies to provide food. This is in addition to security and safety measures around the stage and audience.

To finance the event, a number of national businesses have expressed a willingness to sponsor this project. The majority of the costs could be met through ticket sales. In addition, we could charge traders to rent stalls inside the grounds of the festival.

There is no doubt that the festival will bring problems. These include but are not limited to noise around the site; litter and damage around town; disruption of transport and local services. However, there are also benefits. The event, which will bring the local community together, should also attract a large number of people from outside the town which will, in turn, bring in revenue to the local economy and make it easier to promote our town on a national and international basis.

I think it's a brilliant plan, and we should do it. If we chat to the locals, they'll be fine about it.

1. Is the content of the report relevant? Why/Why not?
2. Does the writer use a lot of the same language as the input?
3. Where in the report would you put these five subheadings?

> Financing the event   Introduction
> Possible impacts   Practical considerations
> Recommendations

4. Look at the conclusion. What do you think is wrong with it?
5. Rewrite the conclusion using these words.

> in close consultation with   local community
> not go ahead   recommend
> without whose support

5 The following paragraph needs linking to reach a logical conclusion. Put the sentences in the correct order and then think of ways to link them. What would be a good subheading for this section?

1. Young people's needs for entertainment have been neglected in the past.
2. There are few events for young people.
3. They could volunteer with the organisation if they can't afford the entry tickets.
4. The event can provide opportunities for all of them to participate.
5. There are several reasons to hold the festival here in Hoopers Hill.

6 Read the language box and add two more examples from the report in Ex 4.

explore language   ↪ p144

Build ideas so that they lead towards a suggested conclusion. Use the first sentence in each paragraph to show how your ideas develop.
the aims of this report are …
1 ....
2 ....

7 Complete the sentences with these phrases.

> broadly speaking   I would suggest   should   the majority   we would recommend

1. In conclusion, we found that .... of residents were in favour of the event.
2. ...., the concerns could be addressed with careful planning.
3. .... that the event go ahead.
4. To minimise the risk of accident, ... closing the roads around the event.
5. I believe a working group .... be set up to help ensure the event goes smoothly.

Write on

8 You are going to write a report on a food festival. Read the task and think of the headings you will need. Then make notes under those headings.

> You are part of a local committee that has been asked to evaluate the possibility of holding a food festival in your town. You have been asked to write a report for the mayor.
>
> Your report should include:
> - information about the practical challenges of hosting the event
> - ways of publicising the event
> - suggestions about the possible long-term impact of the event.
>
> Write your report in **220–260** words.

9 Work in groups of three to debate the idea. One person argues in favour of holding the food festival and the other argues against. The third person should ask questions and challenge the speakers to defend their ideas, then decide whether to hold the festival or not.

10 Plan your report. Think about:
- your audience and tone.
- the subheadings you need.
- the conclusion you are going to reach.

11 e Write your report in 220–260 words.

SWITCH ON

As I see it

1 Work in pairs. Select five objects in the room which are each mainly one colour. Follow these steps.

   1 Individually, write down the colour you see for each object.
   blue
   Add an adjective to help you describe it more clearly.
   sky blue
   Now add one more adjective.
   soft sky blue
   2 Compare what you have written with your partner.
   3 What does this tell you about how you experience what you are looking at?

2 ▶ Watch the clip. Which part of Africa is home to the Himba tribe?

3 ▶ Watch again. Work in pairs.
   1 List the four Himba colour names and what colours they include.
   2 In one sentence, summarise the test the Himba people are asked to take.

4 Write a brief summary comparing and contrasting how the Himba and Westerners perceive colour. Give an example.

5 Work as a class. Has the video changed how you think language affects understanding? If so, how?

Project

6 Work in small groups to brainstorm English colour idioms.
   1 Choose your favourite colour idiom. Research its origin, what it means and examples of how and where it features in popular culture.
   2 Present your findings to the class in whatever form you think best (e.g. slides, a class presentation, a short online presentation, a roleplay of a short scene using the idiom).

INDEPENDENT LEARNING

Feedback

1 Look at the four situations below. Which are good and bad examples of giving feedback? Why? How would you change them?

   1 Another student looks at a review you have written and says, 'I like your ideas. It would be nice to read more information because your opinions are really interesting.'
   2 You have just completed a speaking activity and your teacher says, 'I find it really hard to understand you. I'm not really sure I know what you were talking about.'
   3 You and another student are giving each other feedback on a speaking activity you have just done. You say to your partner, 'I think you don't use very long sentences. And you keep repeating the same words over and over.'
   4 Your teacher hands back an essay you have written and says, 'You have some good ideas, but you use the same grammar structures a lot. Next time, can you try to use some different structures and different ways of expressing your ideas?'

2 Read the feedback tips. Work in pairs and show each other a piece of your work. Practice giving each other feedback.

> **When giving feedback:**
> - give positive feedback first and then talk about areas where the other person could improve.
> - always try to give at least one idea for how they could make their work better.
> - always be polite. Use cautious language (e.g. *You could ...* rather than imperatives).

3 Think about the feedback you have received. Complete the sentences to make them true for you:
   1 It was helpful for me to get feedback on my work because ....
   2 I think I could improve this piece of work by ....
   3 I would find it useful to get more feedback on ....

UNIT CHECK

Wordlist

Senses
concept (*n*)
deceptive (*adj*)
disgusting (*adj*)
evident (*adj*)
illustration (*n*)
impression (*n*)
insight (*n*)
mouthwatering (*adj*)
perception (*n*)
sensation (*n*)
transparent (*adj*)

Adjective + noun collocations
different perspective
false impression
main attraction
media coverage
utter disbelief
valuable insight

Noun suffixes
annoyance
approval
brilliance
declaration
denial
departure
disclosure
distraction
intrusion
pressure
refusal
temptation

Speculating
either … or (*phr*)
I guess (*phr*)
probably (*phr*)
I suppose (*phr*)

Structuring a report
broadly speaking (*adv + v*)
finance smth (*v*)
go ahead (*phr v*)
in close consultation with (*phr*)
local community (*adj + n*)
majority (*n*)
practical consideration (*adj + n*)
possible impact (*adj + n*)
publicise an event (*v + n*)
recommendation (*n*)
without whose support (*phr*)

Other
a good case in point (*phr*)
beat (*n*)
bumf (*n*)
catering tent (*n*)
crowd (*n*)
deafening (*adj*)
facepalm (*v*)
facilities (*n*)
headline act (*n*)
serendipity (*n*)
sing along (*phr*)
Wow! (*interjection*)

Vocabulary

1 🔊 2.14 Listen to five people. What word from the *Senses* section of the wordlist does the beep represent?

1 ....
2 ....
3 ....
4 ....
5 ....

2 🔊 2.15 Listen and check your answers.

3 Complete the sentences with nouns from the *Noun suffixes* section of the list.

1 It's hard to resist the .... to eat chocolate!
2 Her .... to co-operate with the police got her into trouble.
3 The trains always pause before .... and arrival.
4 You have to get the headmaster's .... to start a new club.
5 The .... of independence in my country was signed over 100 years ago.
6 To my ...., the school canteen had run out of chicken nuggets.

4 Complete the blog with words from the *Other* section of the wordlist.

> The festival was fun. There was a huge
> [1].......................... of people there – mostly my age –
> and, of course, the [2].......................... was my favourite
> band, The Mouse Traps. I made sure I got to he
> front well in advance, before they came on, so
> I had a good view. The sound was [3]..........................
> and I could feel the [4].......................... of the music
> pounding in my chest. I loved it!
>
> Not everything at the festival was as good
> though. The toilet [5].......................... were gross and
> there were huge queues. The [6]..........................
> only sold burgers, so not much there for us
> vegetarians. Still, I could forgive this for a chance
> to [7].......................... to my favourite songs for an hour.

5 You have been asked to write a report on holding a fundraising event in your school hall during lunchtime. Write three sentences that you could include in your report. Use words from the *Structuring a report* section of the wordlist.

33

UNIT CHECK

Review

1 Rewrite the sentences emphasising the highlighted information. Use relative clauses or inversion.

1 It doesn't matter **what you do**, there will always be some local opposition.
....
....

2 The local community didn't say they were against the festival **at any time**.
....
....

3 **I don't understand** why the council want the festival to be held inside.
....
....

4 It isn't **in any way possible** to say if a decision has been reached or not.
....
....

5 We spoke to a lot of the locals **and a lot of them** said that they would come.
(clue: use 'of whom')
....
....

2 🔊 2.16 Listen and check your answers. What kind of festival were the people discussing? Do you think it should go ahead?

3 Read the article. Use the word given at the end of some of the lines to form a word that fits in the gap in the same line.

Colour-blindness

Colour-blindness affects around 4.5 percent of the population, mostly males. This figure is just an estimation though, as many sufferers go undiagnosed, and ¹.......................... the problem **DOUBT**
is bigger than many believe. Most colour-blind people experience redgreen-blindness, where there's usually an ².......................... of brown **INTRUDE**
colours in their vision. Research has offered
³.......................... insight into how colour-blindness **VALUE**
is passed on genetically, but we also need studies of the practical problems. The
⁴.......................... of colour-blind people say that **MAJOR**
their condition has caused some kind of difficulty or challenge. Most of the ⁵.......................... of **CONVENIENT**
being colour-blind are fairly minor, but in some countries you can't get a drivers' licence if you're colour-blind. Charity groups have been trying to ⁶.......................... the problems. Many **PUBLIC**
of the challenges can be overcome with better
⁷.......................... of the issues. Because it's hard to **AWARE**
imagine how other people see colours, there are many ⁸.......................... around how colour-blind **CONCEIVE**
people see the world.

4 Work in pairs and discuss the questions. Use the prompts to help you.

1 What do you dislike most about the weekends?
What I ...
2 What do you think gives a false impression of schools?
What ...
3 What one thing would you never give up for money?
At no time ...

5 Write a paragraph expressing your views from Ex 4. Swap with a partner and check your paragraphs. Did you use the target language?

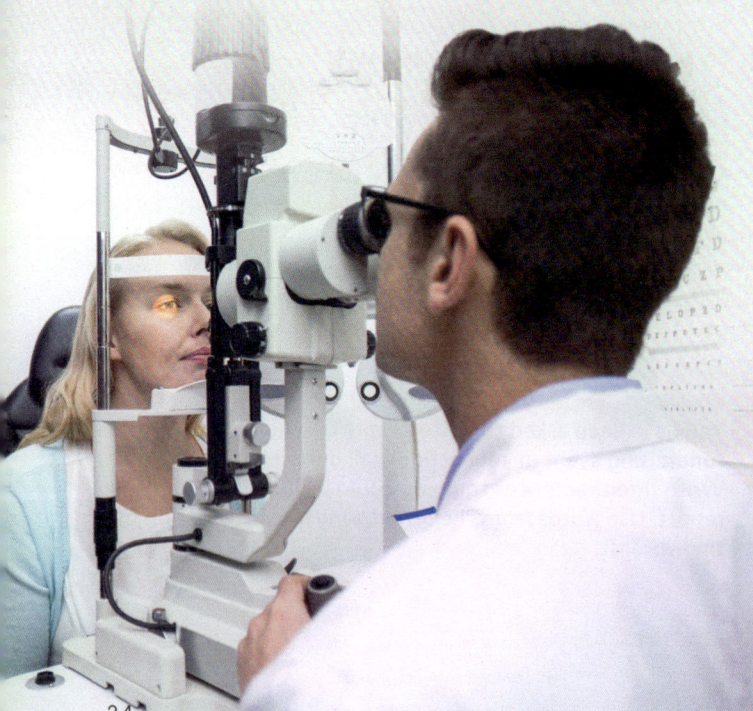

> "Everyone has **a story** to tell."

Look at the photo and discuss the questions.
1 Who has had a big influence on your life?
2 Who or what do you think generally influences people of your age? Why?
3 Who do you influence? How?

3

Influence

READING
topic: teen stereotypes
skill: understanding cohesion
task: gapped text

GRAMMAR
the passive
reporting verbs and the passive

VOCABULARY
the media; collocations
words with similar meanings

LISTENING
topic: false beliefs
skill: understanding idiomatic language
task: multiple-choice: longer text

USE OF ENGLISH
key word transformation
multiple-choice cloze

SPEAKING
topic: influences on children
skill: conversational strategies
task: collaborative task

WRITING
topic: young people and science
skill: organising paragraphs
task: essay

SWITCH ON ▶
video: fashion followers
project: blogging campaign

3 Influence

READING

Power up

1 Work in pairs and discuss the questions.
1. What is the stereotype of a typical person of your age in your culture?
2. How do the media tend to portray teenagers?
3. Do you think this is a fair portrayal? Why/Why not?

2 Read the heading and first sentence of each paragraph in the article. What is the article about?

Read on

3 Read the exam tip and complete the task.

> **exam tip: gapped text**
>
> Writers use substitution (e.g. *this, them, such, one*) and synonyms/paraphrasing to connect ideas in a text and avoid repetition. They usually refer backwards or forward to another word/phrase/idea in the text and help to create cohesion.
>
> Find two examples each of substitution and synonyms/paraphrasing in the first two paragraphs of the article.

4 Look at the words in bold in paragraphs A and D. Which might refer back to a previous paragraph? Which refer back to an idea in the same paragraph?

5 Decide which paragraph (A or D) fits gap 1. Use your answers to Ex 3 and 4 to help you.

6 **e** Read the article. Choose from the paragraphs (A–G) the one which fits each gap (1–6). There is one extra paragraph which you do not need to use.

7 Find words or phrases in the article that mean the following.
1. described or shown as (para i)
2. doing things that aren't sensible (para ii)
3. by quite a large degree (para iii)
4. not wanting to know about (para iv)
5. looking for (para v)
6. having a lot of effect (para vi – two words)
7. only interested in yourself (para A)
8. less powerful (para D)

A And **this particular stereotype** is not the only one our teens have to worry about. There's also **the one** of the lazy, crazy, wild teenager that is often seen on television. Many shows have been made that represent teens as self-centred people who care very little about the people and world around them.

B Such research suggests that teenagers are being used by producers who are simply looking for the next big thing to bring in large numbers of viewers. They appear to be more concerned with this than with showing the youth of today in a fairer and more just way.

C However, they intend to achieve such a transformation by using alternative approaches to their parents. Rather than traditional politics, today's teens see charities, social enterprises and most importantly, collaboration online as more influential these days.

D **This research** comes at a time of high unemployment for 16–24 year-olds who are not in education, employment or training (so-called NEETs). A weakened economy, a lack of skills and an increase in retirement age mean that **they** are competing for fewer jobs against older people with more skills and experience than **them**.

E So, it seems that young people today are socially active and want to make a difference to the world they live in. They care about others in their community and volunteer their time to help them. And yet none of this is featured in the media.

F The majority of teachers also ticked the same box, describing young people as 'caring' and 'enthusiastic'. It turns out that many teens volunteer in the community by helping staff at old people's homes or by organising community campaigns.

G This is because the media are only interested in stories such as these. You're unlikely to find news about young people that contain more positive words such as 'caring', 'helpful' or 'the perfect student' unless it's to describe a young person who tragically lost their life.

Sum up

8 Answer the questions.
1. What opinion is put forward in this article?
2. What evidence is provided to support this opinion? Is it persuasive?
3. What conclusion is put forward?

Speak up

9 Work in groups and discuss the questions.
1. Do you agree with the opinion put forward in the article? Why/Why not?
2. What negative stereotypes are there about teenagers in your country? Do they influence the way teenagers behave?
3. How do the media portray these other groups: old people, people from other cultures, wealthy people?

Media stereotypes are unfair, say teens

i. The media's unfair portrayal of teenagers is having a negative effect on their lives, according to research. Eighty-one percent of 14-17 year-olds who took part in a survey carried out by Demos said they believe their age group is being portrayed in a false light by the media, with many suggesting this will have an impact on them finding work in future.

1

ii. Such a situation is unlikely to be helped by the negative stereotypes that surround young people in the news. If you search for 'teenager' on current affairs websites, you'll find the majority of articles contain words such as 'violent', 'threatening' or 'irresponsible' amid those stories on the topic of crime and other illegal activities.

2

iii. The organisation Women in Journalism discovered this when they examined the language in news articles, and yet the truth is that few 14-17 year-olds get into trouble with the law. The number of offenders under eighteen has actually decreased considerably over the last decade, but still the commonly accepted negative image of young people as criminals persists.

3

iv. Despite the existence of this stereotype, it was found to be untrue by the Demos research. Adults may assume that they are uninterested in politics and other such things but in fact, eighty percent of young people answered yes to the question of whether this generation is more concerned with social issues than previous ones. This will come as no surprise to those who work with young people.

4

v. This indicates young people do support others. They also believe they have a stronger sense of personal responsibility than previous generations despite the media image of self-obsession. The Demos report findings showed that young people are keen to make a difference to society and want to create positive change in some way. Many reported actively seeking ways to do this.

5

vi. In fact, eighty-seven percent of teenagers believe that social media is an effective way to support social issues and push for change. Over a third have signed a petition online. Just under a third have used social media to raise awareness of a cause and nineteen percent have donated money online. Teachers also agreed that sharing opinions on social networks is as impactful as using more traditional platforms.

6

vii. Youth worker Rebecca Jones thinks this needs to change. She says, 'We all should take responsibility and start to share our positive experiences with the polite, friendly, helpful teens of this world. If we use social media to voice our views on the wonderful things these people can do, perhaps we can make a difference to the world and their lives.'

> ❝ 87 percent of teens believe that social media is an effective way to support social issues and push for change. ❞

3 Influence

GRAMMAR

1 Read the grammar box and look at the passive forms in the example sentences. What tense is used in each one?

explore grammar → p146

the passive

We use the passive when:

1 we don't know who did the action or it's understood who did the action and we want to focus on the action or object.

Teenagers believe their age group **is being portrayed** in a false light by the media.

2 we want to avoid taking responsibility or apportioning blame.

Many shows **have been made** that represent teens as self-obsessed.

3 we want cohesion between clauses in a text. This means starting consecutive clauses with the same subject or starting a clause with the object from the previous clause. In both cases, it forces the use of the passive form.

While this stereotype exists, it **was found** to be untrue by research.

They care about others and volunteer their time. And yet none of this **is featured** in the media.

2 Work in pairs. Is it ever OK to tell a small lie? If so, in what situations?

3 Choose the best options to complete the facts about lying. Both options are grammatically correct but one is more appropriate.

WHY AND WHEN WE LIE: ten facts

1 None of us are completely honest. On average, **we tell ten lies / ten lies are told by us** each week.

2 In one study, participants talked to a stranger for ten minutes. **Three lies caught them out / They were caught out in three lies**, despite them being convinced **they'd told the truth / the truth had been told**.

3 Lying starts at a young age. By the time a child is three, **they'll have told their first lie / their first lie will have been told**.

4 There's a myth that children cover their mouths when lying but **no one has proved it / this has never been proved**.

5 Early childhood lying is not necessarily a bad thing. **It may be linked to good social skills / Good social skills may link it** later in life.

4 Complete the rest of the facts. Put the words in brackets in the correct order and into the correct active or passive form. Do any of the facts surprise you?

6 Our ability to detect a lie is not much better than guess work, according to research. ………………………………… (it / establish) as just fifty-four percent.

7 People think that ………………………………… (give away / lies / we / our body language / with), but because we all behave differently, it's actually hard to do.

8 Of course, machines can do the work for us. ………………………………… (detect / they) our lies since the early twentieth century, but they are still not completely reliable.

9 ………………………………… (alternative methods / currently / investigate) to see if these methods can detect lies more accurately than a lie detector.

10 The perfect lie detector machine is so unlikely that even by the end of the century, ………………………………… (create / it / still / not).

game on

Complete the sentences with two truths and one lie. Your partner will ask you questions about them. Can he/she spot the lie?

1 A family nickname I've often been called is …
2 A prize I was once given is …
3 A dream I hope will have come true by the time I'm thirty is …

Speak up

5 Work in groups and discuss the questions.

1 Is it possible to tell when someone is not telling the complete truth? If yes, how? If no, why not?
2 How would the world be different if we were unable to lie?

A white lie is one that we tell because we don't want to upset someone or make them angry.

VOCABULARY
the media

1 Choose the correct words to complete the sentences in the quiz. Where is the stress in each word?

What are your **online reading habits?**

Decide if each sentence is mostly true (3 points), sometimes true (2 points) or not true (1 point).

1. My understanding of the news mostly comes from reading **viral / virus** stories online.
2. I share news stories about people in the public **ear / eye**, even if I've not read them.
3. I tend to believe the **propaganda / revelations** that the media print about celebrities.
4. **Balanced / Sensational** headlines catch my eye and I regularly click on them.
5. I'm not **objective / subjective** when I read news stories and pay attention only to certain bits.
6. I prefer to read news stories that are **biased / disclosed** to my point of view.
7. I don't usually assess the source of a news story to decide if it's **exclusive / legitimate**.
8. I never do research to see if emotional **editorial / human-interest** stories I read are true.

2 Do the quiz in Ex 1. Keep a note of your score and turn to page 171 to read the results. Then work in pairs and share your results. How accurate are they?

3 🔊 **3.1** Why do you think people believe fake news stories online? Listen to an expert discussing this. What does he say about these things?

- reading headlines
- repetition of stories
- checking sources
- confirmation bias
- related stories

collocations

4 Choose the correct words to complete the language box.

explore **language** ↪ p160

collocations

A collocation is a pair or group of words that typically go together. For example, journalists ¹**collect / gather** news, they don't ²**collect / gather** it. News can be ³**extremely / highly** happy, but not ⁴**extremely / highly** happy.

5 🔊 **3.2** Match a word on the left with a word on the right to form a collocation. Listen again and check your ideas.

contribute	critically	expose	analyse	figure	the lie	money
fall for	go	high-	profile	a trick	viral
		publicise			their website
		public			

6 Complete the sentences with collocations from Ex 5. You might need to change the form of the words.

1. I once embarrassed myself by .... and believing something that wasn't true.
2. I've .... to a good cause before.
3. When I read someone's opinion, I .... it rather than just believe it.
4. I think the media does a good job of .... that people tell.
5. I'd hate to hang out with .... people. There'd be photographers everywhere.
6. I know how to create an attractive .... and .... it.
7. The only news I read are stories that .... on social media.
8. I think it's harder for .... to maintain their privacy these days.

7 Work in pairs. Which statements in Ex 6 are true for you? Give more information.

Speak up

8 Work in pairs and discuss the questions.

1. Have you ever believed a fake story? What was it?
2. Whose responsibility is it to stop fake news spreading on social media? Why?
3. How could people learn to spot fake stories better?

3 Influence

LISTENING

Power up

1 Work in pairs. Think of something you once believed and then discovered was false. What was it? Why do you think you believed it? How did you feel when you learnt the truth?

Listen up

2 Read the exam tip and answer the question.

> **exam tip: multiple choice: longer text**
>
> Because the meaning of idiomatic language isn't always obvious from the individual words, it's important to use the context to help you understand the meaning.
>
> What is the meaning of the highlighted idiom?
>
> My parents often disagree but when it comes to me, they only ever speak with one voice.

3 3.3 Listen to five speakers using the idioms below. How else could you express the meaning of each one?

1 take something on board
2 stick in your mind
3 a hidden agenda
4 turn a blind eye to something
5 set the record straight

4 You are going to listen to two experts. They will use the idioms in Ex 3. Read the questions (but not the options) in Ex 5. What topic will the speakers talk about?

5 3.4 Listen to the podcast. For questions 1–6, choose the answer (A, B, C or D) which fits best according to what you hear.

1 Paul created his website in order to
   A learn why false beliefs persist.
   B inform a book on dishonesty.
   C collect a list of untrue ideas.
   D expose incorrect information.

2 According to Sally, all types of false beliefs or misinformation
   A are treated equally in the believer's mind.
   B should be corrected immediately.
   C are influenced by a person's fears.
   D are best analysed in a laboratory setting.

3 According to Sally, the results of a study in Australia showed that
   A false beliefs are connected to a person's principles.
   B misinformation affects a person's view of politics.
   C some types of actions affect a person's existing belief.
   D accurate information is seen as less influential than false beliefs.

4 Paul and Sally agree that correcting misinformation is best achieved through
   A quoting facts and evidence.
   B identifying a person's beliefs.
   C creating a feeling of self-assurance.
   D making people more tolerant.

5 Why does Paul quote the example of raw milk?
   A to explain a theory about staying healthy
   B to point out a possible medical problem
   C to prove a point about science
   D to justify a proposed course of action

6 What does Sally suggest can prevent the spread of false beliefs?
   A the use of online networks
   B a pact between politicians
   C a consensus among experts
   D the opinions given by celebrities

Speak up

6 Work in pairs and discuss misinformation in politics, health and business. Think about:
- who might spread misinformation in each case
- why they might spread it
- what effect the misinformation might have on people.

USE OF ENGLISH 1

1 Read the language box and complete the example sentences with the correct form of the words in brackets. Check your answers in audioscript 3.4.

explore **language** → p146

reporting verbs and the passive

We can use the passive with reporting verbs (e.g. *say, believe, think*) to report what people say, believe, think, etc. in a general way, without stating who.

To refer to the same time period, we can use:

- *it* + passive reporting verb + *that* clause
  It **1**................................. (say) that there are health benefits to drinking raw milk.
  It **2**................................. (once / falsely / claim) that Obama didn't have a US birth certificate.

- subject + passive reporting verb + (*not*) *to*-infinitive
  Once false information **3**................................. (believe / be) true, it sticks in people's minds.

To refer back to a previous time period, we can use:

- subject + passive verb + (*not*) *to have* + past participle
  Obama's mother **4**................................. (still / think) by some **5**................................. (give) birth to him outside the USA.

2 Write statements using the prompts.

Fact or fiction?

1. Mount Everest / understand / be / highest mountain in the world. But is it?
2. it / often / believe / body heat / mostly disappear / through the head. But does it?
3. Elvis Presley / understand / have / naturally black hair. But did he?
4. blood without oxygen / know / be / blue. But is it?
5. the Great Wall of China / believe / be / the only man-made object visible from space. But is it?
6. people / consider / have / more than five senses. But do they?
7. Einstein / believe / do / badly at school. But did he?
8. water / report / drain / in different directions on each side of the equator. But does it?

3 Work in teams. Decide if the statements in Ex 2 are fact or fiction. Try to get as many correct answers as possible.

4 🔊 3.5 Listen and check your answers to Ex 3.

5 e Complete the second sentence so that it has a similar meaning to the first sentence using the word given. Do not change the word given. Use between three and six words.

1. The media often wrongly say that people should drink eight glasses of water a day.
   REPORTED
   It .... by the media that people should drink eight glasses of water a day.

2. The first cola customers thought cola provided medicinal benefits.
   BELIEVED
   Cola .... medicinal benefits by its first customers.

3. People have suggested that shaving causes hair to grow back thicker.
   CLAIMED
   It .... causes it to grow back thicker.

4. Parents often tell their children that going outside with wet hair will cause a cold.
   SAID
   Wet hair .... cause a cold if children go outside with it.

5. Some people still think we use just ten percent of our brains.
   THOUGHT
   It .... we use just ten percent of our brains.

6. People used to think that if you swallowed your chewing gum, it stayed in your stomach.
   ONCE
   Chewing gum .... in your stomach if you swallowed it.

Speak up

6 Work in pairs. What other similar popular modern myths or superstitions have you heard of? What influence have they had on you, if any?

'A lie gets halfway around the world before the truth has a chance to get its pants on.' (Winston Churchill)

3 Influence

USE OF ENGLISH 2

1 Choose the correct word in each question. Why is the incorrect option wrong?

1 What **appeal / attraction** do vloggers have for young people?
2 What **consequence / influence** do they have on you or your peers?

2 Read the language box and use the information to check your answer to question 1 in Ex 1. Then use a dictionary to check your answer to question 2.

explore language

words with similar meanings

To recognise small differences in the meaning of similar words and check words they go together with, use the example sentences and collocation information in a dictionary.

appeal: The film **has great appeal** for young audiences.
attraction: Being your own boss **is** one of the **attractions of** owning your own business.

3 Work in pairs and discuss the questions in Ex 1.

4 Choose the correct words to complete the sentences. Why are the incorrect options wrong?

1 A vlog is a fairly new **aspect / form** of television.
2 A vlogger's **audience / crowd** tends to be young adults.
3 One striking **feature / element** of a successful vlog is interesting content.
4 Vlogs are **considered / regarded** as a key source of information by some.
5 Vlogs probably have less **meaning / significance** for the older generation.
6 **Clients / Consumers** are influenced by what vloggers buy and talk about.
7 The recent launch of a vlogger's book was a huge media **activity / event**.
8 Free video websites **allow / approve** ordinary people to make a name for themselves.

5 ⓔ Read the article. Decide which answer (A, B, C or D) best fits each gap.

Vloggers for hire ▶

Vloggers are rapidly replacing celebrities as the people to follow online with many of them known for their expertise in fashion, make-up, music and gaming. They have a simple ¹............ : they're fun and entertaining, and you may aspire to be like them. Because they are persuasive public ²............ , vloggers make money from advertising, often charging ³............ running into the thousands. Companies are jumping at the ⁴............ to get these next-door-neighbour-type people to tell the world about their goods but if vloggers aren't careful, the system will break down.

The best ⁵............ to discover a brand is through a real-life friend. Word of mouth is still highly ⁶............ when it comes to brand awareness. Since a vlogger is just like a friend, their recommendation can have the same effect as a face-to-face friend. The problem is that many vloggers have become popular because of their honesty and authenticity. If they start promoting ⁷............ simply because they're being paid, fans will ⁸............ this and stop watching.

1	A attraction	B appeal	C charisma	D quality
2	A movers	B figures	C profiles	D citizens
3	A rates	B costs	C scales	D degrees
4	A opening	B occasion	C access	D chance
5	A source	B way	C method	D means
6	A influential	B powered	C dominant	D worthwhile
7	A objects	B articles	C products	D pieces
8	A glimpse	B concentrate	C tell	D spot

6 Read the exam tip and check your answers to Ex 5.

exam tip: multiple-choice cloze

When you've completed the task, read through the text a final time to check that all the words you've chosen fit, both in meaning and use.

Speak up

7 Work in pairs and discuss the questions.

1 How ethical is it for vloggers to take money to promote products?
2 Who or what influences what you purchase the most?

Someone who tries hard to sell you something gives you 'the hard sell'. The opposite is 'the soft sell'.

SPEAKING

Power up

1 Look at the diagram. How could you use these words and phrases to discuss the question?

broaden their minds   have admiration for   influential   inspire   reassure
a role model

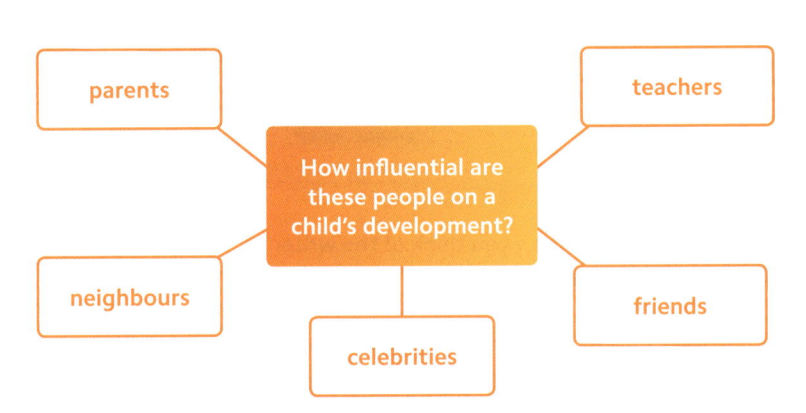

- parents
- teachers
- neighbours
- friends
- celebrities

How influential are these people on a child's development?

2 Work in pairs. Discuss the question and prompts in the diagram. Use the words in Ex 1 to help you.

3 🔊 3.6 Listen to two students discussing the question in Ex 1. Which ideas do they mention that you didn't?

4 Match the first half of each phrase (1–6) with the second half (A–F).

1	Let's start	A	on parents.
2	Would you agree	B	say something?
3	Shall we move	C	what we were saying,
4	Getting back to	D	mean exactly?
5	I know what	E	with that?
6	What do you	F	by talking about parents.
7	Sorry, can I	G	you mean but …
8	So, we've decided	H	onto the next one?

5 🔊 3.7 Listen again and check your answers to Ex 4. Which word has the main stress in each phrase?

6 Read the language box. Match the functions with the phrases in Ex 4. Can you think of any more phrases for these functions?

explore language

conversational strategies

A conversation involves each speaker taking turns to speak. Set phrases can help us to start and end a conversation and manage it in between. Learn phrases to:
- begin the discussion
- ask for agreement
- change the subject
- redirect the discussion
- disagree politely
- ask for clarification
- interrupt politely
- come to a conclusion.

Speak up

7 Work in pairs. Discuss the question and prompts in the diagram again. Follow the instructions below. Use the phrases in Ex 4 to help you manage the discussion.

Student A, you're very talkative and you try to dominate the conversation. Make sure your partner sticks to the topic.

Student B, you don't always stick to the topic and often go off track. Make sure your partner doesn't dominate the conversation.

8 e Work in new pairs. Turn to page 171 and complete the task. Use the phrases in Ex 4 to help you manage the discussion.

Speaking extra

9 Work in pairs and discuss the questions.

1 Who do you think has had the biggest influence on these things in your life? How?
   - your character
   - your hobbies
   - your taste in music
   - your taste in fashion
   - your temperament
   - your skills

2 Some people say that being an eldest child, a middle child, the youngest child or an only child can shape who you are. Do you agree?

3 What form of media has had the biggest influence on you? Why? How?

3 Influence

WRITING

Power up

1 Work in pairs and discuss the questions.

1. To what extent do the following influence the interests of boys and girls?
   - parents
   - friends
   - the media
2. Some research suggests girls have less confidence than boys, which continues into adulthood. Do you think this is true? What could be the reasons?

Plan on

2 Work in pairs. Read the task and think of one suggestion for each of the three prompts.

> In your class, you have watched a television debate about how to encourage young women to feel more confident. You have made the notes below:
>
> How can young women be helped to become more confident?
> - parental support
> - encouragement at school
> - influence of the media
>
> Some opinions expressed in the discussion:
>
> 'Parents can point out more female role models to their daughters.'
>
> 'Despite people saying girls talk all the time at school, research suggests boys do more talking in a mixed group.'
>
> 'The media continue to reinforce old-fashioned gender stereotypes.'
>
> Write an essay for your teacher discussing **two** of the ways in your notes. You should **explain which way is more effective** in encouraging young women to be more confident, **giving reasons** in support of your answer.
> Write your essay in **220–260** words.

3 Read the essay. What do you think of the writer's ideas? What is the main point of each paragraph?

Typically at school, girls are more academically successful than boys, with many going onto university and successful careers. However, despite this success, girls and women continue to suffer from lower confidence levels than boys and men. This essay suggests two possible ways to overcome this problem.

¹The first is to provide confidence-building activities for girls at school. ²This is because although more academically successful, girls are known to be quieter in class when it comes to classroom discussions. ³Girls still often resort to traditional behaviour and let the boys take control of the conversation. ⁴Confidence-building activities at a secondary school age to target girls specifically will give them confidence to speak their mind throughout their school life.

In addition to this, the media could do more to improve girls' self-assurance by spending less time focusing on their physical appearance, for instance, celebrating a singer's dress sense. This focus simply reinforces the view that girls only exist to look pretty. If more time were spent on celebrating the achievements of women in a range of fields in and out of work, girls might feel they could achieve the same and could result in more equal confidence levels among both sexes.

To sum up, both schools and the media could do more to help young women develop the confidence they need to be successful in life. From my perspective, the media has the greatest influence on how girls see themselves and I believe that if they changed their perspective on women, it would have the greatest effect on women's self-esteem.

Plan on

4 Look at paragraph 2 in the essay. Match each sentence (1–4) with its purpose (A–C). Does paragraph 3 follow a similar pattern?
- **A** give a reason or explanation
- **B** come to a conclusion
- **C** state the main idea

5 Read the language box and check your answers to Ex 4.

explore language

developing ideas in a paragraph

To present and develop your ideas in a paragraph, start by stating your main idea. Then provide reasons, explanations and examples to support this idea. End with a concluding sentence that says why the previous information is important or what the impact of a course of action will be.

6 Put the sentences in the correct order to form a paragraph. Follow the structure in the language box.
1. This gender difference may prevent girls from feeling they can relate to the role models.
2. The reason they need to do this is that male role models seem to have greater coverage by the media.
3. Parents could make a conscious effort to highlight positive female role models to their daughters.
4. So, if daughters are shown achievements made by women, they may feel they too can be successful.

7 Find a phrase in the essay which introduces:
1. an opinion.   3. an example.
2. a reason.   4. a conclusion.

8 Complete each gap with one word to create a cohesive paragraph.

Girls should be encouraged to set higher career goals than ¹................. currently do while at school. ²................. is because research suggests that when asked what their salary will be at different future ages, girls give a much lower figure than boys. It is known that equal pay in some industries still does not exist and girls may contribute to ³................. because of ⁴................. low expectations. Having the confidence to set higher goals could give ⁵................. the opportunity to change ⁶................. .

Write on

9 Read the task on page 172. Then read the exam tip. Work in groups and complete the task in the exam tip.

exam tip: essay

To help you think of solutions, first think of reasons for the problem.

What stops young people from studying sciences at university? Make a list of ideas. Then use these to think of solutions.

10 Share your best idea with the class. Which two ideas are the best overall?

11 Prepare to write your essay. Complete the paragraph plan with key words and phrases.

Paragraph 1: introduction	
Paragraph 2: first idea and reasons	
Paragraph 3: second idea and reasons	
Conclusion: which idea is best and why	

12 e Write your essay in 220–260 words. Develop your main ideas well in your paragraphs.

Improve it

13 Work in pairs. Read your partner's essay and answer the questions about content and organisation.
1. Can you identify your partner's main points easily? What are they?
2. Is each paragraph organised well so that each main point is developed clearly?
3. Are the ideas in each paragraph linked appropriately with substitution words?

14 Work in the same pairs. Share your answers to Ex 13 with your partner. Say one thing you liked about the essay and one thing that could be improved.

15 Revise your essay in light of your partner's feedback. Read it yourself and check you are happy with the content, organisation and use of language.

Punctuation matters: 'Let's eat Grandma!' 'Let's eat, Grandma!'

SWITCH ON

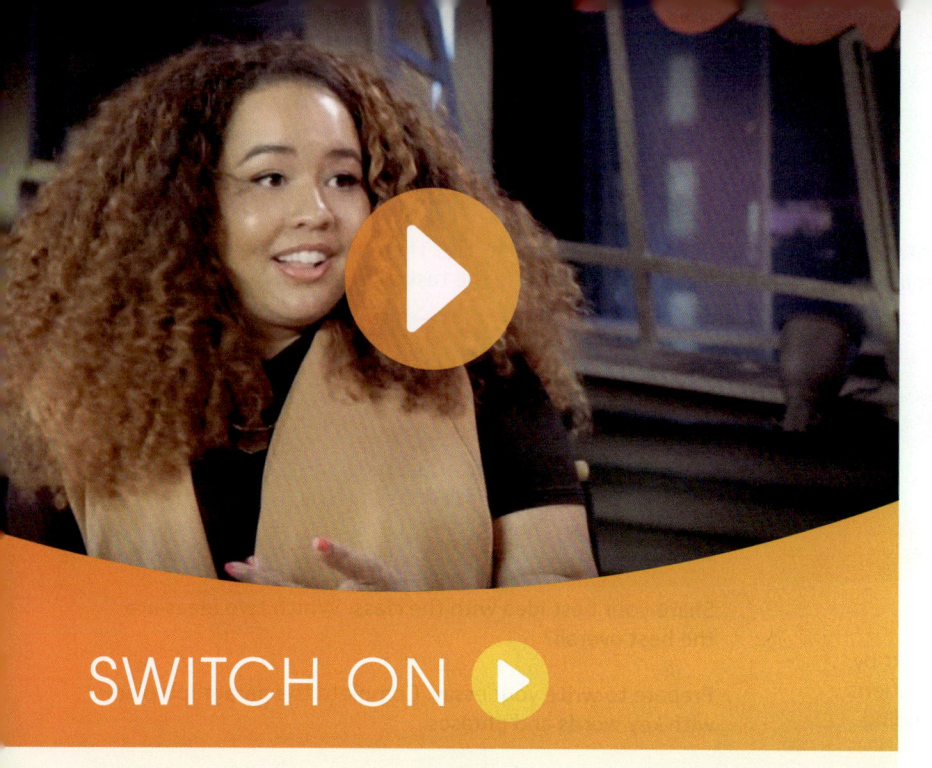

Fashion followers

1 Work in pairs and discuss the questions about bloggers and vloggers.
   1 Who are the most influential ones that you know?
   2 Who is their main audience?
   3 In what way do they influence their audience?

2 ▶ Watch the clip. What are the two things Gabi wanted to do with her blog?

3 Work in pairs. List what Gabi considers to be the advantages of being her own boss.

4 ▶ Watch again. What are Gabi's views about 'trolling' (offensive online comments)? How would you react to trolling?

5 Work in small groups. Think about a viral video that has influenced a lot of people. Write a short paragraph describing what it is and the effects of it.

Project

6 Work in pairs or groups of three. You are influential bloggers who have decided to work together to promote a product or brand.
   1 Decide on the product or brand you want to promote for a digital marketing campaign in the blogging world.
   2 Choose your areas of expertise and do some research.
   3 Plan your digital marketing campaign (e.g. *social media, hashtags, banner ads* etc.).
   4 Present your campaign to the class.
   5 Vote on the most original campaign.

INDEPENDENT LEARNING

Skill assessment

1 Look back at the work you did in Units 1–3. Write two things that you did well in each skill area.

Reading	
Writing	
Grammar	
Vocabulary	
Listening	
Speaking	

2 Think about the skills in Ex 1. Which one is your favourite? Which do you enjoy the least? Why?

3 Work in groups and discuss your least favourite skills. What makes them difficult for you? What tips can you give each other?

4 Write down the tips that you will find useful to help you improve in those skills in the future.

UNIT CHECK

Wordlist

The media
biased (adj)
disclose (v)
editorial (n)
exclusive (adj)
human interest (n)
in the public eye (phr)
legitimate (adj)
objective (adj)
propaganda (n)
revelation (n)
sensational (headline) (adj)
subjective (adj)

Collocations
contribute money (v+n)
critically analyse (adv+v)
expose a lie (v+n)

fall for a trick (phr v+n)
go viral (v+adj)
high profile (adj+n)
publicise a website (v+n)
a public figure (n)

Idioms
a hidden agenda (phr)
set the record straight (phr)
stick in your mind (phr)
take smth on board (phr)
turn a blind eye (phr)
with one voice (phr)

Words with similar meanings
activity (n)
allow (v)
appeal (v)

approve (v)
aspect (n)
attraction (n)
audience (n)
chance (n)
client (n)
consider (v)
crowd (n)
customer (n)
element (n)
event (n)
feature (n)
form (n)
meaning (n)
method (n)
rate (n)
regard (v)

significance (n)
way (n)

Other
aspiration (n)
broaden your mind (phr)
dig (v)
have admiration for (phr)
influential (adj)
inspire (v)
ironic (adj)
outweigh (v)
reassure (v)
regard (for) (n)
role model (n)
self-centred (adj)
show in a better light (phr)
transformation (n)

Vocabulary

1 Complete the sentences with words or phrases from the *The media* and *Collocations* sections of the wordlist. Change the form of the word where necessary.

1 The recent .... about my favourite actor have really shocked me.
2 I love my English teacher but then I'm .... because she's also my aunt!
3 I'd hate to be in the .... People stare at you when you go out.
4 If you want to know if this news story is ...., go to a reliable news site.
5 I know you're only joking. I won't .... for that trick again!
6 The president has given an .... interview with one of the daily papers.
7 A video of my sister snoring has gone .... It's all over the internet.
8 You'll only get people looking at your website if you .... it.

2 🔊 3.8 Listen to eight people. What word from the *Idioms* and *Words with similar meanings* sections of the wordlist does the beep represent?

1 ....   5 ....
2 ....   6 ....
3 ....   7 ....
4 ....   8 ....

3 🔊 3.9 Listen and check your answers to Ex 2.

4 Replace the highlighted words in each sentence with a word or phrase from the *Other* section of the wordlist.

1 It's important to learn about different cultures to expand your understanding of the world.
2 My uncle's overcome a lot of problems in his life. I have a lot of respect for him.
3 To succeed in life, it's good to have someone to look up to and copy.
4 He's much better behaved these days. In fact, the change is incredible.
5 I need to do research to find more information for my essay.
6 The positives are greater than the negatives.

47

UNIT CHECK

Review

1 Complete the news stories with the correct passive form of the verbs in brackets. Use the time expressions to help you choose the correct tense.

1 Huge footprints .... (recently / spot) in the Himalayas.
2 A strange animal .... (see) in a lake in Scotland yesterday.
3 Amazing drawings .... (just / find) by a scholar flying over Peru.
4 Two girls .... (recently / photograph) with fairies.
5 Planes .... (regularly / lose) over the North Atlantic Ocean.
6 Strange buzzing noises .... (currently / investigate) in New Mexico.
7 Sightings of a large cat in the outback .... (report) to police yesterday.
8 Sailors were surprised yesterday when they found a British ship in the Atlantic Ocean which .... (completely / abandon).

2 Do you recognise any of the stories in Ex 1? Do you know anything more about them?

3 Read the article and complete the gaps with one word only.

The Beale Papers

Even when a mystery is exposed ¹................ a lie, we want to believe it. The Beale Papers is ²................ of these mysteries. Supposedly, in the 1820s, $43m worth of treasure ³................ buried in Virginia by Thomas Beale, who left three coded messages with a friend before disappearing. At no time after that ⁴................ he get in touch, so after twenty-three years, the friend passed the messages to another friend. In twenty years, that man solved just one of the codes. It listed the treasure, much of ⁵................ was gold and silver. The others were said ⁶................ list the location and owners.

Eventually, the friend published a leaflet detailing the story and including the codes. So ⁷................ thousands of attempts to break the other two codes have failed. This may be because it's a hoax. According to experts, several words used in the broken coded message were not in existence at the supposed time of writing. Plus, the codes and leaflet are believed to have ⁸................ written by the same person.

4 Complete the second sentence so that it has a similar meaning to the first sentence using the word given. Do not change the word given. Use between three and six words.

1 Some people believe that a monster lives in Loch Ness.
   THOUGHT
   A monster .... in Loch Ness.

2 The photographer who took the most famous Loch Ness monster photo wanted to be anonymous.
   BY
   The most famous photo of the Loch Ness monster .... wanted to remain anonymous.

3 On hearing the name Loch Ness, people immediately imagine the monster.
   WHENEVER
   People immediately think .... the name Loch Ness.

4 We now know that the famous Loch Ness monster photo is a fake.
   UNDERSTOOD
   The famous Loch Ness monster photo .... a fake.

5 Most of the one million visitors to Loch Ness each year come to see the monster.
   OF
   Loch Ness attracts a million visitors each year, ... order to see the monster.

6 The Loch Ness monster turned Loch Ness into a tourist attraction.
   MAKE
   What the Loch Ness monster .... Loch Ness into a tourist attraction.

5 Write a short paragraph on a strange mystery you are familiar with or research one and share it with the class. Include at least one passive form, one reporting verb with the passive and an example of substitution. Say:
- what it is
- why it's a mystery
- how this mystery has affected people.

"I'm not into stuffy hotels."

Look at the photo and discuss the questions.
1 What kinds of travel or holiday experiences do you enjoy most?
2 What makes a good travel companion?
3 What do you take photos of when you travel?

4 Going places

READING
topic: online travel photos
skill: recognising points of view
task: multiple matching

GRAMMAR
participle clauses
prepositions with -ed forms

VOCABULARY
tourism; verb + noun collocations
prefixes (*dis-, mis-, pre-, re-, over-, under-*)

LISTENING
topic: virtual reality travel
skill: listening for clarification
task: sentence completion

USE OF ENGLISH
open cloze
word formation

SPEAKING
topic: journeys to school
skills: putting forward a clear argument; using formal English
task: discussion

WRITING
topic: dream study trip
skill: adding ideas
task: formal letter

SWITCH ON ▶
video: alone at sea
project: young adventurers

4 Going places

READING

Power up

1. Look at the photo in the article. Where do you think it was taken?

2. Work in pairs. Turn to page 172 and look at the photos. Then discuss the questions.
   1. Have you seen photos like this online?
   2. Why do you think people take them?
   3. Have you ever altered your photos? If so, how? If not, why not?

Read on

3. Read the title of the article and the introduction. What do you think the article will be about? Read it quickly to check your ideas.

4. Match the sentences (1–4) with the topics (A–D). Highlight the synonyms or paraphrases that helped you.
   1. People know photos are edited these days and there's no real harm.
   2. A fake vacation is so much less hassle than the real deal.
   3. Who wants to waste a whole day squashed in an airline seat for hours?
   4. Faking a vacation is like watching TV – they're both just a form of escape.

   A real and fake holidays
   B falsifying images of yourself
   C fake holidays and other forms of distraction
   D typical holiday experiences

5. Match these functions with sentences 1–4 in Ex 4. Which words helped you?

   a comparison   a contrast   a criticism   a justification

6. Highlight the topic and function in these points.
   1. a difference in accounts of a holiday
   2. a comparison of how we feel about our own and other people's photos
   3. a description of how an unreal environment inspires real emotions
   4. a suggestion that using social media influences our choice of social activities
   5. a contrast between the motivations of two people
   6. a failed attempt at falsifying a holiday that captured the public imagination
   7. a justification for trying to mislead others
   8. a comment on the environmental damage of re-creating holiday experiences
   9. a positive result from another person's empathy
   10. an opinion that realistic images require knowledge of technology

7. Read the exam tip. Then look at the two highlighted sentences in the article. Which best matches point 1 in Ex 6?

> **exam tip: multiple matching**
> In this task you have to match ten points with information in a text. Sometimes you can find similar information in two different sections of the text. Read both sections and the point again carefully. Only one will exactly match the topic and function.

8. Read point 2 in Ex 6 again. Match it with information in the article using the advice below.
   1. Think of possible synonyms for key words.
   2. Scan the article for the synonyms you predicted or others.
   3. Read that section of the article carefully to see if the function also matches.

9. e Read the article again. For questions 1–10 in Ex 6, choose from the paragraphs (A–D) the one that mentions each point. The paragraphs may be chosen more than once.

10. Find words or phrases in the article that mean the following.
    1. attempts to do something (para A)
    2. realistic or believable (para B)
    3. accept that something is true (para B)
    4. became involved in something (para C)
    5. become unclear and difficult to see (para C)
    6. understanding how important or good something is (para D)

Sum up

11. What were the different reasons the people in the article used fake photographs? Which did you sympathise with the most? Why?

Speak up

12. Work in pairs and discuss the questions.
    1. What kinds of photos do you post of yourself online?
    2. Would it ever be OK to post fake photos? If so, in what circumstances?
    3. What location would you choose for a fake holiday? Why?

Did you know Reiner Riedler even managed to find a ski resort in Dubai, with real snow?

#Fakingit

We all post carefully selected photos to show us in the best light for our social media feeds. But is this honest? And where could it lead?

A A collection of badly-edited fake holiday photos on one woman's social media account were so poor they turned into a series of hilarious images that quickly became an internet hit. Sevelyn Gat had dreamt of taking a holiday in China for years. Knowing she couldn't afford the real trip, she decided to create a set of fakes. [1]She posted a photo of herself, edited to make it look as though she was on the Great Wall, with comments saying that she was thrilled to be there. Except she'd never left home! Her pretty poor efforts to deceive her friends led to a new hashtag going viral. A series of images appeared online showing exotic locations with Gat's image poorly stuck on top. It ended well for Gat, though, when her story was picked up by fellow Kenyan, Sam Gichuru, a businessman. Recognising that Gat's actions were just a result of her determination to dream big, he felt inspired to pay for a real trip to China. He also gave Gat a job interning at his business.

B Gat isn't the only one whose fake holidays have stirred interest on the internet. Dutch student Zilla van den Born took things further, faking an entire five-week holiday across Southeast Asia. Working from her flat in Amsterdam, both she and her boyfriend possessed the computer know-how necessary to create a set of very convincing photos. Gat's amateur efforts were clearly nothing compared to this set of fakes. If Gat was a dreamer, van den Born had much wider aims, hoping to demonstrate just how far we are using social media to manipulate the image of ourselves that we share with the world. Fabulous social media lifestyles have become a reality that many people aspire to. Van den Born, like almost everyone these days, is familiar with the fact that photos of models and lifestyle bloggers are carefully constructed to distort reality. However, she feels that while many happily blame models for creating unrealistic expectations with their fake photos, they fail to acknowledge that we all regularly post photos online to show ourselves in the best light.

C With fake images filling our screens, it wasn't long before the professionals got in on the act. Journalist Gideon Jacobs decided to post a series of photos showing a road trip across America that never happened. His reason for creating the fake trip was to show how disconnected people today are from real life and enjoying the moment. In the past, cameras were used to record special moments as they naturally occurred. These days, we are more likely to choose to have an experience, such as attending a party, because we feel that it will produce a positive online image. Telling our own personal story online has taken over from living it. Jacobs reused images that had already been shared by other people, and so real geographic location tags had been automatically added to the images. [2]The use of photos with location data made the vacations seem convincing, but the captions beneath told another story, making it clear that the holiday was fictional, not fact. The result of Jacobs' project is intentionally confusing. Even his own mother didn't realise he'd never left home. It illustrates his point that the line between fiction and reality has begun to blur.

D Fake holidays don't only exist online – it's also possible to have a fake holiday in the real world. Leisure companies have created amusement parks based on foreign lands, set up beaches in the middle of cities, and even brought the desert into shopping centres. Inspired by pictures of these holiday destinations, Reiner Riedler decided to photograph people enjoying these plastic paradises thousands of miles from the original sites. After talking to the subjects of his photos, Riedler soon realised that the feelings associated with these artificial locations are anything but fake. People visiting pop-up beaches in busy European capitals reported genuinely enjoying the experience. Avoiding reality, whether you're on vacation or just imagining you are, seems to lead to genuine happiness. Turning ordinary places into fictitious worlds requires a massive technological effort, though. As Riedler points out, manufacturing these illusions places a huge unnecessary burden on our limited natural resources. We should be appreciating what occurs naturally around us, not shipping other worlds in.

Whatever your views on the merits or otherwise of these fake destinations, it is clear that when it comes to social media, it is becoming increasingly difficult to believe what we see.

4 Going places

GRAMMAR

1 Read the grammar box and complete the participle clauses. Then check your answers in paragraphs A and D of the article on page 51.

explore grammar → p148

participle clauses

We can use a participle clause to join two clauses using fewer words. We form them with the present or past participle. We use the present participle if the verb is active, and the past participle if the verb is passive.

A We can shorten relative clauses.

Her pretty poor efforts to deceive her friends led to a new hashtag ~~which went~~ [1] .... viral.

She posted a photo of herself ~~which had been edited~~ [2] .... to make it look …

B We can join two clauses. Note the subject of both clauses must be the same.

~~Because he recognised that~~ [3] .... Gat's actions were just a result of her determination to dream big, he …

~~Because he was inspired~~ [4] .... by pictures of these holiday destinations, Reiner Riedler …

2 🔊 **4.1** Listen to part of a documentary on an unusual holiday destination. Answer the questions.
1 Where is Dharavi?
2 What is life like for people who live there?
3 What do tourists think of the area?

3 🔊 **4.2** Complete the participle clauses in the sentences using these verbs. Listen and check your answers.

arrive   bring in   employ   locate   pass down

1 .... in the city of Mumbai in India, it's home to almost a million people.
2 There are so many .... from poor rural areas daily.
3 It's also an economically active area, ... up to a billion US dollars a year.
4 The pottery and textile workers continue a tradition .... over more than a century.
5 Jobs have appeared in the recycling industry, ... around a quarter of a million people.

4 Read the first part of a text about slum tourism. What concerns are mentioned?

Slum tourism – for better or worse

Many people are opposed to slum tourism, [1]**questioning / questioned** the ethics of privileged people [2]**paying / paid** to witness the suffering of others. However, not everyone agrees. [3]**Pointing / Pointed** to the realities of modern global economics, many experts believe that tour companies [4]**basing / based** in slums are here to stay, and that's not necessarily a bad thing. Researchers [5]**studying / studied** slum tourism in South Africa found that slum tourism is not necessarily an exploitative money-maker [6]**imposing / imposed** by outsiders.

5 Choose the correct participles to complete the text in Ex 4.

6 Rewrite the highlighted clauses in the second part of the text using participle clauses.

On the contrary, researchers found that communities often adopted tourism themselves, [1]*because they saw it* .... as a way of taking the regeneration of their neglected neighbourhood into their own hands. Many in Rio de Janeiro's Rocinha favelas were positive about tourism, [2]*and they used words* .... like 'splendid' and 'phenomenal' to describe the influx of tourists. In central Bangkok, Thai researchers looked at government plans [3]*that threatened* .... to destroy a 100-year-old slum. They found that residents [4]*who lived there* .... were able to use tourism to their benefit, to protect their homes. [5]*When they witnessed* .... responsible slum tourism in action in this way, researchers concluded that it could bring substantial benefits to impoverished communities.

Speak up

7 Work in pairs. Do you think that tourism is a good thing for a town? Would you like to have more tourists in your neighbourhood? What are the advantages and disadvantages?

game on

Take turns to go around the class and describe an imaginary holiday. Add more information using participle clauses.

Student 1: I left home early.
Student 2: Leaving home early, I drove to the station.

If you can't remember the story, you're out of the game!

There's a street in Dharavi called Blue Dog Street. Can you guess how it got its name? → page 174

VOCABULARY

tourism

1 🔊 **4.3** Listen to a woman talking about how two friends started a slum tourism company. How did they meet?

2 🔊 **4.4** Listen again and complete the sentences with the correct words.

1. Krishna was working when some British .... came in.
2. Chris and his friends were trying to avoid the .... parts of the city.
3. Chris loved India so much he decided to .... his trip.
4. Krishna didn't think tourists coming to Dharavi could .... the culture.
5. Chris was sure people didn't just want a .... holiday.
6. Krishna was shocked as they .... around the slum.

verb + noun collocations

3 Match the first half of each sentence (1–5) with the second half (A–E).

1. Reality tours **considered the**
2. Few travellers **came into**
3. Krishna didn't think locals **posed a**
4. The kindness of locals **created an**
5. Many guests **gained**

A **contact** with extreme poverty.
B **insight** into their work ethics.
C **impression** on everyone.
D **threat** to visitors.
E **implications** of their actions.

4 Read the language box and complete the task. Then complete these sentences with nouns from the collocations in Ex 3.

1. Experts will need to examine the .... of the new proposals.
2. It is important authorities establish .... with community leaders.
3. It is unlikely they will issue a .... to remove residents by force.
4. The locals conveyed a positive .... when they spoke about the area.
5. Similar projects could provide a good .... into the lives of others.

explore language

collocations

Words that you already know may have collocations that you're not aware of. Extend your knowledge by noting collocations down when you see them or finding new ones in your dictionary.

Look up 'tour' in a dictionary. How many collocations can you find?

5 Read the text quickly. Would you enjoy this kind of holiday? Why/Why not?

DAY 3 We were outside of Mumbai, far from the crowded ¹landmarks of the ᴬbustling city, staying in a beach hut in the fishing village of Mandrem. To get to the ᴮremote village, we had to follow miles of bumpy ²backroads, but it was worth it. The ᶜunspoiled ³coastline had no hotels or restaurants, and was a temporary home to just a handful of people. Spreading out before us were five kilometres of ᴰdeserted beaches, just empty sands, a few crabs and a green frog that lived in our toilet. On our ⁴trek among the sand ⁵dunes, close to the shore, we saw a turtle nest with rope around it to keep visitors away. On the first night, we caught sight of an eagle drifting in on the wind currents from ᴱdistant lands, miles away. It was a heavenly break from the crowds.

6 Match these definitions (A–E) with the nouns (1–5) in the text.

A a long and difficult journey
B the area where the sea meets the land
C small roads that are not used very much
D small hills made of sand near the sea or in the desert
E something that is easy to recognise and helps you to know where you are

7 Match the adjectives in the text (A–E) with these phrases.

empty of people   far away   hard to get to   natural   very busy

Speak up

8 Work in pairs and discuss the questions.

1. Do you think it's better to visit the famous sights or go to deserted places on holiday? Why?
2. Would you be interested in taking a tour of a slum? Why/Why not?
3. Where do you take friends or family members when they come to visit you? Why do you go there?

4 Going places

LISTENING

Power up

1 Work in groups. Which of these places have you heard of? Have you visited any of them? Which would you like to visit in real life and which would you prefer to visit virtually? Why?

the Himalayas   the Brazilian rainforest   the Maldives
Machu Picchu   the Egyptian Pyramids
the Great Barrier Reef   the Serengeti   space

Listen up

2 4.5 Listen to Marisa talking to a group of students about her experience of a virtual reality balloon ride. What did she see? How did she feel?

3 Look at the first gap in Ex 5. What could the missing word be?

4 4.6 Read the exam tip. Then listen to the first part of Marisa's talk again and complete gap 1 in Ex 5 with a word. Why is the answer NOT 'manufacturing' or 'tourism'?

exam tip: sentence completion

To choose the correct answer and not a distractor, listen for words and phrases that express contrast (e.g. *rather than …, I was going to … but …, I expected … but …*). Remember to write the words you hear.

Read the example sentence and question. Then choose the correct words in 1–2 below.

'I thought the trip would be fun rather than disappointing.'

The man described the trip as ....

1 The distractor is: **fun / disappointing**.
2 The answer is: **fun / disappointing**.

5 4.7 Listen to the whole talk again. Complete each gap with a word or short phrase.

Taking a *virtual* balloon ride

Marisa is convinced that virtual reality will not always be linked to the ¹........................ industry.

Marisa selected her virtual reality destination using a ²........................ .

Marisa uses the word ³........................ to describe how she felt about the experience.

Marisa was surprised by how ⁴........................ the landscape was in the Serengeti.

Marisa speculated that it was the ⁵........................ season because she could see wild animals.

Marisa believed the experience to be real despite an inability to ⁶........................ .

Marisa's only criticism was that the virtual trip caused her to feel ⁷........................ .

Marissa claims that virtual reality will improve ⁸........................ for tourists.

6 Work in pairs. What do the words in bold in the description mean?

I looked at the **picturesque** view. The horizon was **sparkling** so much I actually had to **squint**. I could **make out** something below us. At first I thought it was **bushes** but then realised it was a huge **herd** of wildebeest.

Speak up

7 Work in pairs. Imagine you have taken a balloon ride over a place you know well. Describe what you saw. Use these words and the words in Ex 6 to help you.

agricultural   grass(y)   hillside   polluted   rocky   roof   sandy
scenic   valley   vegetation

USE OF ENGLISH 1

1 Work in groups. In what ways is a virtual experience (e.g. a roller coaster ride) different to a real-life experience? Think of at least four ideas, both positive and negative.

2 4.8 Listen to a podcast about virtual experiences. Work in groups and discuss the final question the presenter asks.

3 4.9 Read the language box. Then listen again and complete the examples with prepositions.

explore **language** → p160

prepositions with *-ed* forms

We use *-ed* forms in participle clauses and passive verbs, or as adjectives. They are often followed by a preposition

stunned **1**.......................... the amazing view
identified **2**.......................... a technology
thrilled **3**.......................... exciting experiences

4 Complete the statements with these words. Do you agree with the statements? Why/Why not?

adopted   armed   combined   dissatisfied   related

1. People will learn more about the world if .... with VR equipment.
2. Learning is more fun when VR is .... by schools.
3. There are a number of potential problems .... to VR.
4. VR .... with social media will change communication.
5. Some people might live solely in a virtual world if .... with the real world.

5 e Complete the second sentence so that it has a similar meaning to the first sentence using the word given. Do not change the word given. Write between three and six words.

1. Dissatisfaction caused Paul to complain about his headset.
   WITH
   Paul .... so he made a complaint.
2. The mix of virtual reality and education could be quite powerful.
   COMBINED
   When virtual reality .... the potential to be quite powerful.
3. If schools adopt virtual reality, students will enjoy huge benefits from it.
   BY
   If virtual reality is .... hugely from it.
4. The word 'virtual' describes anything on the internet.
   AS
   Anything connected .... virtual.
5. Last year my school created a department for technology.
   DEDICATED
   Last year a department .... created at my school.
6. The benefits persuaded school leaders to invest in VR.
   CONVINCED
   School leaders were so .... invested in VR.

6 Read the exam tip. Then look at audioscript 4.5 and find four examples of *-ed* form + preposition collocations.

exam tip: key word transformation

Exploit reading texts by highlighting useful collocations (e.g. *-ed* form + preposition) so you actively notice them. This will help you with exam tasks like key word transformation.

Speak up

7 Work in groups. How could virtual reality be exploited in your school? List as many ideas as possible. Share them with the class.

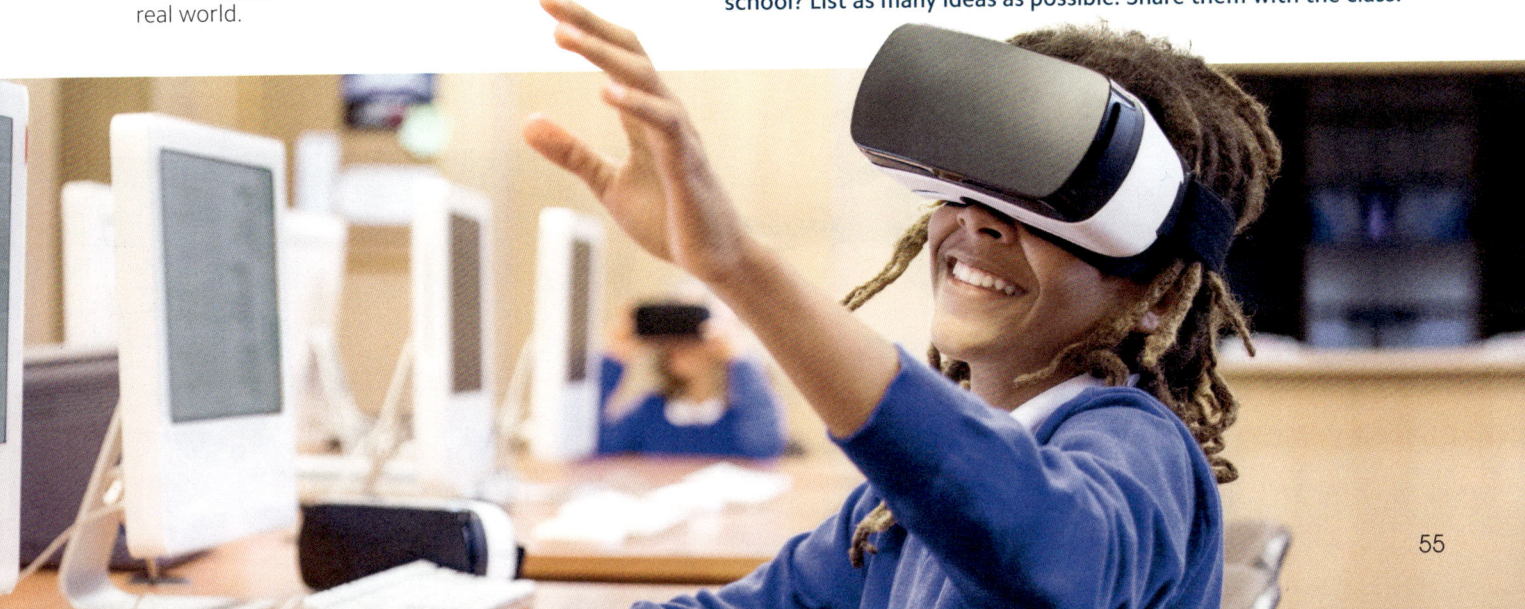

4 Going places

USE OF ENGLISH 2

1 Work in pairs. Look at the photo below. What kinds of things can go wrong on a journey?

2 🔊 4.10 Listen to a news story. What went wrong with the journey?

3 Read the language box. Complete the table with these words.

| again | before | not | not enough | too much | wrongly |

explore language → p160

prefixes

prefix	meaning	example
dis-	1	dishonest
mis-	2	mistrust
pre-	3	pre-order
re-	4	redevelop
over-	5	overpay
under-	6	underpay

4 Add a prefix to each of these words. Some words go with more than one prefix.

| age | arranged | belief | courage | estimate | historic |
| lead | miss | state | taken | understanding | view |

5 🔊 4.11 Listen to the news story again. Which words from Ex 4 do you hear?

6 Complete each gap in the topics below with a prefix. More than one answer might be possible.

1 a ....understanding you had during a trip
2 a tourist attraction for which you ....paid
3 a trip away you had to ....arrange at the last minute
4 a place you visited that was ....crowded
5 a place you would ....courage other people from visiting

7 Work in pairs. Talk about each topic in Ex 6 for one minute.

8 Read the article about GPS. What is the writer's opinion of this technology? Do you agree?

Is GPS making us stupid?

We've all seen headlines like 'Woman drives into river after GPS error'. Just the other day an American tourist drove for five hours across Iceland when his GPS ¹.......................... sent him in the wrong direction. It was only after the man had suffered much ².......................... during the 266-mile journey and arrived at his destination that he realised his GPS had ³.......................... him.

So, is GPS making us all stupid? Certainly, some experts believe we're too ⁴.......................... on it. They say that, because our mental map making skills are now ⁵.......................... , our navigation skills are insufficient. Map-reading skills haven't been taught in mainstream lessons for years, but experts suggest they should be ⁶.......................... into lessons.

Is this an old-fashioned idea or a sensible suggestion for helping young people become ⁷.......................... thinkers and cope better when technology fails? Without navigation skills, it's possible they'll be ⁸.......................... from applying for certain jobs or, at the very least, risk the same fate as the American tourist in Iceland.

CORRECT
COMFORT
LEAD
RELY
DEVELOP
INTRODUCE
DEPEND
COURAGE

9 e Read the article in Ex 8 again. Use the word given at the end of some of the lines to form a word that fits in the gap in the same line.

Speak up

10 Work in pairs. Imagine a story of your own 'worst journey'. What happened to you? Use prefixes where possible.

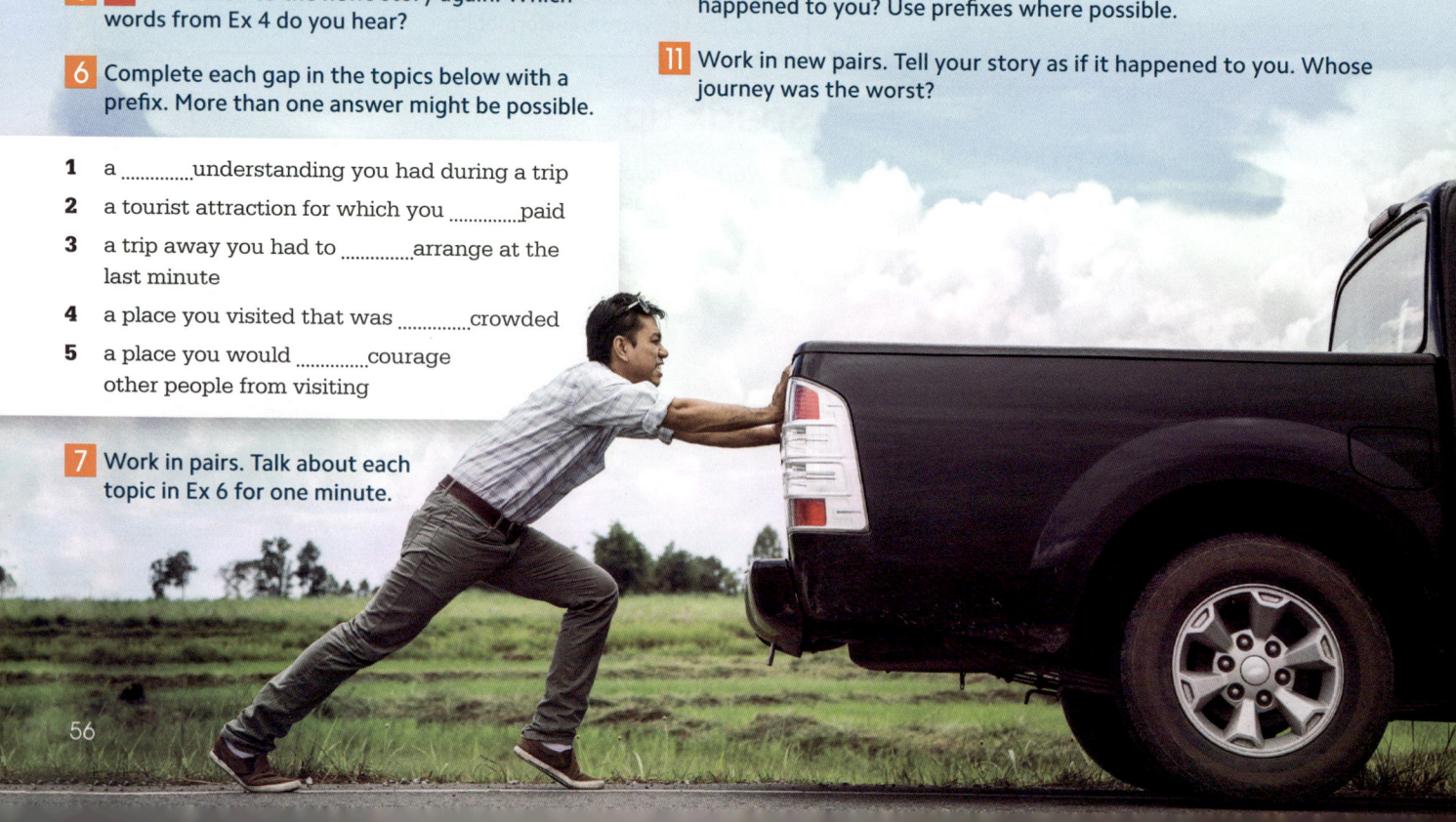

11 Work in new pairs. Tell your story as if it happened to you. Whose journey was the worst?

SPEAKING

Power up

1 Work in groups. Look at the photos of children going to school. Who has the best, worst and most interesting journey to school? How do these journeys compare with your own journey to school?

2 Read the discussion questions. What topic do they cover? Choose two questions and discuss them with a partner.

1. How easy is it for children to get to school in your country?
2. How could more people be encouraged to walk or cycle to school?
3. How important do you think it is for people to use public transport?
4. Some people think that governments should do more to increase the use of public transport. What do you think?
5. Is it always better to use public transport? Why/Why not?
6. What do you think public transport companies could do to make long journeys more interesting for passengers?

3 🔊 4.12 Listen to Hayley and Mark discussing question 2 in Ex 2. Who provides the clearest argument? Why?

4 Match each highlighted phrase that Hayley uses (1–5) with its function (A–E). Which words in the phrases are stressed?

1. **Personally, I think** the local government should build more cycle paths.
2. **The main reason for this is that** at the moment kids have to cycle on the roads.
3. **To give an example,** where I live there are regular cycling accidents.
4. Cycle paths mean children get to and from school more easily and, **above all,** more safely.
5. **What do you think?**

A introducing a reason
B introducing an example
C giving an opinion
D inviting an opinion
E emphasising a key point

5 Match these phrases with the functions in Ex 4 (A–E).

It seems to me that …   What's your view?   Let me give you an example.
… since …   What that means is …   For instance, …   The key thing is that …
As I see it, …   How do you feel about it?   This is due to …

6 Read the exam tip. Then look at the audioscript and add phrases to make Mark's argument clearer. Work in pairs and compare your ideas.

> **exam tip: discussion**
>
> To give a clear, logical argument, state your opinion and then give reasons and examples. Use phrases to organise and emphasise your ideas so the listener can follow them clearly.

Speak up

7 Work in pairs and answer question 1 in Ex 2.

Student A, give an opinion, a reason and an example. Invite Student B to give his/her view.

Student B, respond to Student A's view, give your view, a reason and an example.

8 🅔 Work in pairs and discuss the answers to questions 2–6 in Ex 2.

Speaking extra

9 Work in groups. Invent a perfect form of transport for travelling to school. It could be for your area or one of the areas in the photos. It has to be convenient, safe, comfortable and environmentally-friendly.

1. Create an illustration of it. Decide what it's called, how it works and what its benefits are.
2. Present your ideas to the class. Vote on the best invention.

4 Going places

WRITING

Power up

1 Work in groups. The people in the photos have travelled abroad to study and learn a new skill. Imagine you could do the same. Follow these steps.

1. Think of a skill you'd like to learn (e.g. learn to cook, ride a unicycle) but don't tell your classmates.
2. Take turns to mime the skill. Your classmates have to guess what the skill is.
3. The first group to mime and guess all the skills wins.
4. Tell your group where you'd like to learn the skill you mimed and why. Find out if they're interested in the same thing as you.

Plan on

2 Read the competition advertisement below. What three things do you need to write about in your letter? How do you think you can make your letter persuasive?

3 Read the letter on page 59 and answer the questions.

1. Does the writer include all the relevant information?
2. How many paragraphs does he use? What is the topic of each paragraph?
3. How does he make his letter persuasive?
4. What phrases does he use to start and end his letter?
5. Is his language formal or informal? How do you know?

free study ABROAD

The Worldwide Study Programme (WSP) is offering a prize of a two-month course in a country of your choice. Why not learn to make pizza or ice cream in Italy, play the sitar in India or learn some of the skills used by stunt artists in Hollywood? To enter, write us a letter and tell us where you'd like to study and why, what skill you'd like to learn and why we should pick you. The most persuasive letter will win.

Write your letter 220–260 words.

Win your dream study trip!

Dear Sir or Madam,

I am writing to enter the competition to win a place on a course abroad. I would like to put my name forward as not only would I benefit from the prize, but I would also be able to help others as a result.

If I were to win the prize, I would choose to do an app development course in California. This is because I have an idea for an app that I would like to create but I do not currently have the technical skills to create it myself. I believe that the course abroad would allow me the opportunity to learn the technical skills that I need to do this myself with some support. Furthermore, it would allow me to meet and learn from people in Silicon Valley, California, who have expertise in this area and could help me in my future career.

I believe you should select me because I am extremely outgoing and enjoy meeting new people and collaborating in a team. In addition to this, I volunteer each weekend to help run the under-tens football team. I hope to launch an app where other young people can volunteer for an hour each week and be matched to a community activity that suits their skills. As a result, the course abroad would benefit the local area where I live.

I hope that you find my application attractive and look forward to hearing from you in due course.

Yours faithfully,

Alex Panos

4 These sentences are too informal for a formal letter. Rewrite the highlighted parts using more formal language. Use the letter above to help you.
1 I'm writing because I want to win your competition.
2 I want to do a course in marine biology.
3 The course abroad would give me the chance to learn more about the Pacific Ocean.
4 I reckon you should pick me because I like sea animals.
5 I hope you think my application's good.
6 I'll wait for your reply.

5 Read the language box and add two more linkers from the letter.

explore **language**

adding ideas

Use a variety of linkers of addition to join similar ideas and add information. Try to use one or two in each paragraph.
not only … but … , ¹............................ , ²............................

6 Link the sentences using the words in brackets.
1 I have a keen sense of humour. I enjoy performing on stage. (as well as that)
2 I would like to drive a racing car. I would like to win races. (not only … but …)
3 I really enjoy outdoor activities. I am keen to learn survival skills. (in addition to)
4 One day I want to be a journalist. I want to write novels. (as well as)
5 I enjoy physical activities. I want to push myself out of my comfort zone. (furthermore)
6 Learning to cook will help me be creative. I would become more independent. (what's more)

Write on

7 Turn to page 173 and read another advertisement. What could you write about? Make notes under these headings.
- Place and reasons
- Benefits for my future
- Why choose me

8 Work in groups. Turn to page 173 and follow steps 1–4.

9 Plan your letter. Think about:
- your audience and tone
- how to start and end your letter appropriately
- the number of paragraphs and topic of each one
- how to link your ideas.

10 e Write your letter in 220–260 words.

Improve it

11 Read your letter. Which of the four points in Ex 9 have you addressed well? Are there any improvements you could make?

12 Look back at your last two pieces of written work. What grammar and vocabulary errors did you make? Check if you've made any of these errors in your letter.

SWITCH ON

Alone at sea

1 Work in groups.
1 Talk about someone you know who has wanderlust (a strong desire to travel).
2 Where do they want to go? Why?

2 ▶ Watch the clip. Work in pairs and answer the questions.
1 How far does Mike have to travel to go all the way around the world? Write your answer.
2 What happens to Mike in the Pacific Ocean and how does he fix the problem?

3 List three examples of Mike being proactive. Then work in pairs and compare your lists.

4 Work in pairs. You are getting ready for a similar trip. Discuss what you plan to take with you:
- to eat and drink
- to keep you warm and dry
- to stop you getting bored
- to remind you of home.

Project

5 Work in groups to create a slideshow or presentation about a young adventurer and their achievements.
1 Research some young people who have undertaken inspirational journeys.
2 Decide which person's story to tell and how to tell it.
3 Decide how to structure the story and create your slideshow or presentation.
4 Present your work to the class.
5 Write down what you've found most inspiring about the stories you've heard.

INDEPENDENT LEARNING

Reading and writing

1 Work in pairs and discuss the questions.
1 In what ways will the reading skills you practised in this unit help you in the future? What was the most valuable thing you learnt? Why?
2 Did you and your partner approach the letter writing task in the same way or in different ways? What approach could you try next time to see if it works? Why?

2 Look at the tips from Units 1–4 for improving your reading and writing skills. Which ones do you think are the most useful? Which would you like to focus on practising?

<u>Reading</u>
- identifying attitude
- recognising opinion
- understanding cohesion
- recognising points of view

<u>Writing</u>
- developing an argument
- making your ideas sound less definite
- building ideas towards a conclusion
- adding ideas

3 Complete the sentences with your own reading and writing goals.
1 One thing I will do to make sure I improve my reading skills is ....
2 One thing I will do to make sure I improve my writing skills is ....
3 Outside of class, I would prefer to practise by ....

UNIT CHECK

Wordlist

Verb + noun collocations
contact
come into contact with sb
establish contact with sb
impression
convey an impression
create an impression
implication
consider the implications
examine the implications
insight
gain insight
provide insight
threat
issue a threat
pose a threat

Tourism
backpacker (n)
backroad (n)
bustling (adj)
coastline (n)
deserted (adj)
distant (adj)
dune (n)
extend a trip (phr)
landmark (n)
package holiday (n+n)
remote (adj)
soak up the atmosphere (phr v + n)
touristy (adj)
trek (v)
unspoiled (adj)
wander around/along (v)

Prefixes
disbelief (n)
discomfort (n)
discourage (v)
dismiss (v)
misunderstanding (n)
mislead (v)
mistaken (adj)
prearrange (v)
prehistoric (adj)
preview (n)
rearrange (v)
reintroduce (v)
restate (v)
review (v)
overestimate (v)
overstate (v)
overview (n)
underage (adj)

underdeveloped (adj)
underestimate (v)
understate (v)

Other
blur (v)
burden (n)
bush (n)
convincing (adj)
effort (n)
get in on the act (phr)
herd (n)
hilarious (adj)
integrity (n)
make smth out (phr v)
overlook (v)
picturesque (adj)
sparkling (adj)
squint (v)

Vocabulary

1 Complete the sentences with verb + noun collocations from the wordlist.

1. You really should .... of what you do before you act.
2. Arriving late won't .... that you want people to like you.
3. When you take up a new sport, you often .... new people.
4. I'd love to .... into what my dog's thinking!
5. It's wrong to .... to people, even if you don't mean it.

2 🔊 4.13 Listen to six people. What word from the *Other* section of the wordlist does the beep represent?

1. .... 4. ....
2. .... 5. ....
3. .... 6. ....

3 🔊 4.14 Listen and check your answers.

4 Complete the blog with words from the *Tourism* and *Prefixes* sections of the wordlist. You may need to change the tense of verbs.

> Some young people aren't interested in going on organised ¹........................ holidays. Backpackers often prefer to get off the beaten track and avoid the ²........................ parts of a country. They're also happy to suffer the ³........................ of a cheap, basic hotel to travel on a budget. However, don't ⁴........................ the difference between backpackers and holidaymakers who have everything ⁵........................ for them when it comes to activities. Even backpackers tend to visit ⁶........................ cities, full of people, where they can ⁷........................ the culture in museums and galleries or ⁸........................ around the back streets.

5 Write a similar blog entry in favour of package holidays.

UNIT CHECK

Review

1 Complete the text with prepositions.

> In the 1950s residents of the Galapagos Islands, bothered ¹.................... the effects of tourism, made some changes. They made the decision, armed ².................... research, to turn the Islands into a national park. At first, local wildlife was protected not ³.................... park managers but ⁴.................... personnel at a research station. However, now the wildlife protection is accomplished ⁵.................... the establishment of the Galapagos National Park. In 2011 the number of nights a cruise ship can stay was reduced ⁶.................... four every fortnight. In 2010 the Islands were removed ⁷.................... the list of World Heritage endangered sites.

2 Read the text. Use the word given at the end of some of the lines to form a word that fits in the gap in the same line.

> The coral reefs around the world have been under attack for many years from pollution, climate change and as a result of ¹.................... to the point of emptying previously ².................... seas. However, new research looking into the effects of sun cream have produced results with startling ³.................... . Swimmers produce large amounts of sun cream. Recently, research which was ⁴.................... in coral reefs showed that young corals were killed off at an alarming rate after exposure. Just one drop in an entire Olympic-sized swimming pool caused damage. ⁵.................... that between 4,000 and 6,000 tonnes of sun cream enter coral reef areas, that's a major problem. The coral loses its colour, which eventually ⁶.................... new growth. But the whole process is unnecessary as many sun creams ⁷.................... on non-toxic substances are widely available. Many areas, such as Hawaii, have found the evidence so ⁸.................... that they have decided to ban the use of toxic sun cream products on their beaches.

FISH
SPOIL

IMPLY

TAKE

GIVE

COURAGE

BASE

CONVINCE

3 Complete the second sentence so that it has a similar meaning to the first sentence using the word given. Do not change the word given. Use between three and six words.

1 The tour operator would ensure our money went to local people so we booked with them.
   ENSURING
   We booked with the tour operator, ... to local people.

2 We always felt comfortable.
   TIME
   At .... uncomfortable.

3 We had no contact with local people, which was disappointing.
   LACK
   We .... contact with local people.

4 We had the most fun when we went on a day cruise.
   ENJOYED
   What we .... on a day cruise.

5 The local representative came to visit and he knew a lot of facts.
   ARMED
   The local representative was .... facts when he came to visit.

6 We only chose restaurants where they served fish they caught fresh.
   SERVING
   We only ate at restaurants .... fish.

4 🔊 4.15 Listen to four stories about bad holiday experiences. Predict the ending of each story.

5 🔊 4.16 Complete the sentences with a suitable word or phrase. Listen to check your answers. Did you guess the endings correctly?

1 Mum offered me a sandwich but, ..., I decided to put the sandwich down for a minute.

2 I twisted my ankle .... The next day I cut my foot ....

3 I spent last summer working the vacation, ... the grass in the neighbours' houses down our street.

4 We got there in the afternoon, ... but happy, but .... my bedroom, I saw …

62

"You get back from life what you put in."

Look at the photo and discuss the questions.
1 What does 'community' mean to you?
2 How do you think school prepares people to be part of a community?
3 What is the best piece of advice another person gave you? Why did you like it?

Citizenship

5

READING
topic: reviews of a self-help book
skills: locating opinions on the same topic in a text; recognising points of view
task: cross-text multiple matching

GRAMMAR
modal verbs in the past
emphasising comparatives and superlatives

VOCABULARY
working with phrases
dependent prepositions; phrasal verbs and phrases

LISTENING
topic: good and bad gifts
skill: listening for ideas expressed in different ways
task: multiple matching

USE OF ENGLISH
key word transformation
multiple-choice cloze

SPEAKING
topic: community work
skill: using a variety of phrases
task: long turn

WRITING
topic: family and friends
skill: writing effective introductions and conclusions
task: essay

SWITCH ON ▶
video: sweet treats
project: animal communities

5 Citizenship

READING

Power up

1 Work in pairs. What kind of advice do you usually find in self-help books or videos? Do you ever read self-help books or watch videos? Why/Why not?

2 What tips have self-help books suggested in these situations? How might the animal in the photo help? Turn to page 173 and check your ideas.

  A You are having a serious conversation with someone and you want to lighten it to make it more interesting.

  B You want to make sure that your wallet or purse will be returned to you if you lose it.

  C You need to do some creative work and you have no ideas.

3 How helpful do you think these tips are? Do you think self-help books can be useful or a waste of time?

Read on

4 Read the text quickly. What is it about?

5 Read the task and identify the topic of each question. Find the sections of the text where each reviewer discusses each topic.

   Which reviewer:
   1 has a similar opinion to reviewer A on Wiseman's use of other sources?
   2 shares reviewer D's opinions on the way Wiseman presents his ideas?
   3 expresses a different opinion to reviewer B on the practicalities of Wiseman's tips?
   4 agrees with reviewer A on the possible impact of reading the book?

6 Look at the highlighted sentences in sections A–C of the text. Which reviewers agree with each other? Which one disagrees?

7 Find the sentence in section D that covers the same topic. Does reviewer D say the same thing or something different?

8 **e** Read the exam tip and complete the notes. Then read the text again and complete the task in Ex 5. For questions 1–4, choose from the reviewers (A–D).

> **exam tip:**
> **cross-text multiple matching**
> Once you have located the information in each section, make some notes to keep track of what each person says so you can compare the information more easily.
>
> Complete the notes with words from the highlighted sections of the article.
> A should have been ..... selective .....
> B useful, chosen .... examples
> C too many ....
> D carefully filtered out the rubbish

9 Look at the opinions from the text. Do the reviewers have similar opinions?

   1 What do you think of most self-help authors?
      Section A: … the self help industry, with so-called experts weighing in on topics …
      Section C: If you are naturally suspicious of the usual self-help formula homespun anecdotes and …
   2 What did you think of the book?
      Section A: … all those minutes could be better spent making real changes to the things that matter or reading a more solid self-help book. …
      Section D: However, this book contains dozens of useful nuggets of information with science on their side …

Sum up

10 What advantages of Wiseman's book were mentioned in the reviews? Do you agree that they are benefits?

Speak up

11 Work in pairs. Look at the titles of real lifestyle and self-help books on page 173. Which looks the most interesting? How do you think they might help their readers?

59 Seconds:
Think a little, change a lot.

A In the 1980s, people couldn't have predicted the success of the self-help industry, with so-called experts weighing in on topics from passing exams to achieving a dream body. In *59 Seconds*, Richard Wiseman compiles and reviews various research papers and recommends activities that take less than a minute to implement and improve one aspect of your life. In the book's conclusion Wiseman provides his top ten scientifically supported techniques. These brief summaries are helpful, given the large number overall in the book, but I felt he could have been a little more selective in his use of sources. Some are clearly just one-minute jobs. However, others require considerably more time than his title implies or may be impractical for regular use. In my opinion, all those minutes could be better spent making real changes to the things that matter or reading a more solid self-help book.

B Popular psychologist Richard Wiseman's new book suggests that tiny alterations to our day-to-day lives can make a huge difference to our overall happiness. Some of his suggestions are relatively simple, but that just means that it's hardly life-changing stuff. Anything meaningful will clearly take more than a minute. Unfortunately, there's not a lot to a fifty-nine-second tip, and so the constant repetition of ideas also starts to get on the nerves after a while. Even so, Wiseman's attempts to simplify the evidence from scientific journals and turn them into small gems of life-changing advice is a useful approach and he's certainly chosen some fascinating examples. I'd go for it – reading this book is unlikely to make any real difference to your life, but it will at least improve the quality of your party conversations!

C If you are naturally suspicious of the usual self-help formula of homespun anecdotes and upbeat promises, Richard Wiseman's *59 Seconds* seems a useful read. Undoubtedly, psychology has identified many clues to success, but I couldn't help feeling that Wiseman was trying to summarise too many experts in this one book. It may be worth flicking through to remind yourself that minor changes in behaviour can produce results, but you could use your time more wisely. How do you become blissfully happy? Apparently, nodding your head often should do it. Others might not appreciate your new-found cheerfulness though – the word *annoying* comes to mind. Nevertheless, Wiseman rightly warns that, although his techniques are best used cautiously and with consideration, many seem perfectly achievable in the minute. Wiseman includes a four-step worksheet that will help readers to achieve their goals, which is time-consuming, but worthwhile. And who ever went wrong by smiling too much?

> How do you become blissfully happy? Apparently, nodding your head often should do it.

D Richard Wiseman is on the campaign against self-help books which, he argues, make harmful claims not backed up by research. In this book, Wiseman has carefully filtered out the rubbish and just left advice that's backed up by scientific evidence. He might be exaggerating the 'less than a minute to implement' claim, however. For example, research suggests that putting a potted plant on your desk should increase your creativity by fifteen percent, but going out to buy a plant takes more than fifty-nine seconds. Some early self-help groups might have been trying to make a quick profit, but Wiseman admits that others, like Dale Carnegie who was popular in the 1980s, must have been onto something as his insights have been validated by research. Wiseman's frequent summarising can get a bit repetitive. However, this book contains dozens of useful nuggets of information with science on their side, and reminding yourself of such tried and tested insights is hardly a waste of time.

5 Citizenship

GRAMMAR

1 Find the modal verb and main verb in these sentences. Which verb tells you that the events are in the past?

Some early self-help groups might have been trying to make a quick profit.

In the 1980s, people couldn't have predicted the success of the self-help industry.

2 Read the grammar box. Complete the rules with these verbs.

couldn't have known   might have been studying
needn't have worried   shouldn't have lied

explore grammar → p150

modal verbs in the past

We use modal verbs in the past:

A to speculate or make deductions about the past (e.g. *may/might have, couldn't/couldn't have, can't have, must/had to have*).

You ¹.. about the mistake.

B to criticise or express regret about the past (e.g. *should/shouldn't have*).

You ².. to your mum.

C to talk about things that were and weren't necessary (e.g. *needn't have/ didn't need to*).

I ³.. after all!

We use continuous forms to show that the action was ongoing or was interrupted.

Jack ⁴.. all weekend. He had a big test this week.

3 🔊 5.1 Listen to a talk on 'crowd psychology' and 'the bystander effect'. What are they?

4 🔊 5.2 Choose the best verb form to complete the sentences. Listen again and check your answers.

1 People around young children **had to play / had to have played** some role in that criminal behaviour.
2 Those children **might have seen / might have been seeing** a lot of crime around them.
3 That **can't have been / couldn't have been** good for them.
4 People who **could / must** have easily intervened in a situation just walk on by.
5 You **must have ignored / could have ignored** it, but you knew no one else was around.
6 You **might have thought / might have been thinking** that someone else **must have opened / must have been opening** the door already.

5 🔊 5.3 Look at the sentences in Ex 4 again and think about how the modal verbs are contracted in speech. Listen and practise saying the sentences.

6 Work in pairs. Have you ever experienced crowd psychology or the bystander effect? Do you think we should try and overcome them?

7 Match the first half of each sentence (1–5) with the second half (A–E).

1 You really **should have**
2 I tried to help,
3 I left the pizza money on the table so
4 John offered to pay the pizza guy,
5 I **could have** kicked myself

A but I **needn't have** bothered.
B it **ought to have** been there when you got home.
C so I **didn't need to** do it myself.
D done more to help that woman!
E when I found out I'd made that mistake!

8 Match the modal verbs in bold in Ex 7 with these functions.

criticism of others   regret about the past   speculation
something that was unnecessary, but you did it
something that was unnecessary so you didn't do it

game on

Play in groups of three. Think of a past regret. The other two students in the group can ask twenty yes/no questions to try and work out what the past regret was. Who can guess first?

A: (I shouldn't have eaten a whole bar of chocolate at the weekend.)
B: Is it something you should have done?
C: Did it involve other people?

Speak up

9 Work in pairs. Read about John's problem and speculate about what he did to solve it. Then turn to page 173 and check your ideas.

> John was told that there were three boxes in the kitchen, but all three were labelled incorrectly. One was labelled 'Apples', another 'Oranges' and the last one was labelled 'Apples and oranges'. John took just one fruit from one of the boxes and then labelled all three correctly.

VOCABULARY
working with phrases

1. 🔊 **5.4** Listen to four people describing criminals. Which do you think was the least intelligent? Why?

2. 🔊 **5.5** Read the sentences. What do the phrasal verbs in bold mean? Listen again and check.
   1. Vandalism **gets to me** every time.
   2. I was sure he was just **fooling around**.
   3. They weren't exactly **jumping at** the chance.
   4. He wasn't going to **settle for** just a small amount.
   5. My uncle calmly told them to **hang back** a bit.
   6. The police thought someone was **winding them up**.
   7. I decided to **stand up to** the guy.
   8. I thought he must have been **having me on**.

3. Read the text. How were the criminals detained?

4. Read the language box below. Then match the phrasal verbs in bold in the text (1–6) with their definitions (A–F).
   - A attempt to use physical violence in return
   - B not do anything to help or prevent something bad
   - C felt upset, shocked or frightened
   - D becoming impossible to control
   - E hold someone so they are not able to move from a position
   - F helped

explore language

phrases

Pay attention to how new phrases are formed and how they are used in sentences.

Look at the phrase 'alarm bells' in the text. What kind of word comes after it? What word does the text use instead of the usual 'can't bring yourself to do something?' Why?

5. Find these phrases in the text. What do they mean?

   alarm bells rang   composed herself   coming to terms with
   kicking themselves   on her conscience   stuck to her guns
   unable to bring themselves to   wrapped up in the moment

6. Cover the text and just look at the phrases and phrasal verbs in Ex 4 and 5. Can you retell the story?

Speak up

7. Work in pairs. Do you think the granny did the right thing? Think of the problem from the perspective of the jewellery shop owner, the police and the granny's family. What would they say? What would you have done?

Hero granny
takes on the bad guys

When a group of masked men started attacking a jeweller's shop in a busy high street, one granny looking on decided she couldn't **¹stand by** and do nothing – she didn't want that event on her conscience, and so she ran to the rescue. Alarm bells rang for the OAP when she saw a group of men walking around the jeweller's with a sledgehammer in their hands. Without thinking, she ran across the road. 'I was just so wrapped up in the moment, I didn't think about my own safety,' said the pensioner, who cannot be named. What the men were doing was wrong, and she stuck to her guns and started hitting the men with her handbag to make them stop. Thankfully, unable to bring themselves to **²fight back**, the men sped off on mopeds. But when one of them fell, the woman, thought to be in her seventies, composed herself yet again and tried to **³pin the man down**. A large group of onlookers **⁴came to her aid**, and between them, they were able to detain the man until the police arrived. Coming to terms with what she'd just done, the granny **⁵was** clearly **shaken up**, but pleased with her efforts to prevent the situation from **⁶getting out of hand**. No one was injured in the raid and all of the gang members were later caught and arrested. The event was filmed and viewed online around the world – there's no doubt the criminals will be kicking themselves for being brought down by a granny.

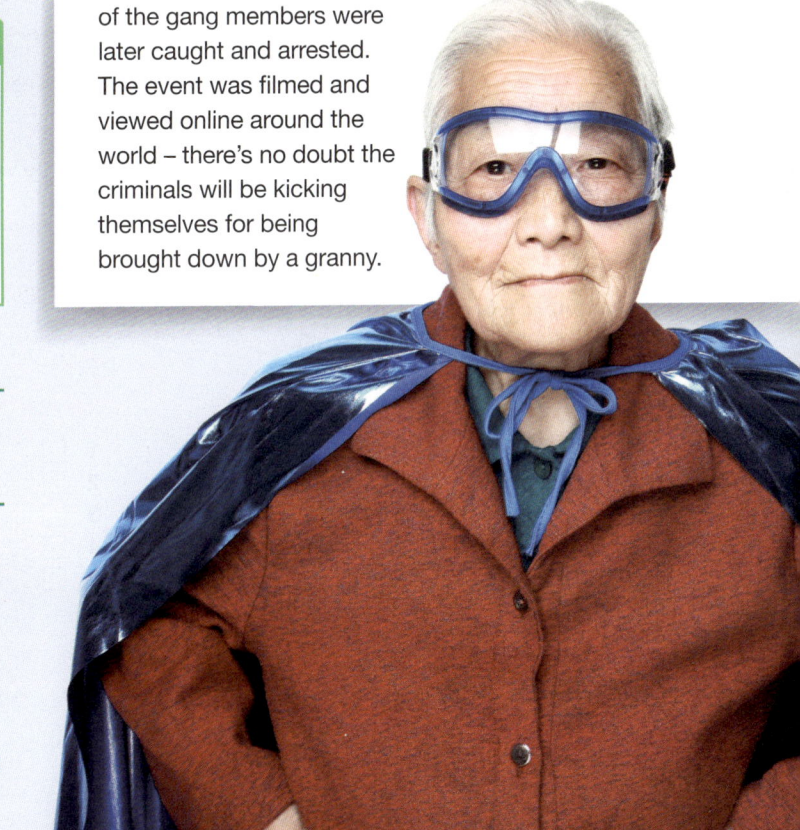

5 Citizenship

LISTENING

Power up

1 Work in pairs and discuss the questions.

1 If you had to receive one of the gifts in the photos, which one would you least hate? Why?
2 What's the best gift you've ever received? Why?
3 When do people give gifts in your culture?
4 Why do you think gift-giving is a feature of society?

Listen up

2 🔊 5.6 Listen to a girl describing the worst gift she's ever been given and answer the questions.

1 How did she feel about receiving it?
2 What does she think would make choosing a gift for someone easier?

3 🔊 5.7 Read the exam tip. Then listen to a boy talking about gift-giving. In what order does he answer the questions in Ex 2?

> **exam tip: multiple matching**
>
> Don't expect to always hear the speaker answer the Task 1 question first. Sometimes speakers will answer the Task 2 questions first.

4 Read the two tasks in Ex 5. What do you have to listen for in each task? Check that you understand options A–H.

5 e 🔊 5.8 You are going to hear five people talking about the worst gift that they have ever received. Listen and complete the tasks.

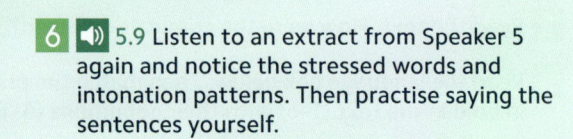

6 🔊 5.9 Listen to an extract from Speaker 5 again and notice the stressed words and intonation patterns. Then practise saying the sentences yourself.

Every year I got these thick woolly socks from my aunty. I was thirteen! I was never sure if she'd got me mixed up with someone else. Every year I hoped she'd get something different. Thank heavens my mum never made me wear them!

Speak up

7 Work with a partner. What's the worst gift you've ever been given? Why? Do you agree that 'it's the thought that counts'? What advice would you give to someone buying gifts? Why?

Task 1

For questions 1–5, choose from the list (A–H) how each speaker felt about receiving the gift.

A unaffected by the disappointment
B amused by the timing of the gift
C keen to avoid offending the giver
D relieved to get revenge
E upset by the thoughtlessness
F resigned to using the item
G uncertain if gift was for another person
H let down by a loved one

Speaker 1 1 ☐
Speaker 2 2 ☐
Speaker 3 3 ☐
Speaker 4 4 ☐
Speaker 5 5 ☐

Task 2

For questions 6–10, choose from the list (A–H) what each speaker thinks would make choosing a gift easier.

A keeping the receipt
B buying something practical
C personalising the gift
D keeping the packaging simple
E getting professional advice
F spending less money
G getting the same gift as before
H asking the receiver what they want

Speaker 1 6 ☐
Speaker 2 7 ☐
Speaker 3 8 ☐
Speaker 4 9 ☐
Speaker 5 10 ☐

In a survey, one third of mums were named as the best gift-giver, compared to only 0.17 percent of grandads!

USE OF ENGLISH 1

1 Complete the sentences about gift-giving in your own words.

A If all else fails, it's far better to give …

B By far the worst gift I ever got was …

C I think … is just as good as getting something expensive.

2 Read the language box. Complete the rules with these words. Then match sentences A–C in Ex 1 with the rules.

as … as comparatives   *-er/more* comparatives   superlatives

explore language → p150

emphasising comparatives and superlatives

We use 'far', 'a great deal' (formal) and 'way' (informal) to emphasise ¹…………………… .

We use 'by far' to emphasise ²…………………… .

We use 'just', 'nowhere near', 'nothing like', 'half' and 'twice' to emphasise ³…………………… .

3 🔊 5.10 Listen to a story about a boy called Josh. What happened to him?

4 Read a newspaper story about Josh's experience. Complete it with these words and a suitable comparative form of the adjectives in brackets. There may be more than one possible answer.

nothing like   far   just   nowhere near   a good deal   way

Fined for missing a birthday party!

In the past, birthday parties were ¹……………… (complicated) as today – a few party games and some cheese sandwiches. Life was ²……………… (easy) than it is today! These days kids are ³……………… (likely) to end up in a ski centre, at a recording session or on a driving experience as at a party at home. But if you think the last party you went to was pretty awful, it'll be ⁴……………… (bad) as Josh Walton's last experience. His family was threatened with court action when he failed to turn up.

Josh had been invited to a friend's party at a local ski centre, but on the day, his parents decided that it would be ⁵……………… (good) for him to spend the day with his grandparents. Josh's parents were shocked when he came home from school the next Monday with an angry demand for a £16 'no show fee'. The conversation between the parents took place on social media, with neither side agreeing to back down. A party at home would have been ⁶……………… (controversial)!

5 Complete the second sentence so that it has a similar meaning to the first sentence using the word given. Do not change the word given. Use between three and six words.

1 I know that it was wrong to lie to my mum.

SHOULD

I know that ………………………………… my mum the truth.

2 I think the DJ was much more expensive than the one that we had last year.

TWICE

The DJ was ………………………………… the one that we had last year.

3 Anna didn't get to the party, and I'm sure it was because the weather was too bad.

PREVENTED

The bad weather ………………………………… to the party.

4 The party was a good deal better than I thought it would be.

NOTHING

The party was ………………………………… I expected.

5 David wasn't around when I decided to go home, so it's possible he left before the end.

MIGHT

David ………………………………… until the end of the party.

6 The leisure centre party venue is much smaller than the one at the ski centre.

NOWHERE

The leisure centre party venue ………………………………… the one at the ski centre.

exam tip:
key word transformation

Reread the completed second sentence to make sure the sentence makes sense grammatically.

Look at sentence 1 in Ex 5 again. If you write 'I know that I should have my mum the truth', does that make sense? What verb could you add before 'my mum' that would make sense?

Speak up

6 Why do you think both mums in the missed birthday party situation thought they were doing the right thing? Who did you sympathise with more? Why?

Did you know the average cost of attending someone else's wedding party in the United States is $673?

5 Citizenship

USE OF ENGLISH 2

1 In what ways can young people help in a community? How do you think people feel when they do community work?

2 🔊 5.11 Listen to a story about a girl who helped others. What positive thing happened as a result?

3 🔊 5.12 Read the news story and complete it with these words and suitable prepositions. Listen again and check your answers.

appalled	ashamed	capable	contrary	eager
impressed	intent	subject		

Many people were **1**........................ the mess the local play park was in, and felt **2**........................ themselves for letting it get so bad. But one girl, Caitlin Davis, got together with a group of fellow pupils who were **3**........................ a chance to help out in the neighbourhood. They cleared the rubbish and repainted. Local builders volunteered staff, who were more than **4**........................ fixing the play equipment to safe building standards. It turned out well for Caitlin, too. The local council were so **5**........................ the project that they offered Caitlin a £1,000 grant. The money was **6**........................ her carrying on with the project in another park. It just goes to show that **7**........................ popular belief, young people are keen to help others. Caitlin says that she is **8**........................ making sure this project makes a real difference to the community.

4 Complete the questions with words and prepositions from Ex 3. Then work in pairs and discuss the questions.
1. What selfish acts have you done that you are most .... ?
2. Do you think that receiving charity money should be .... terms and conditions?
3. Are we .... feeding everyone on the planet or is it impossible?
4. What acts of kindness are you most .... ?

5 e Read the exam tip and answer the question. Then read the text and decide which answer (A, B, C or D) best fits each gap.

exam tip: multiple-choice cloze
Use prepositions to help you rule out possible answers.
Look at gap 1 in the text below. Which word can be followed by 'of'?

Test your vocabulary and win free rice for someone who's hungry

Want to help someone today? Everyone's **1**........ of doing their bit. The people at the United Nations' Food Programme website are so **2**........ on working to address global education and hunger, they've created a website to feed the world. The concept is simple: answer questions and for each correct answer, the UN will **3**........ ten grains of rice to a person who needs it. Whether you're the president of a company or a street child living in poverty, **4**........ time in your education is the most direct route to improving your life. **5**........ to popular belief, a website like this can make a difference to hungry human beings, giving them the energy they need to be **6**........, healthy people able to contribute economically. You can relax in the **7**........ that somewhere in the world a person is eating the rice you provided. And if you were wondering whether the project can really make a difference, it has already raised enough to feed millions of people. Just imagine how **8**........ anyone would be with results like that!

	A	B	C	D
1	gifted	capable	talented	competent
2	determined	committed	absorbed	intent
3	donate	trust	tip	provide
4	spending	occupying	investing	filling
5	Contrary	Besides	Conversely	Aside
6	advantageous	productive	rewarding	favourable
7	conscience	understanding	familiarity	knowledge
8	influenced	impressed	inspired	impacted

Speak up

6 How could you help people every day? Use these ideas or your own. Which do you think does more good? Is this kind of help always welcome?
- offering to do chores
- listening to people
- asking people what they need help with
- sending someone a text to cheer them up
- volunteering

'No one ever became poor by giving.' (Anne Frank)

SPEAKING

Power up

1 Work in pairs and discuss the questions.
1. What kinds of problems can people in a town or city solve if they work together?
2. Have you ever raised money for a charity or helped with a local group? If so, how?
3. If you were asked to do one thing to improve your community, what would you do?

2 🔊 5.13 Listen to Susie and Eric discussing the questions in Ex 1. Which student sounds a bit unfriendly? Why?

3 Replace the highlighted words in Eric's answers with these phrases.

> For the life of me, I can't remember the reason.
> I know singing in the choir sounds a bit dodgy.
> I guess you could check out what's going on at the town's website.
> I never got round to going.
> That's not a question kids my age give a lot of thought to.

1. Dunno, really. I guess we have celebrations in the town square for the big festivals. ....
2. Nice. Never been. You'd need to ask my mum. ....
3. I had to sing in a ... what's the word? Well, outside the shopping centre. Dunno why. ....
4. Yeah. But I like it. ....
5. Probably. Look online. ....

4 Work in pairs. Ask and answer the questions.
1. What do you do in your free time?
2. What problems are there in your home town?
3. What do people do together in your town?
4. What would you like to change about your home town?

5 🔊 5.14 Listen and match the speakers (1–3) with the photos (A–C).

6 Read the exam tip. Then work in pairs and compare the photos. If you don't have the vocabulary to describe what's happening, think about how you can paraphrase.

> **exam tip: long turn**
> Remember that you can use informal language, but keep it interesting by varying it.
>
> Match these informal phrases with the photos (A–C).
> 1. This is definitely one of the good guys. He must've been sorting through those boxes for ages!
> 2. There are a load of blokes, I suppose – it's kind of hard to tell who that is beneath the costume.
> 3. This is the kind of thing that would drive me nuts, out there clearing up some other guy's mess.

Speak up

7 e Work in pairs. Turn to page 176 and complete the task.

Speaking extra

8 Work in pairs. Turn to page 173. Would you like to get involved in this community project? Why/Why not?

Why don't prawns give to charity? Because they're a little 'shellfish'!

5 Citizenship

WRITING

Power up

1 Work in pairs and discuss the questions.
1. What do families tend to argue about? How do they help each other?
2. If you could ask each family member to do one thing for you, what would it be?
3. What might your family want you to do more of for them?

Plan on

2 Work in pairs. Read the task below and answer the questions.
1. When is it better to compromise? What shouldn't people compromise on? Why?
2. How can people show respect for others? What is the effect of being critical?
3. How could people help family or friends? Who benefits from helping? How do you feel when others help you?

> You have attended a talk on how people can support each other more in relationships. You have made the notes below:
>
> How can people support each other more in relationships?
> - compromising
> - respecting
> - helping
>
> Some opinions expressed in the talk:
>
> 'Sometimes you have to agree to disagree otherwise you never get anywhere.'
>
> 'Nobody became happy criticising others – it's so destructive.'
>
> 'The little things we can do for each other every day make people feel special.'
>
> Write an essay for your teacher discussing **two** of the ways in which people can support each other more in relationships. You should **explain which way is more important, giving reasons** in support of your answer.
>
> You may, if you wish, make use of the opinions expressed in the talk, but you should use your own words as far as possible.
>
> Write your essay in **220–260** words.

3 Read the introduction to an essay. Then match the functions below (A–C) with the sentences in the introduction (1–3).

> ¹Constant disagreement is often cited by experts as the biggest complaint in any kind of relationship. ²To have successful friendships and family relationships, people need to be more supportive of each other. ³This essay will consider the positive impact that helping others and showing respect can have in building strong bonds with those around us.

A Introduce the main idea or argument.
B Preview the structure of the essay.
C Get the reader's attention.

4 Read the sentences from a student's introduction for the task in Ex 2 and put them in the best order (1–3). Think about the functions in Ex 3.

A This essay will consider ways to be supportive in two key areas: showing respect and compromising.

B While it can be easy to argue or criticise when things go wrong, being supportive and reliable are the keys to any successful relationship.

C Positive relationships with those around you may not make you richer or healthier, but they will make you happier.

5 Read the sentences from the student's first main paragraph and put them in the best order (1–3).

A In fact, I would go as far as to say a person who does not respect the people around them will probably have very few friends.

B By far the most important quality in a relationship is respect.

C It shows that you value the other person and understand that people are different, but that does not necessarily mean better or worse.

6 Read the language box and complete the task.

explore language

You can use a range of phrases to express the strength of your opinion.

Complete the sentences with phrases that you have learnt in this unit.

1 .... the most important thing in any relationship is respect.

2 It can be .... meaningful to help with the small, day-to-day matters as to make grand gestures.

7 Complete the paragraph with these phrases. Notice how they help the student to structure her ideas.

above all   besides   it is worth bearing in mind that
plays a vital role in   underline the fact that

Learning to compromise on minor issues also ¹............................. developing good relationships. ²............................. no one will agree with you all the time on every issue. ³............................., even if they do agree, it may not mean that you are both right. ⁴............................., good friends should be prepared to 'take one for the team' and do some things they do not enjoy. Many successful people ⁵............................., in life, a team victory is just as good as a personal one.

8 Read three possible conclusions (1–3) to the essay. Match them with the conclusion types below (A–C).

1 In conclusion, there are many reasons why investing time and effort in loved ones is important. If you fail to build strong enough relationships now, you never know when you might regret that decision in the future.

2 To sum up, supporting others requires a lot of patience. Nobody finds it easy to ignore their own selfish desires, and putting others' needs first is challenging. It can only be done if you bear in mind that selfishness is rarely ever attractive, and make a small effort every day to be the kind of person you admire.

3 As has been illustrated in this essay, relationships need a lot of effort to make them work. However, any time invested is usually rewarded in ways that will surprise the giver.

A a positive prediction about the future
B a warning about something bad that might happen
C a suggestion for how you can improve a situation

Write on

9 You are going to write a similar essay. Turn to page 174 and read the task. How will you structure your main paragraphs?

10 Work in groups of three and discuss your ideas. What evidence can you use to support your opinions?

11 Plan your essay. Think about:
- your introduction and conclusion
- paragraph organisation
- ways of drawing attention to your main points.

12 e Write your essay in 220–260 words.

Improve it

13 Work in pairs. Choose one of the main paragraphs from your essay and follow these steps.

1 Copy the sentences in a random order and give them to your partner.
2 Can your partner put the sentences back in the correct order?
3 If not, what could you do to make the order of ideas clearer?

SWITCH ON

Sweet treats

1 Work in pairs. Think of some ways in which animals help humans in everyday life.

2 Watch the clip. Work in pairs and answer the questions.
  1 What is the name of the bird that collaborates with the Masai boys?
  2 Where does the bird lead the boys?
  3 How does the bird signal that they are near the target?
  4 What happens to the boy when he retrieves the sweet treat?

3 ▶ Watch again. How do the boys fulfil their part of the bargain? And what would happen if they did not?

4 Work in pairs. Explain these expressions from the video:
  • follow my leader
  • getting hotter
  • hit the jackpot
  • part of the bargain

5 Work in groups. Debate this motion.
'Man exploits animals for his own gain; animals never benefit'.

Project

6 Work in small groups. Create a presentation comparing animal communities. Follow these steps.
  1 Research how bees work together in a hive to create their food and one other animal community of your choice.
  2 Compare the two animal communities. How are they similar and different?
  3 Decide how you will present your information.
  5 Present your information to the class.

INDEPENDENT LEARNING

Listening and speaking

1 Complete the sentences to make them true for you.
  1 The listening skills I have worked on in this unit are …
  2 The listening skills I am good at in general are …
  3 It is important to continue working on my listening skills because …

2 Work in pairs and follow these steps. Make notes on your ideas.
  1 Make a list of the biggest challenges for you when doing listening practice.
  2 Has there been a particular listening task so far that has been more difficult than others? Why do you find it hard?
  3 Suggest tips for each other on how to improve your listening skills in these areas. You can look back at exam tip boxes to help you.

3 How confident do you feel about your speaking skills so far? Number the skills 1–7 (1 = the skill you feel most confident in, 7 = the skill you need to improve most)

using stress and intonation to sound interesting ☐

using polite language to talk in a formal situation or to someone you don't know well ☐

using specific words or phrases to speculate about what is happening ☐

using set phrases in the right way ☐

giving reasons and examples to support your opinions ☐

using phrases to organise your ideas when you are speaking ☐

using phrases to speculate or express how likely or unlikely something is ☐

4 Write down words and phrases from Units 1–5 that you can use in the future to improve the speaking skills you would like to work on.

UNIT CHECK

Wordlist

Phrasal verbs of attitude and opinion
fool around
get to sb
hang back
have sb on
jump at smth
settle for smth
stand up to sb
wind sb up

Phrases and verbs of attitude and disagreement
alarm bells ring (*phr*)
be on sb's conscience (*phr*)
be unable to bring yourself to do smth (*phr*)
come to sb's aid (*phr*)
come to terms with (*phr*)
compose yourself (*v*)
fight back (*phr v*)
get out of hand (*phr*)
kick yourself (*phr*)
pin sb down (*phr v*)
shake sb up (*phr v*)
stand by and do nothing (*phr*)
stick to your guns (*phr*)
wrapped up in the moment (*phr*)

Dependent prepositions
appalled at
ashamed of
capable of
contrary to
eager to
impressed by/with
intent on
subject to

Other
cheer sb up (*phr v*)
do chores (*phr*)
volunteer (*v*)

Vocabulary

1 🔊 **5.15** Listen to four people. What phrasal verb does the beep represent?

1 .... 3 ....
2 .... 4 ....

2 🔊 **5.16** Listen and check your answers.

3 Complete the sentences with words or phrases from the *Dependent prepositions* and *Other* sections of the wordlist.

1 We were all very .... the quality of her work.
2 I felt .... myself for being so careless.
3 Our bins haven't been emptied for weeks. We feel really .... the local council.
4 I help my parents .... around the house but I don't enjoy it!
5 My son's .... help with the basketball match. He loves sport.
6 We need people to .... to deliver meals to the elderly.
7 Chatting to my neighbour always seems to .... and leave a smile on his face.
8 He often asks me to do the work for him, although he's more than .... doing it himself!

4 Complete the blog comments with phrases from the wordlist. You may need to change the tense and pronouns.

Who would win in a fight? YOU DECIDE.

» **Gandalf the Grey vs Dumbledore**

Steff: Dumbledore's a bit weak and it seems he can't ¹..................... to enter into any fight, to be honest. And he just seems to ²..................... while school kids do all his fighting. Gandalf ³..................... his friends' aid in every battle.

» **Pirates vs ninjas**

Max: Duh! Seriously? Ninjas, of course. Pirates are just a bunch of lazy no-hopers. Ninjas are always cool – they're able to calm down and ⁴..................... so they can make sensible choices, even in the middle of a fight.

» **A gorilla vs ten fully grown men**

Stinkboy: The gorilla would win. Gorillas don't tire easily, plus they'd be so ⁵..................... that they wouldn't think twice about whether they were doing something wrong. Perhaps if all the men ran at him at the same time, they could ⁶..................... to the floor.

5 Write your own blog entry on one of these epic fights or choose your own. Use at least three phrases from the wordlist.
- Hulk vs Superman
- great white shark vs giant squid

UNIT CHECK

Review

1 🔊 5.17 Listen to a boy talking about parties. What is his opinion?

2 🔊 5.18 Complete the sentences with these words and a suitable comparative form of the adjectives in brackets. Listen again and check your answers.

---
far   just   nowhere near   twice   way
---

1 They're .... (good) as everyone expects them to be.
2 Movies make them out to be .... (exciting) they ever are.
3 Most kids are .... (likely) to talk to someone new at a big party as they are sitting in the library or at home.
4 These days you're .... (likely) to end up with a bunch of strangers on the doorstep as before.
5 It's .... (interesting) staying at home and hanging out with friends.

3 Read the article. What four things can counteract the bystander effect?

Counteracting the bystander effect

A society where strangers help each other is a desirable thing, so what can counteract the bystander effect? In a study, researchers asked an actor to lie on the street and pretend to be sick. Many people walked past, and they [1].......................... but they didn't. Several bystanders thought the man [2].......................... too much, and that they [3].......................... anything even if they'd wanted to. However, the researchers asked another actor to pretend to help and as soon as just one person stepped in, almost all the other people then tended to join in. It seems that some form of knowledge, such as medical training, makes people more willing to help.

Previous personal experience is also important. Survivors of an accident or a tragic event often say they felt they [4].......................... more on that occasion and were more likely to lend a hand in the future. It [5].......................... bad luck on the day of the study that the people were in a bad mood. The people who walked past [6].......................... positive about themselves that day because people in a good mood tend to help more.

4 Read the article again and complete it with these words and a suitable modal verb in the past.

---
just   be   do   drink   feel   help   stop
---

5 Complete the second sentence so that it has a similar meaning to the first sentence using the word given. Do not change the word given. Use between three and six words.

1 Not going to the party was a mistake.
   SHOULD
   I .... the party.
2 I'd expected my friend's birthday party to be so much more fun.
   NOWHERE
   My friend's birthday party was .... I'd expected.
3 We attended a launch party for the new film shot last year.
   WHICH
   We attended a launch party for the new film .... last year.
4 People always say that my town's annual fair is the best party for miles.
   BELIEVED
   The annual fair in my town .... the best party for miles.
5 The number of visitors doubled this year.
   TWICE
   There were .... compared to last year.
6 Because my mum allowed me to stay up, I was able to go to the party.
   HAVING
   I was able to go to the party, ... up by my mum.

6 Look at the photo. What do you think might have happened? Write five sentences using modal verbs in the past. Then work in pairs and compare your ideas.

"I love that the city never sleeps."

Look at the photo and discuss the questions.

1 What three words best describe city life for you?
2 How does city life compare to rural life in your country?
3 How has the place where you live shaped who you are in terms of your character, your interests, your dreams, etc.?

Urban tales

6

READING
topic: modern ruins
skill: understanding connected ideas
task: gapped text

GRAMMAR
past and present narrative tenses
phrasal verbs

VOCABULARY
describing city life; compound words
adjective suffixes

LISTENING
topic: street fashion
skill: understanding agreement and disagreement
task: multiple choice: longer text

USE OF ENGLISH
open cloze
word formation

SPEAKING
topic: important features of a city
skill: coming to a conclusion in a minute
task: collaborative task and discussion

WRITING
topic: a film with an important location
skill: using higher level vocabulary
task: review

SWITCH ON
video: Banksy's school visit
project: art planning

6 Urban tales

READING

Power up

1 Work in pairs and discuss the questions.
1 How modern is your city? Are there any old buildings that aren't used anymore?
2 Do you think older buildings add character to an area or should they be pulled down? Why?
3 How do you feel when you look at the building in the photo? Why? Use these words to help you.

crumbling   debris   decay   grand   impressive
luxurious

2 Read the heading and subheading of the article. What two questions do you hope the article will answer? Work in pairs and compare your ideas.

Read on

3 Read the article. Does it answer your questions from Ex 2?

4 Read the exam tip. Complete the examples with the words in bold in the article. Can you think of any more examples for each category?

exam tip: gapped text
Look for linkers and other organisational phrases to help you identify how the ideas in a text are organised and how the information in paragraphs is connected.

addition	not only that but, ..., ... / ....
comparison	similarly, ... / ....
contrast	in contrast, ..., ... / .... / ....
cause	since, ..., ... / ....
effect	thus, ... / ....

5 e Read the article again and choose from the paragraphs (A–G) the one which fits each gap (1–6). There is one extra paragraph which you do not need to use.

Sum up

6 Answer the questions.
1 What reasons in the article support tours of Detroit's ruins?
2 What reasons are given that oppose them?
3 Would you like to go on the tour? Why/Why not?

7 Find words or phrases in the article that mean the following.
1 the state of being unable to pay your debts (para ii)
2 left by its owners (para ii)
3 failure to look after something or someone (para iv)
4 fall down because a building is weak or damaged (para vi)
5 accept or admit something is true (para C)
6 completely dark (para E)

Speak up

8 Work in pairs and discuss the questions.
1 Is it important for a city to look attractive? Why/Why not?
2 How attractive is the area where you live? How could it be improved?
3 How do you think people will view modern buildings in 100 years from now?

A Debris **like** this makes urban exploration physically dangerous. **In addition**, we could be fined for trespassing, which is why all tour participants are required to sign a form to say they take full responsibility for their actions.

B **Due to** increased competition in the motor industry, the demand for workers in Detroit began to fall. **Unlike** New York, people in Detroit chose to live out in the suburbs, which **resulted in** a city spread far and wide that affected people's abilities to find work near home.

C The locals believe that if less time were spent talking about Detroit's historical past and more time on the potential of its future than it would be much easier to attract investment from outside sources. Although others do acknowledge that its history is something that can be built upon.

D However, it turns out that people do have an interest in preserving Detroit's history, **even though** it may not always feel like it. A grand, old theatre, currently used as a car park, will soon be renovated. **While** the new owners will use it for big events, not plays, the ornate ceiling will be protected.

E It is certainly not an easy task and we all have to crawl on our hands and knees but once in, we stand up straight. It appears to be pitch black at first but our eyes soon adjust to the lack of light and we start to take in the scenery around us.

F **Despite** this comparison, the two situations are different **as** Detroit's problems are man-made. The ruined buildings here represent the best of human innovation and craftsmanship, **not to mention** the worst of human greed. They also represent the dreams of all those who travelled to the area to find work in the mid-1900s.

G **Nevertheless**, not everyone has this same desire to explore the buildings in this way. Many locals feel frustrated that the buildings focus on their negative past and not the positive potential of their future.

LOOKING FOR BEAUTY IN DECAY

Go on a tour of Detroit's ruined buildings with journalist Elspeth Thompson.

i The rapid growth of Detroit as the automobile capital of the world in the first half of the twentieth century made it a very significant city. Art deco skyscrapers, luxury hotels and impressive theatres were built to accommodate its growth as well as demonstrate its wealth. It was a time of huge investment, which did not last.

1

ii The decline of the city meant grand buildings of the early twentieth century were abandoned. When the city was going through bankruptcy in 2013–14, its urban decay made headlines. People who had seen the news wanted to see it for themselves, in the same way that visitors to Italy want to see the volcanic destruction of Pompeii.

2

iii It is this destruction of ideological hopes that has brought me here one Sunday in May, on a tour of an old hotel. Along with a group of nine others, I would like to see the decay up close and reflect on what it all means. So, here I am, armed with my camera, ready to make my way through the side entrance of the building.

3

iv Next, we walk down a corridor and go through a set of faded doors. We are now standing in what looks like a once grand dining room. The high ceilings are still colourful in places and they are incredibly ornate. However, **thanks to** neglect, the ceiling and walls are crumbling and there is concrete all over the floor, **as well as** wood and old items of furniture.

4

v Yet, this has not deterred the people on the tour today. We take photos and admire the workmanship, materials and money that must have gone into the building all those decades ago. We find the beauty among the dirt and graffiti. It might sound surprising but it isn't hard.

5

vi I start to get annoyed myself. I'm angry at the way the building has been left to collapse. A fellow tour participant tells me of the first time he felt this way on a tour. 'I'm standing in this beautiful old theatre looking at this exquisite architecture,' he says, 'and I notice a huge piece of ornate ceiling which has fallen to the floor and I realise that no one cares.'

6

vii In a similar spirit, the David Whitney Building, a skyscraper in the downtown area of the city, was renovated in 2014 and now comprises a boutique hotel and luxury residences. The building's website describes it as 'The grandeur of Detroit's past. The promise of its future'. Let's hope projects like these **lead to** more people seeing the city's true beauty.

What do these cities have in common: Kolmanskop, Namibia; Bodie, USA; Ghost Island, Japan? → p175

6 Urban tales

GRAMMAR

1 Read the grammar box. Complete the example sentences with the correct form of these verbs.

fall   go   notice   see   stand   want

explore grammar → p152

past and present narrative tenses

We generally use past narrative tenses to tell stories about the past.
When the city ¹_____ through bankruptcy in 2013–14, its urban decay made headlines. People who ²_____ the news ³_____ to see it for themselves.

We can use present narrative tenses to make a story more engaging or when we are when describing a book or film.
'So, I ⁴_____ in this beautiful old theatre looking at this exquisite architecture,' he says. 'and I ⁵_____ a huge piece of ceiling which ⁶_____ to the floor'.

2 ▶ 🔊 6.1 Watch or listen to five people talking about their experiences of visiting a new city. Which speakers use the past narrative? Which use the present narrative?

3 ▶ 🔊 6.2 Choose the correct verb forms in the sentences. Watch or listen again and check your answers.

1. The only window ... was fine, but then they**'d had / were having** a party downstairs till about 5 a.m.
2. They were so confused it **was / was being** so embarrassing. We **can't / couldn't** get a spoon to save our lives!
3. **I'm / was** on my bike, cycling along with my boyfriend and we**'re trying / 'd tried** to get to the beach.
4. We end up at the beach but it's the wrong beach and we **went / 've gone** about three miles the wrong way.
5. Nobody **had spoken / spoke** English apart from one person. ... And he **was wearing / wore** a Boy Scout uniform.
6. You know, I was twenty-one. Nobody **had called / called** me 'sir' before!
7. So, when I **was travelling / had travelled** by myself in Milan ... I **got / 've got** food poisoning.
8. In the end I just sort of **pretended / was pretending** to throw up on him and he **gave / 'd given** me some pills.

4 Work in pairs. Use the photos and your imagination to tell an engaging story about a young boy who was lost in a city. Follow these steps.

1. Put the photos in a logical order.
2. Tell the story using either past or present narrative tenses but be consistent.
3. Use the words under each photo to help you.

5 🔊 6.3 Listen and compare your story with the true story.

Speak up

6 Work in pairs and discuss the questions.

1. When Saroo moved to Australia, what do you think he found most surprising, difficult and frightening?
2. How would you cope with moving to a city like Mumbai, with a completely different culture?

A 1,000 miles away, wander the streets, threats

B rescue, orphanage, Australia, adopted

C grow up, locate, satellite images, landmarks, success

D Saroo, four-year-old, Indian train station, lose brother

VOCABULARY

describing city life

1 Put the letters in order to form words related to city life. Each first letter is in bold. Which words relate to the photo below?

tonw**d**own   go**m**s   bu**s**rbus   pak**s**ecrsyr

2 Choose the correct adjectives to complete the sentences. Then work in pairs and decide which adjectives you could use to describe your city.

1 I'd describe my area as **industrial / upmarket** as it has loads of factories and very few **bustling / green** areas.
2 The air in this area is pretty clean now but **civic / neighbouring** areas are still **fashionable / polluted**.
3 This district's been **industrialised / redeveloped** and is full of trendy, modern flats with **communal / pedestrian** gardens rather than private ones.
4 We recently moved to a **congested / suburban** area. After midnight the streets are **deserted / metropolitan** and quiet.

compound words

3 Read the blog about a city app, ignoring the gaps. Would you like to use this app? Why/Why not?

4 Complete the blog by adding these words to make compound words.

built-   construction   housing   industrial   inner-   never-   roof   run-   sky   water

5 Read the language box. Which words in Ex 4 are compound nouns? How are they formed? Which are compound adjectives?

explore language

forming compound words

Compound nouns are made up of an adjective + noun (e.g. *industrial estate*) or two nouns (e.g. *rooftop*). They are sometimes written as one word and sometimes as two separate words. Compound adjectives are often written with a hyphen (e.g. *run-down*).

6 🔊 6.4 Match a word from each group to make compound words. Listen and check your answers.

back.   convenience   high-   market
noise   pedestrian   traffic   world-

crossing   famous   jam   place
pollution   rise   streets   store

Speak up

7 Work in pairs. Complete the tasks using as many words from this page as possible.

1 Compare the area where you live to another area.
2 Describe what you would see if you took a different route to school one day.

Taking a 'dérive'

Frustrated by walking the same ¹_____ city streets every day, 1940s Parisian artists took unplanned routes named 'dérive'. Last week my friend and I used an app to try it ourselves. Our normal route home from school takes us through a ²_____ estate with blocks of flats but the app's route took us through a neighbouring ³_____ estate. The factories there are quite ⁴_____ down but looking at the ⁵_____ tops, I noticed a beautiful old chimney worthy of a photo. I uploaded it and immediately got some likes. In contrast, nearby was a ⁶_____ site where a new glass-fronted office block was going up. Next, the app guided us along the ⁷_____ front. I'd been there many times but never looked at it closely. I took photos of the pretty ⁸_____ line across the river.

The dérive has made me appreciate this ⁹_____ up area of the city more. In fact, I might even stop complaining about the ¹⁰_____ ending walk to school.

What difference can a hyphen make? 'Look, there's a man-eating fish!' 'Look, there's a man eating fish.'

6 Urban tales

LISTENING

Power up

1 Work in pairs and discuss the questions.

1 What or who influences what people wear? How?
2 Are you influenced by the same things? Why/Why not?
3 How would you define 'street fashion'?

Listen up

2 6.5 Listen to four conversations about fashion. Decide if each pair agrees or disagrees with each other.

3 6.6 Read the exam tip. Listen again and complete the examples in the tip.

> **exam tip: multiple choice: longer text**
>
> Listen for adverbs or other phrases to help you identify agreement or disagreement. Don't forget to listen out for a 'but', as people often express some agreement before they disagree!
>
> ¹.......................... high street fashion is often different to catwalk fashion.
>
> Yeah, friends are ².......................... influential but …
>
> Yeah, ³.........................., that's how trends spread.
>
> Fashion magazines have an impact but not ⁴.......................... on people my age.

4 6.7 You are going to listen to a fashion trend forecaster, Danielle, and a fashion retailer, Richard, discussing how fashion is created. For questions 1–6, choose the answer (A, B, C or D) which fits best according to what you hear.

1 How does Danielle feel about the way new fashions are established?
   A frustrated by how long it takes
   B convinced that normal consumers are the key
   C irritated by the amount of research required
   D aware of the need to involve all forms of media

2 Richard believes that designers ultimately want to
   A gain financial benefits.
   B establish a reputation.
   C use sustainable resources.
   D produce high quality goods.

3 What does Richard suggest should be a priority for a successful fashion retailer?
   A consulting a colour forecaster
   B working with a fabric manufacturer
   C using a designer's portfolio
   D having a clear strategy

4 Richard and Danielle both think that fashion shows indicate
   A whether fashion forecasts were correct.
   B what designers will be most popular.
   C whether retailers purchased well.
   D what consumers will demand.

5 What does Danielle say about the accuracy of her forecasts?
   A She has caused problems for designers.
   B She has made few incorrect predictions.
   C She has plenty of regrets.
   D She has influenced many people.

6 How do Danielle and Richard both feel about the influence of social media on fashion?
   A worried about its effect on their work
   B nervous that it gives out too much information
   C unsure about its long-term effect on established fashion houses
   D irritated with the way it gives everyone a chance to predict fashion trends

Speak up

5 Work in groups. To what extent do you agree or disagree with these statements?

1 The clothes you wear show the world who you are.
2 You buy fashion but you own style.
3 Fashion is a waste of time, money and resources.

USE OF ENGLISH 1

1 Complete the conversation with the correct form of these phrasal verbs.

come through (x2)   go on (x4)   kick off (x2)   mess up (x2)

A: Did you know that the process of identifying fashion trends can ¹ .... for two years or more?

B: Can it? ² ...., tell me how.

A: Well, trend experts ³ .... the process by doing tonnes of research on what's happening around the world. They then make forecasts and once those have ⁴ ...., designers create their collections.

B: Really? I didn't know all that ⁵ .... behind the scenes. I just thought the new ideas all came from designers.

A: Yeah, I suppose that's because we only hear about trends when fashion show season ⁶ .... and then clothes ⁷ .... sale in the shops. I wonder if the experts ever ⁸ .... their predictions and upset the designers!

B: From what I've read, no, they don't ⁹ .... very often. Most ¹⁰ .... the process with their reputations intact!

2 Read the language box and answer the questions.

explore **language**   → p152

phrasal verbs

Some phrasal verbs can be both transitive and intransitive. The meaning may stay the same or it may be different.

I know you have the answer, but don't **shout it out** to everyone! (transitive)

When I saw her take the wrong coat, I **shouted out**. (intransitive)

Which phrasal verbs in Ex 1 are transitive? Which are intransitive? Which ones have a different meaning when they have an object?

3 Read the sentences and add an object where necessary.
1. I carry my phone because I can't fit .... in my pocket.
2. I love to dress .... up for special occasions.
3. I try to wear what others wear so I can fit .... in.
4. If I'm cold, I put on a thick cardigan to warm .... up.
5. When I wear something new, I always show .... off.
6. If my feet are cold, I get out some socks and warm .... up on a radiator before putting them on.
7. I sometimes show .... off when I'm with people I don't know because I'm nervous and want them to like me.
8. I think babies look silly when their parents dress .... up in animal costumes.

4 Work in pairs and dicuss. Are the sentences in Ex 3 true for you? Why/Why not?

5 Read the blog. Do you agree with the author's views?

Life gets better when you give up trying to be *cool*

At some point in our lives, we all want to be cool so we fit ¹ .... But while some people are naturally cool, the rest of us are working hard just to make sure that we are. The problem ² ...., the cool people are enjoying their lives because they're being true to themselves while the rest of us are miserable copying them. But we can turn ³ .... situation around. Happiness comes when you give up being cool.

⁴ .... fashion, for example. Is it worth you putting ⁵ .... through the pain of trying to live ⁶ .... to the standards of everyone else just to blend in? It wasn't until I realised that literally ninety percent of my closet was filled with fuzzy pink sweaters that I finally faced up ⁷ .... the fact that this was me. It was ⁸ .... fashionable nor cool, but it represented the way I see myself. As soon as you wear clothes for you and not somebody else, you stop worrying about what's cool.

6 e Read the blog in Ex 5 again and complete the gaps with one word only.

Speak up

7 Complete the questions with one word in each gap. Then work in pairs and discuss the questions.
1. Who do you look up .... when it comes to fashion? Why?
2. In your view, what is the worst fashion item that a designer has dreamt .... ? Why?
3. Would you encourage a friend with an extreme style of fashion to blend .... more? Why/Why not?

Why did the golfer have an extra pair of trousers? In case he got a hole in one!

6 Urban tales

USE OF ENGLISH 2

1 Work in pairs and discuss the questions.
1. Would you describe the area where you live as trendy? Why/Why not?
2. What fun or exciting events happen where you live? Describe them.

2 🔊 6.8 Listen to a news story about an event in Reykjavik, Iceland. What happened and why?

3 🔊 6.9 Read the language box and complete the examples with these words and a suffix. More than one answer might be possible. Listen again and check your answers.

access   chill   co-operate   exception   notice
photograph   rest   thank

explore language ➔ p161

adjective suffixes

We can use the following suffixes to turn verbs and nouns into adjectives. We may need to omit or change letters when we add the suffix.

-able	preferable, ¹............................
-ible	reversible, ²............................
-ly/-y	costly, ³............................
-less	worthless, ⁴............................
-ive	preventative, ⁵............................
-al	optional, ⁶............................
-ful	dreadful, ⁷............................
-ic	strategic, ⁸............................

game on

Work in pairs. Think of as many more examples for each suffix in the language box as possible in two minutes.

4 Read the article about another unusual city event. What's your opinion of the event? Why?

The city that banned men

It was a girl's night out of the kind never seen before as women in Bogota, Colombia had fun on the orders of the mayor. The ¹............................ event was the idea of the mayor, who felt it would be ²............................ for women to enjoy time with friends at women-only concerts and open-air parties. Men had to stay home and look after the children – not easy for those who are usually ³............................ when it comes to childcare. They were banned from even setting foot outside their homes without a special pass.

After the event, while women were positive about it, men were less ⁴............................. Some believed it was ⁵............................ while others claimed the mayor was being ⁶............................ in spending a lot of money on this event when other issues were more urgent.

Despite the controversy that this ⁷............................ initiative has attracted, it seems that people are ⁸............................ the mayor will drop it. He has even promised a men-only night in the near future.

CONTROVERSY
BENEFIT

INVOLVE

ENTHUSE
POINT
RESPONSIBILITY

COST

DOUBT

5 ℯ Read the article in Ex 4 again. Use the word given at the end of some of the lines to form a word that fits in the gap in the same line. Then read the exam tip and check your answers.

exam tip: word formation

When you've filled the gaps, don't forget to read the article through one more time to check it makes sense with the words you've written.

Speak up

6 Work in pairs. What fun or exciting event would you like to see in your city? Why? Share your best idea with the class.

SPEAKING

Power up

1 Work in pairs. Match these words with the prompts in the diagram on the right.

architecture   congestion   keep fit
living standards   well-being

2 🅴 In pairs, discuss the question and prompts in the diagram for two minutes.

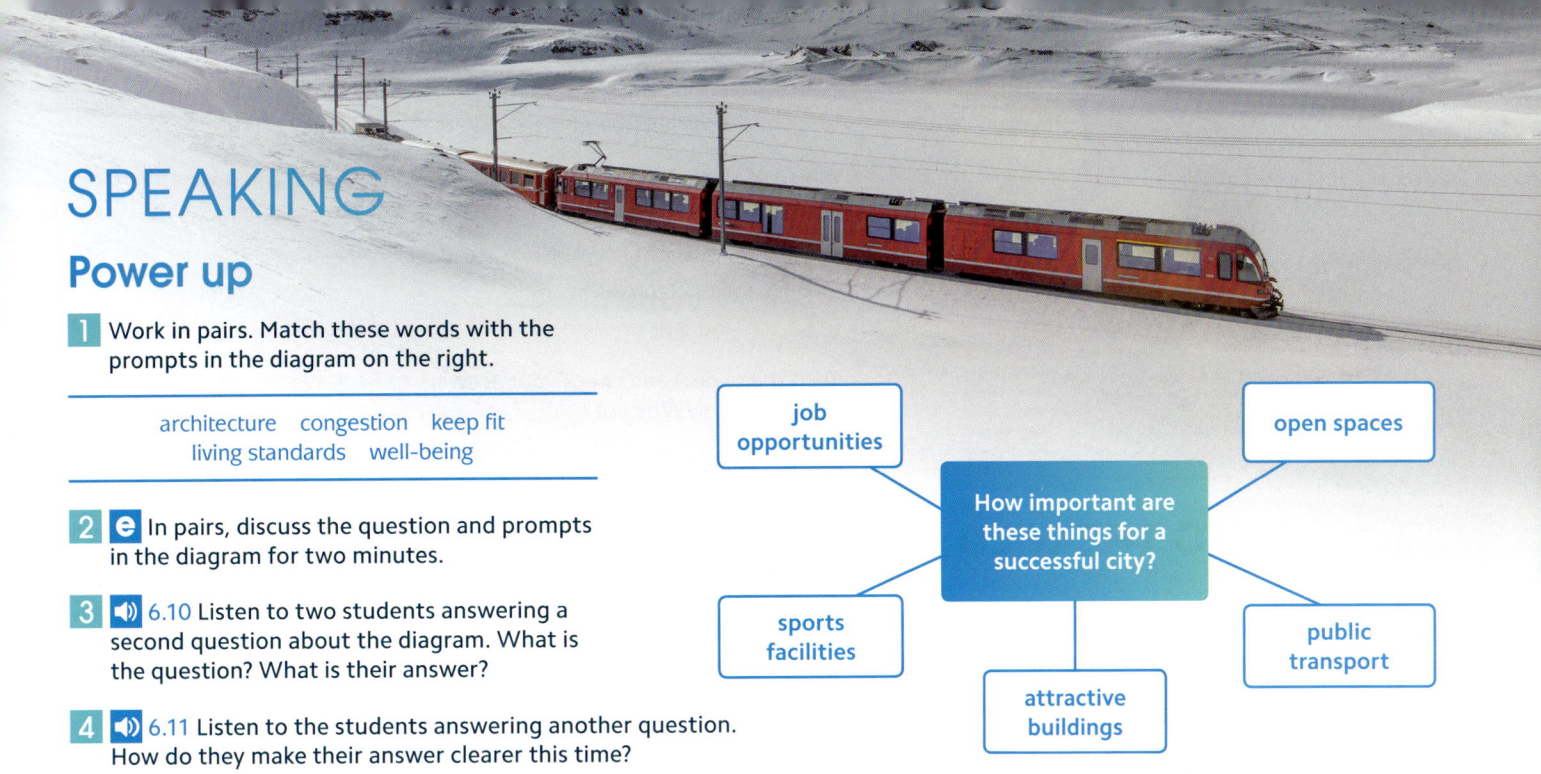

3 🔊 6.10 Listen to two students answering a second question about the diagram. What is the question? What is their answer?

4 🔊 6.11 Listen to the students answering another question. How do they make their answer clearer this time?

Diagram

How important are these things for a successful city?
- job opportunities
- open spaces
- sports facilities
- public transport
- attractive buildings

Speak up

5 Work in pairs. Read the exam tip and complete the task.

> ### exam tip: collaborative task
> In the exam, you won't lose marks if you don't have time for the conclusion or can't agree. However, it's still a good idea to practise speaking for one minute so you can learn to discuss the question and try to come to a conclusion in that time.
>
> Start a timer. Speak together about the prompts in the diagram and stop when you think a minute is up. Check the timer. How close were you?

6 Work in pairs. Decide in one minute which two things in the diagram have the greatest effect on people's daily lives. Summarise your ideas and come to a conclusion. Use one of these phrases to begin your summary.

In short, …   So, …   So, basically then, …   To sum up then, …

7 Work in pairs and discuss three or four of the questions for three minutes. Give reasons. Use these phrases to help you agree and disagree politely.

I completely agree.   I agree to a certain extent/ up to a point/in some ways.
That's a good point, but …

1 What's the biggest problem for people who live in a city?
2 Do you think it's the responsibility of ordinary citizens or the local government to solve urban issues?
3 Why do you think some people prefer living in the countryside to living in a city?
4 How are people who live in cities different from those who live in rural areas?
5 Do you think the pace of city life today creates too much stress?
6 How might cities of the future be different to cities of today?

Speaking extra

8 Work in groups of five. You are all city councillors. Read the agenda. What's the purpose of the meeting?

COUNCIL MEETING
Monday 6 April

Agenda

1 Decide which city initiatives to spend our £1m budget on. Options:
- new music venue (£600,000)
- new children's hospital ward (£650,000)
- street cleaners (£150,000)
- new park (£250,000)
- improved sports centre (£400,000)
- new tram line (£350,000)

9 In your groups, decide who is councillor A, B, C, D and E. Read about your interest and decide which initiative(s) you will support and why.

- Councillor A: You are interested in people's health.
- Councillor B: You want to make the city more fun.
- Councillor C: You want to attract visitors to the city.
- Councillor D: You care about the environment.
- Councillor E: You want to attract business to the city.

10 Roleplay the council meeting. Debate the options and decide as a group how to spend the £1m budget.

6 Urban tales

WRITING

Power up

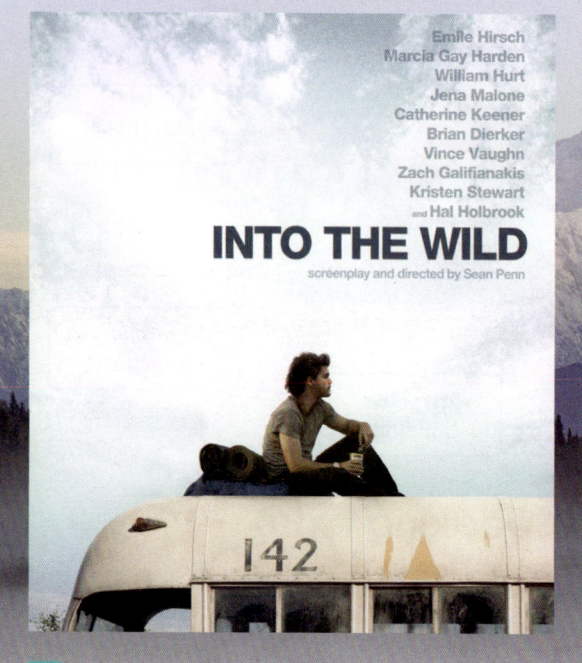

1 Work in groups and discuss the questions.
1. What are three of your favourite films or TV series? Why?
2. Which of these things do you think have the biggest impact on whether the story in a film or TV series is engaging or not?
   - acting
   - action
   - characters
   - lighting
   - location
   - music
   - script
   - special effects
3. How important is location to your favourite films/TV series? Why?

Plan on

2 You see this advertisement on a student website. What two things do you have to write about?

Location, location, location

In some films or TV series the location is central to the story, while others could be set anywhere. We're looking for reviews from you about a film or TV series that you've seen where the location is vital to the plot.

Tell us why the location was so important to the story and the impact the location had on you in 220–260 words.

We'll publish the best reviews on our website.

3 Which of these things do you think should feature in the review? Why?
- title
- full description of the plot
- language of comparison
- formal language
- recommendation(s)
- examples
- rhetorical question(s)

4 Read the review and check your answers to Ex 3. Would you like to see this film? Why/Why not?

Life in the wilderness

What's the first thing that comes to mind when you think of Alaska? Chances are it's snow, ice or the cold. It's a vast, unforgiving landscape which helped create the true story of Christopher McCandless in the film *Into the Wild*.

McCandless has a difficult relationship with his parents, so he leaves home straight after university and spends two years travelling around the USA. He then decides to break from society completely and connect more fully with nature. He heads to Alaska, where winter is making way for spring and the landscape is green and lush. This cleverly mirrors McCandless's own state of mind at the time. As we see him looking for food, everything around him is alive, which suggests he feels this way too.

I hadn't read the book that the film is based on, so I was unaware of McCandless's journey. I found the location to be a stunning backdrop to his tragic story, one essentially about our relationship with nature and each other. While I wanted McCandless to succeed in living off the land in isolation, the film — and Alaska — subtly made me aware that nature is a power unto itself; something that became more apparent as the film headed ominously towards its conclusion.

Without Alaska, the film would have been unable to tell the real-life story of an idealistic young man attempting to escape the ties of normal life. The breathtaking scenery demonstrated that, while we may wish to bond with nature, we cannot control it and are ultimately at its mercy.

5 Work in pairs and discuss the questions.
1. What is the purpose of each of the four paragraphs?
2. Why does the writer start with a question?
3. What is the purpose of the adverbs 'cleverly' (para 2) and 'subtly' (para 3)?
4. Does the writer use a range of tenses and other grammatical structures? Find examples.
5. Does the writer use a range of vocabulary? Find examples.

6 Read part of a review. Complete it with the correct form of the verbs in brackets.

MOVIE REVIEWS

The Shawshank Redemption ★★★★☆

The Shawshank Redemption ¹............... (tell) the story of a man who goes to prison for a crime he says he ²............... (not commit). At the Shawshank Prison, Andy Dufresne **suffers through** life with the help of a man called Red, who ³............... (be) at the jail for some years already. From Red, Andy ⁴............... (learn) how to live a **comparatively comfortable** life there, while all the time he ⁵............... (dream of) life on a **distant beach**.

When watching this film, the prison setting and the dark lighting ⁶............... (make) me feel as if I ⁷............... (experience) everything with Andy. The **strict**, cruel prison warden ⁸............... (cause) me to **worry about** Andy's fate as well as to **understand** what life would be like without personal **freedom**. By the end of the film I felt as if I ⁹............... (be) on a huge emotional rollercoaster. Reactions like this are why the film, not a **hit** on its release, ¹⁰............... (since / become) a classic cult movie.

7 Read the language box. Choose the more advanced words in the examples.

explore language

using higher level vocabulary

Use a range of higher level vocabulary when you write to keep readers engaged.

1 The actor **portrays** / **plays** the character as weak.
2 You'll love it so much that you'll have to **replay it** / **play it again**.
3 The channel **broadcasts** / **shows** a new episode each week.
4 The character is **sent to prison** / **imprisoned**.

8 Replace the highlighted words and phrases in the review in Ex 6 with these more advanced words and phrases.

appreciate   box office success   endures
faraway   be fearful of   liberty   painless
relatively   shore   stern

Write on

9 You are going to write a review. Make notes under these headings.
- Film/TV series name and location
- The location was important
- How it impacted on me

10 Work in pairs. Take turns to tell each other about the film or TV series you are going to review. Use your notes to help you. Ask questions to help each other think of ideas for your review.

11 Plan your review by adding your notes to a paragraph plan. Think about the grammar and vocabulary you will use.

12 e Write your review in 220–260 words.

Improve it

13 Work in pairs. Read your partner's review and make a note of the purpose of each paragraph. Tell your partner if each purpose is clear.

14 Read your review and answer the questions.
1 Do you agree with your partner about the clarity of ideas in your paragraphs?
2 Is the tone appropriate for a review?
3 Do you use present and past narrative tenses accurately?
4 Do you use a range of higher level vocabulary?

15 Use Ex 13 and 14 to help you edit and improve your review.

SWITCH ON

Banksy's school visit

1. Work in pairs. Do you consider graffiti to be art? Why/Why not?
2. ▶ Watch the clip. Name four cities where Banksy's works can be found.
3. ▶ Watch again. Make a note of the different reactions to Banksy's school mural from:
   - headteacher
   - the primary school teachers
   - a young pupil.
4. Work in pairs and answer the questions.
   1. We see two examples of graffiti being preserved. What are they?
   2. What Banksy piece is Westminster Council planning to remove?
   3. Why does gallery curator Andrew Mac think that preserving graffiti is a problem?
5. Work in pairs. Select a piece of graffiti from the video and explain its social commentary message.

Project

6. Work in groups to choose a space for graffiti in your home town.
   1. Research three different legal graffiti walls around the world.
   2. Find out:
      - why the space was allocated
      - is the wall visible or hidden
      - it's location in the town or city
      - how the local people feel about it?
   3. Decide on the best place for legal graffiti, what kind of graffiti you would like to see, and the benefits to the local area.
   4. Present your idea to the class. Use illustrations if necessary.
   6. Vote on the best space for legal graffiti.

INDEPENDENT LEARNING

Grammar and vocabulary

1. Answer the questions about Unit 6.
   1. Which parts of the unit do you think have been most useful? Why?
   2. What grammar and vocabulary have you studied in this unit? How confident do you feel about using them? Choose one of the options below or write your own statement.
      - ☐ I can generally use the grammar accurately when I speak and write.
      - ☐ I make some errors in the grammar when I speak and write.
      - ☐ I find it hard to use the new vocabulary when I speak.
      - ☐ I can use a range of the new vocabulary when I write.
      - ☐ Other: I ....
   3. What grammar or vocabulary from Unit 6 do you think you need to work on? Why?
   4. Below are some strategies learners can use to help them develop their use of grammar and vocabulary. What strategies for learning grammar and vocabulary have helped you while studying Units 1–6? Add them to the list.

   - Use a vocabulary app.
   - Ask a classmate to test you.
   - Talk about something and record yourself.
   - Write a short text and share it online.

2. Look at your answers to question 1 in Ex 1. Then choose two strategies to help you improve in the grammar/vocabulary areas you have chosen. Say how and when you will use them and how you think they will help you.

1
2

UNIT CHECK

Wordlist

Describing city life
bustling (adj)
civic (adj)
communal (adj)
congested (adj)
deserted (adj)
industrial (adj)
industrialised (adj)
metropolitan (adj)
neighbouring (adj)
pedestrian (adj/n)
redeveloped (adj)
residential (adj)
suburban (adj)
upmarket (adj)

Compound words
back street (n)
built-up (adj)
construction site (n)
convenience store (n)
high-rise (building) (adj)
housing estate (n)
industrial estate (n)
inner city (n)
marketplace (n)
never-ending (adj)
noise pollution (n)
pedestrian crossing (n)
rooftop (n)
run-down (adj)
skyline (n)
traffic jam (n)
waterfront (n)
world-famous (adj)

Phrasal verbs
blend in
come through
dream up
dress up
face up to
fit in
kick off
go on
live up to
look up to
mess up
put through
show off
turn around
warm up

Adjective suffixes
accessible
chilly
controversial
co-operative
costly
doubtful
dreadful
enthusiastic
exceptional
inactive
invaluable
irresponsible
noticeable
optional
photographic
pointless
preferable
preventative
restless
reversible
strategic
thankful
worthless

Other
abandoned (adj)
acknowledge (v)
bankruptcy (n)
collapse (v)
neglect (v)
pitch black (adj)

Vocabulary

1 🔊 **6.12** Listen to eight people. What word from the *Describing city life* and *Compound words* sections of the wordlist does the beep represent?

1 .... 5 ....
2 .... 6 ....
3 .... 7 ....
4 .... 8 ....

2 🔊 **6.13** Listen and check your answers.

3 Use the words in brackets to form a word that fits in each sentence. Then check your answers in the *Adjective suffixes* and *Other* sections of the wordlst.

1 The food festival was .... (cost), but it was definitely successful.
2 Some of the music was .... (dread) though.
3 It was .... (notice) that people disliked it.
4 The play facilities made the festival .... (access) for children.
5 We were .... (thank) it didn't rain.
6 I won a prize but it was only a .... (worth) plastic toy.
7 The food we had was .... (exception). I've never tasted better!
8 Tickets were .... (cost) and therefore .... (controversy).

4 Replace the highlighted words in the sentences with the correct form of a word/phrase from the *Phrasal verbs* and *Other* sections of the wordlist. You may need to add an object.

1 The food festival started at around lunchtime.
2 Last year the organisers made a mistake with the festival.
3 Organisers made the event successful after last year's failed event.
4 I was made to experience the pain of listening to the awful band for hours.
5 I was so tired when I left the festival that I was ready to fall over.
6 The lack of lighting made it hard to see as we left the site. It was very dark.
7 It was sad to see so many deserted buildings near the festival site.
8 Next year organisers will have to make sure they meet people's expectations.

UNIT CHECK

Review

1 Read Zak's anecdote about a misunderstanding in Tokyo. Complete it with the correct past form of the verbs in brackets. Who do you think the dentist really was?

A couple of years ago my parents and I ¹.......................... (visit) my sister in Tokyo, where she ².......................... (work). My parents ³.......................... (go out) for the day, leaving me with my sister.

Unfortunately, while we ⁴.......................... (have) lunch, I ⁵.......................... (break) my tooth. My sister had to go to work, but she pointed me in the direction of a dentist. I set off to try and find it. I was in a lot of pain and it felt as if I ⁶.......................... (walk) for ages by the time I ⁷.......................... (find) the right place, or so I thought. Anyway, it was a kind of studio in the back garden of a house. I ⁸.......................... (cannot) speak Japanese and I ⁹.......................... (forget) to get my sister to write me a note in Japanese, so I used lots of gestures to convey the fact I had tooth pain. He told me to lie down on this bed, not a typical dentist chair. While I ¹⁰.......................... (lie) there, I ¹¹.......................... (get) a sense that something wasn't quite right. Suddenly, he leant over and produced this needle from the table next to him and started waving it near my ear. I quickly ¹².......................... (get up), ¹³.......................... (make) my apologies and ¹⁴.......................... (find) my way home.

2 🔊 6.14 Listen and check your answers to Ex 1. Who was the man?

3 Zak is now telling the story using the present narrative tense to make it sound more exciting. Complete it with the correct present form of the verbs in brackets.

So, my sister ¹.......................... (live) in Tokyo and one week my parents and I ².......................... (decide) to visit her. One day my sister and I ³.......................... (have) lunch when I hear this horrible crunch and realise I ⁴.......................... (break) a tooth. My sister ⁵.......................... (cannot) take me to the dentist because she has to go to work and my parents ⁶.......................... (go out) on a day trip, so she ⁷.......................... (direct) me to a dentist. By the time I arrive, I ⁸.......................... (walk) for around twenty minutes, which seems further than she suggested, but still I go in. The guy can't speak English and I ⁹.......................... (not ask) my sister to write down any instructions, so I use gestures to explain the problem. He ¹⁰.......................... (ask) me to lie down on this chair, which I do. While I ¹¹.......................... (lie) there, I start to feel a bit uneasy. And that's when he suddenly ¹².......................... (produce) this really long, thin needle and ¹³.......................... (start) moving it towards my ear. I ¹⁴.......................... (panic), sit up, bow my head in apology and get out of there as fast as I can!

4 🔊 6.15 Listen and check your answers to Ex 3.

5 Read the blog and complete the gaps with one word only.

Communicating in a **foreign land**

New post   2 July

I was twenty-one when I first went travelling on my own. I ¹.......................... never been to Thailand before. In fact, I didn't even know where it was; I just wanted an adventure. When I landed in Bangkok, I was mobbed by people wanting to befriend me. I genuinely didn't know what to do, so I got on a bus. As it turned ².......................... , unfortunately, it was a bus going nowhere ³.......................... my destination. Nobody spoke English apart from an eleven-year-old child wearing a Boy Scout uniform. He must have ⁴.......................... heading to a scout meeting. He said, 'Can I help you, sir?' Nobody had called me 'sir' before and at no ⁵.......................... had I thought it would be by an eleven-year-old in a foreign country. The boy explained to me I was ⁶.......................... the wrong bus and told the driver ⁷.......................... had happened. The driver stopped, wrote down the correct information and eventually I got there. That experience helped me over the next three months. Whenever I didn't understand something, I found that kindness and a smile ⁸.......................... a long way.

6 Write a short amusing anecdote about you or someone you know in the narrative past or present. Share it with the class. Whose is the funniest?

> "I throw myself into everything I do."

Look at the photo and discuss the questions.
1 Read the quote. How true is it for you?
2 How else would you describe your attitude to life?
3 What three traits do you most admire in people? Why?

7

Mind and body

READING
topic: a girl's view on tidiness
skill: understanding writer purpose
task: multiple choice

GRAMMAR
subject-verb agreement
quantifiers

VOCABULARY
health and diet; phrasal verbs of food and drink
similar words

LISTENING
topic: becoming more competitive
skill: predicting words you might hear
task: sentence completion

USE OF ENGLISH
open cloze
multiple-choice cloze

SPEAKING
topic: exercise and relaxation
skill: linking ideas
task: long turn

WRITING
topic: changes to a canteen
skill: expressing ideas in a neutral way
task: proposal

SWITCH ON ▶
video: Pepper the robot
project: robot analysis

7 Mind and body

READING

Power up

1 Work in pairs and discuss the questions.
1 Do you and other members of your family ever argue over tidiness? Why do you think it's a common cause of disagreement?
2 What do you think a messy room says about a person's character?

2 Work in pairs. Read the exam tip and complete the lists with these words. Can you think of any more words to add?

essential   illustrates   negative   similarly

> **exam tip: multiple choice**
> When thinking about a writer's purpose, you can look for clues in the vocabulary and linking words that they use.
>
> | comparing | in the same way, like, ¹............... |
> |---|---|
> | persuading | necessary, must, ²............... |
> | criticising | ineffective, damaging, ³............... |
> | informing | shows, demonstrates, ⁴............... |

3 Read the sentences. What is the author's purpose in each one?
1 One study showed that messy people put on two kilos more weight than their tidy counterparts.
2 Messiness affects the millennial generation and we need to do something urgently.
3 Messy people are unproductive because they waste time locating objects.
4 My desk is messy. I tend to liken it to a daily brain-training workout.

Read on

4 Read the title of the article and the introduction. What idea will the text challenge?

5 Read question 1 in Ex 6. Match the options (A–D) with these purposes.

convincing   raising concern   comparing   informing

6 e Read the article and choose the answer (A, B, C or D) which you think fits best according to the text.

1 In the first paragraph, the writer wants the reader to
  A consider organisation in relation to other things that might matter.
  B understand the effect organisation can have on a person.
  C feel persuaded that organisation will be viewed differently in future.
  D be worried that organisation has failed to attract attention from academics.

2 When speaking about creativity and disorganised desks, the writer implies that
  A she feels that messy desks inhibit genuine creativity.
  B she considers messy people have received unfair treatment.
  C she believes too much attention has been paid to the problem.
  D she thinks messy desks force people to behave a certain way.

3 How does the writer feel about Kathlene Vohs' study?
  A convinced that people will never stop misjudging messy rooms
  B sceptical that she has reached any significant conclusion
  C concerned that the study was biased from the start
  D surprised that she limited the range of the study

4 What is the writer's purpose in describing Albert Einstein and Steve Jobs' desks?
  A to prove a point made previously
  B to recommend a particular course of action
  C to make a distinction between two concepts
  D to entertain the reader with amusing accounts

5 The writer believes that the state of teenage bedrooms illustrates that
  A it is distinct from the way messiness appears in adults.
  B there may be more worrying tendencies behind messiness.
  C there has been too much attention paid to what is a temporary phase.
  D it is an inevitable part of everyone's development.

6 What was the writer's main purpose in writing this article?
  A to justify the point that messiness indicates few other personality traits
  B to argue that messiness could have benefits if embraced in the right way
  C to make the case that individuals are responsible for their own messiness
  D to persuade people that messiness ultimately causes arguments with others

Sum up

7 Find two pieces of evidence in the article that support having a messy room, and two that suggest it is a bad idea.

Speak up

8 Work in pairs. Do you know anyone who is particularly messy? Do you think the mess reflects their creativity? How do you feel when you are in a place that is very messy?

My room was tidy … but then I had to decide what to wear!

MESSY ROOM, MESSY BRAIN?

All our lives organisation has been valued as a direct key to success. Whether at home, school or in your bedroom at camp, organisation is something that has been encouraged in everyone pretty much from birth. Being messy has been equally condemned and made out to be a quick path to failure, right up there with an early life of crime and dishonesty. No amount of counter-argument could say otherwise. I mean, what good can come from being disorganised, right? A study conducted by the University of Minnesota last year suggests that more good can come than you might think.

There has always been a sort of 'urban legend' that has floated around modern society that messy people have high levels of creativity. Frankly, I thought that people with 'messy desks' had to be creative, out of necessity, just to survive their levels of disorganisation. Last week's test in one corner; a page from last month's Sports Now magazine in another; empty drink cans distributed across the surface, like a battlefield. When you habitually fail to put things in their correct place, you're bound to get creative figuring out ways to make everything, I don't know, fit; and fit comfortably. While it might look completely random to strangers, a lot of times a person's mess is very sensible – with respect to him- or herself.

Psychologist Kathleen Vohs set out to put an end to this urban legend. She didn't limit her study to solely the desk. No, Vohs, clearly a creative mind, chose to think outside the desk. Using one messy room and one tidy room, and a series of trials, Vohs concluded that messy rooms encourage more creative thinking – and provided scientific evidence! The question Vohs failed to ask is, 'What exactly do we mean by 'creative thinking', and how will the mess in your room help?' Creative thinking, in its purest form, is thinking outside the lines of 'conventional' reasoning. When considering this, it should be no huge shock that messy rooms containing possessions misplaced from their 'conventional' location increase creativity.

Albert Einstein famously said, 'If a cluttered desk is a sign of a cluttered mind, then what are we to think of an empty desk?' Einstein's desk looked like an angry rival was intent on destroying his workspace – and succeeded. And no wonder Steve Jobs invented iBooks; his desk and office alike were truly disasters. But what does this mean to you? Trash your desks, trash your rooms and hope a touch of genius comes your way? Not exactly. The relationship between messiness and creativity is by no means casual, even if both do tend to occur at the same time. If you are 'messy by nature', perhaps finding a healthy balance between your usual mess and that urgency to clean is the best option. By limiting your sloppy desk, room or habits, you should keep in mind that you might also be limiting your overall creativeness.

> Of course, nobody does messy rooms quite like teenagers.

Of course, nobody does messy rooms quite like teenagers. So are the majority of teenagers misunderstood future creative geniuses? Well, it may just be that teen brains haven't quite got there yet cognitively – when it comes to sticking to clean-up routine. Things like controlling impulsiveness, seeing things from other people's point of view and understanding consequences all take time to be learnt. However, one concern is that there's a darker warning lurking behind the pile of clothes on the floor. That messy room might not be a sign of expressing independence or a lack of cognitive skills; it may be a fundamental indication that the person who owns the bits and pieces in a mess lacks self-control. Why bother with something so trivial? Well, self-control has been shown to be one of the best predictors of future success time and time again.

Ultimately, the only way to judge the effectiveness of your messy creativity is to go out and experiment for yourself. So, go ahead, make it rain with all your important files and paperwork, have fun! See what you come up with afterwards. But if you have a roommate, tell him not to send me any hate mail if your space turns into a zoo while you experiment with this. I am not to blame for any future messes my articles might encourage.

7 Mind and body

GRAMMAR

1 Identify the noun phrases in the sentences. Find the main subject and choose the correct singular or plural form of the verb.

1 Messy rooms containing possessions misplaced from their 'conventional' location **increases / increase** creativity.
2 Finding a healthy balance between your usual mess and that urgency to clean **is / are** the best option.
3 It may be a fundamental indication that the person who owns the bits and pieces in a mess **lacks / lack** self-control.

2 Read the grammar box. Complete the gaps in 1–3 with these words. Choose the correct words in 4–5.

either a singular or plural   a plural   a singular

explore grammar → p154

subject-verb agreement

Some nouns look singular but are followed by a plural verb or vice versa.

Nouns followed by **¹**............ verb: mathematics, series, athletics

Books and film titles are also followed by a singular verb (*X Men 2, Guardians of the Galaxy*).

Nouns followed by **²**............ verb: the media, the police, the Chinese, the disabled

Nouns followed by **³**............ verb: audience, class, staff, headquarters, data

In noun phrases expressing quantity, the verb agrees with the main noun (half the students are … , the majority of the work is …).

In complex noun phrases, the verb agrees with the main subject (often the first noun).

Finding a healthy balance between your usual mess and that urgency to clean **⁴is / are** the best option.

Things like controlling impulsiveness, seeing things for other people's views and understanding consequences all **⁵takes / take** time to be learnt.

3 🔊 7.1 Read the sentences with opinions about why popular team football shirts are so expensive. Choose the correct verb forms. Sometimes both are possible. Then listen and check your answers.

1 The club **take / takes** all the money.
2 The staff at the clubs **is / are** all overpaid.
3 Well, the government **takes / take** its share.
4 A number of people **is / are** involved in making the shirts.
5 The majority of the money **goes / go** to the shirt manufacturers.
6 I reckon the number of people making decent money **is / are** pretty small.

4 Which sentences in Ex 3 do you think are true? Turn to page 174 and check. Do you think the cost of football shirts is fair?

5 🔊 7.2 Listen to the sentences in Ex 3 again and notice the stress patterns. Practise saying the sentences.

6 Read the article. Where do teenagers get their money from in the UK? What do they spend it on?

TEEN SPENDING HABITS

The amount of money that teenagers **¹**............ (spend) on clothing **²**............ (recently / increase) and now equals the amount that they spend on food. A percentage of young people's spending **³**............ (always / go) on footwear and a large proportion of their spending **⁴**............ (continue) to go on sports shoes, but other forms of leisure wear **⁵**............ (start) to become more popular too. The results of this study **⁶**............ (suggest) quite clearly that teens are more interested in their appearance these days. Of the money which is spent on food, the coffee chain Starbucks **⁷**............ (be) a continual favourite among the older teen group. Where teens get their money from **⁸**............ (remain) relatively stable over the years. The majority of teens still **⁹**............ (depend) on their parents for their income, although the gap between pocket money or an allowance and the money that they earn through part-time work **¹⁰**............ (become) narrower in recent years.

7 Complete the article in Ex 6 with the correct form of the verbs in brackets. Use the present simple or present perfect.

Speak up

8 Work in pairs. What do you think are good and bad ways of spending your money? Why?

VOCABULARY

health and diet

1 🔊 **7.3** Listen to a man talking about health habits. Which of these things does he mention? Does he say that they are good or bad for your health?

low-fat yogurt   diet drinks   high-energy drinks   100-calorie snack packs
weight gain   coffee   working out for thirty minutes
taking a nap for twenty minutes

2 🔊 **7.4** Match the first half of each sentence (1–4) with the second half (A–D). Listen again and check your answers. Check that you understand the meaning of the words in bold.

1 If you're completely **knackered**,
2 Sugar gives you an **energy boost**
3 Both taking a **nap** and thinking about
4 Getting your **heartbeat** going

A will make you feel more **alert**.
B **posture** can help to wake you up.
C the **caffeine** in energy drinks might not help.
D but is usually followed by an **energy crash** soon after.

phrasal verbs of food and drink

3 Replace the phrases in bold in the sentences with these phrasal verbs. Then read the language box below and complete the task.

binge out on   cut out   eat out   go easy on   peel off   wind down

1 My parents like to **have a meal in a restaurant**, but I never enjoy it.
2 I always like to have chocolate in the evening to help me to **relax**.
3 I've decided to **stop eating** sugar and fat altogether from my diet.
4 I tend to eat healthily all week, and then **eat too much** junk food at the weekend.
5 I love apples but I don't like eating the skin, so I usually **remove it**.
6 I think as long as you **don't eat too much** meat, you can eat anything you like.

explore **language** ➡ p161

phrasal verbs

Sometimes you can find clues to the meaning of a phrasal verb in the particle. For example, 'take **off**' has the idea of removing something.

Which sentence in Ex 3 has the idea of removing something?

4 Look at the sentences in Ex 3. Which people have healthy attitudes to food? What advice would you give to the other people?

5 Read the article. What health advice does it offer?

Healthy eating habits that are surprisingly unhealthy

When it comes to healthy eating, you may be doing it all wrong. ¹............... regular soft drinks completely and replacing them with diet drinks may sound like a recipe for health, but a long-term study showed that those people who ²............... on diet drinks, thinking they are a healthy option, tend to pile on the pounds. Not that weighing yourself is all that useful. If you want to lose weight, you might think ³............... on certain foods and doing more exercise will help. Running certainly strengthens your ⁴..............., which is good, but pumping iron builds muscle and muscle is heavier than fat. You'll be in better shape, but you might actually be a bit heavier. Another myth is that you simply need to eat less. Small regular amounts of carbohydrates may only contain 100 calories but they may be doing nothing to give you an ⁵............... or help you nutritionally, and nobody feels lively and ⁶............... on a carb-heavy diet. A good tablespoon of peanut butter may do you more good thanks to the protein punch that it packs.

6 Read the article again and complete it with the correct form of a word from Ex 2 or a phrasal verb from Ex 3.

Speak up

7 Work in pairs. Do you think that there is too much pressure on people to eat or look a certain way?

7 Mind and body

LISTENING

Power up

1 Work in pairs and discuss the questions.

1. Rank these reasons for doing sport in order of importance for you.

   achieving a personal best   bonding in a team
   building self-esteem   developing fitness
   developing strength and stamina
   looking good on the beach   providing relaxation

2. You are going to hear a technology reviewer talk about the object in the photo. What do you think it does? How do you think it can help you achieve your sporting goals?

Listen up

2 Alan is an online technology reviewer. He is talking about the object in the photo. Read the exam tip and complete the task. Then think of possible words to complete the sentences below.

> **exam tip: sentence completion**
>
> Try and predict what words you might hear just before an answer is given.
>
> Read the sentences below. Which of these words might you hear before you hear each answer?
>
> alter   appeared as   mistaken for   enhance

Alan says he thinks that the Halo device's appearance could be confused with ¹........................... at first.

Alan thinks that devices like Halo have been used to improve ²...........................
skills effectively.

3 🔊 7.5 Listen and complete the sentences in in Ex 2.

4 🔊 7.6 Listen again. How does Alan use intonation to maintain his audience's interest? Practise talking about the Halo Sport in pairs, using a range of intonation to make your talk sound interesting.

5 e 🔊 7.7 You are going to listen to a man, Alan, talking about his work and the new Halo device. Listen and complete the sentences with a word or short phrase.

Alan didn't show his videos to friends because he felt that making them was just a ¹........................... in the beginning.

Alan says that he spends most time on ²........................... as part of his work as a technology reviewer.

Alan uses the expression ³'...........................' for the kind of video he prefers to post.

Alan compares problems with producing and selling the Halo Sport device with similar problems in the ⁴........................... industry.

Alan advises users to consider the lack of ⁵........................... before buying the Halo Sport.

When thinking about his audience, Alan is conscious that the idea of the Halo Sport would be familiar to ⁶........................... already.

Alan is concerned about the results of using the Halo Sport on people with ⁷..........................., which have been negative.

Alan is always aware of highlighting the importance of ⁸...........................
for any new product.

Speak up

6 Work in pairs and discuss the questions.

1. Would you use a device that changed your brain structure to improve your performance in sports, learning languages, maths, memory, etc.? Why/Why not?
2. Do you think that using the Halo is a form of cheating?
3. Do we need stricter regulation of products like this?

USE OF ENGLISH 1

1 Work in pairs. Do you agree with these statements?
1 **An awful lot of** professional sports stars depend on brain-training.
2 Listening to **a couple of** psychology CDs won't improve your thinking.
3 When there isn't **a great deal of** information on new technologies, we shouldn't use them on our brain.
4 There hasn't been **an awful lot of** research done on long term effects.

2 Read the grammar box and complete the examples with the highlighted quantifiers in Ex 1.

explore grammar → p154

quantifiers

Different quantifiers are followed by different kinds of noun.

Followed by singular countable nouns: each, every, neither, the whole

Followed by plural countable nouns:
¹...................., countless, several, both, none of, upwards of (100)

Followed by uncountable nouns: bags of, ²....................

Followed by uncountable nouns or plural countable nouns: all the, no end of, tons of, heaps of, ³....................

3 🔊 7.8 Listen to a description of future healthcare. What change does the speaker predict?

4 🔊 7.9 Choose the correct words to complete the sentences. Listen again and check.
1 I've got **bags of / countless** time.
2 There's **a great deal of / a couple of** research going on.
3 **All of / The whole of** the researchers assumed humans would deliver healthcare.
4 **No end of / Every** penny counts and technology can reduce costs.
5 There are **no end of / a great deal of** computer algorithms out there.
6 **The whole / All the** projects are interesting.

5 Read the article. What can the Tricorder do?

The Tricorder
Bringing sci-fi health care to life

There still needs to be a great ¹.................... of progress before we get to the healthcare that sci-fi films promised us decades ago. Superman has X-ray vision. Dr Who has a device that ².................... in so handy it can detect health problems and double up as a flashlight. But what absolutely ³.................... of the true sci-fans really want is Dr McCoy's health scanner from *Star Trek*. Portable and light, it can identify no ⁴.................... of different illnesses. Modern medical experts use data and scanning equipment but ⁵.................... of these two technologies have lived up to our expectations until now. The *Star Trek* vision of healthcare could soon become a reality, though, as prize money upwards ⁶.................... $10 million is being offered. Any research group who ⁷.................... in for the competition needs to create a version of Dr McCoy's gadget. Given the existing technology, it should be feasible in the next five years. Companies just need to join ⁸.................... the dots and link data and biotechnology.

6 Read the exam tip and complete the task. Then read the article in Ex 5 again and complete the gaps with one word only.

exam tip: open cloze

Look at the singular and plural forms of words. They give clues about what words are grammatically possible.

Look at gap 3 in the article in Ex 5. Is the noun that follows singular or plural? Which quantifier that fits the meaning is followed by a plural noun: 'every' or 'all'?

Speak up

7 What health apps do you have or would you like to have on your phone? What are the benefits of constantly monitoring the state of your health? Are there any disadvantages?

8 Would you trust healthcare delivered by a robot? Why/Why not?

When does a doctor get really annoyed? When he runs out of patients!

7 Mind and body

USE OF ENGLISH 2

1 Do you think it's ever acceptable to cheat to get what you want? If so, in what situations?

Similar words

2 Read the language box and answer the questions.

> **explore language** → p161
>
> **similar words**
>
> Some words are difficult to remember because they look similar to words in our own language. We call them false friends.
>
> Do you know the English meaning of these words: 'demand', 'lecture', 'sensible', 'gymnasium', 'afraid'? Do you know any false friends in your language?

3 Read about three ethical dilemmas. Discuss the differences in meaning between the pairs of words. Which is the correct word in each case?

Ethical dilemmas

Dan — Add message | Report

Dan is filling in his college application form and he would be ¹**eligible / legible** for a grant if he lived within five kilometres of the college. He doesn't, but his aunt does, and he's thinking about ²**preceding / proceeding** with the application using his aunt's address.

Jack — Add message | Report

Jack hasn't done his homework. He just could be honest and say he got distracted. ³**Alternately / Alternatively**, he could try and ⁴**convince / persuade** his teacher that he was ill.

Roberto — Add message | Report

Roberto has to complete an important assignment. He couldn't be bothered, so he just copied and pasted from a website, then changed the font to look like his work without ⁵**citing / siting** the original. It was still the right information. ⁶**Beside / Besides**, who really checks?

4 Read the texts in Ex 3 again and discuss what you think the students should do.

5 Read the article. What makes people cheat to get ahead? What can reduce cheating?

Why do we cheat?

Cheating is a complex issue. Not ¹........ cheats. Among those who do cheat, few people ever cheat as much as they might be able to ²........ away with. However, most of us are moral hypocrites, ³........ from other people's behaviours that they are unethical, while our own decisions are ⁴........ reason. A great ⁵........ of research has been done on college students, a group that is often tempted to cheat. Researchers have found that students who are involved in athletics are more ⁶........ to cheat than non-sporty types, which suggests that we're influenced by our social context. If you're tired or if there's some level of anonymity, it's also more probable you'll ⁷........ yourself that it's worth cheating. Scientists have found that reminding people of their own ethical values in an 'honour code' reminds them that they are good people. It also gives people both the ⁸........ of being monitored and can reduce cheating.

	A	B	C	D
1	all	either	many	everyone
2	move	go	come	get
3	inferring	suggesting	implying	hinting
4	between	among	within	from
5	number	deal	level	handful
6	opting	likely	preferring	probable
7	demonstrate	prove	convince	sell
8	reaction	sense	emotion	sentiment

6 e Read the article in Ex 5 again and decide which answer (A, B, C or D) best fits each gap.

Speak up

7 Design your own honour code for friendships or sports team mates. What are the five most important things to include in it?

> **game on**
>
> In a group of four, divide into two teams and draw a noughts and crosses grid. You can draw your nought or cross every time you can show you can use these words accurately.
>
> accept/except   adapt/adopt   advice/advise   affect/effect
> almost/most   all together/altogether   already/all ready
> among/between   apart/a part

Nobody's ever sorry that they cheated. They're only ever sorry that they got caught.

SPEAKING

Power up

1 Work in pairs and discuss the questions.
1. When do you prefer to exercise: morning, afternoon or evening?
2. Do you think exercise is important in your life? Why/Why not?
3. Do you enjoy watching sports on television or live? Why/Why not?
4. Which sports are popular in your country right now?

2 🔊 7.10 Listen to two students answering the first question in Ex 1. Who gives a better answer? Why?

3 Read the exam tip and complete the task.

exam tip: interview

Try to link ideas even when you are answering fairly simple questions about yourself.

Match the linkers Susanna uses (1–4) with their function (A–D).

1. inevitably   A additional information
2. alternatively   B a second explanation
3. while   C likelihood
4. besides   D contrast

4 Choose the correct words to complete Roberto's answer.

Well, ¹**of course / inevitably**, the best time to exercise is probably in the morning. I walk my dog every morning before school. ²**Alternatively / Not only that, but** I also play football on a Saturday afternoon or in the lunch hour, which are also good times. ³**Even so / While**, I don't choose those times. I play then, not ⁴**because / why** it's the best time, but because my friends are around ⁵**as / due to** they're out of class at that time. ⁶**Nonetheless / Besides** I don't think anyone really chooses when to exercise. You exercise when you can.

5 Work in pairs. Practise answering the questions in Ex 1 again. Try to use at least three of these linkers.

even so   inevitably   due to the fact that   besides   alternatively

6 Look at the photos. They show people doing sport or other activities in a public place. Work in pairs and discuss the questions.
1. What do the people in photos A and B have in common?
2. How do the photos differ?

7 Work in new pairs. Take turns to compare one of the photos (A or B) with C.

8 Work in pairs. Take turns to answer the questions.
1. What might be easy or difficult about doing exercise in settings like these?
2. Which activity do you think requires the least skill? Why?

9 e Turn to page 177 and complete the task.

Speak up

10 Work in pairs and discuss the questions.
1. What sports facilities do you have in your town?
2. What sport do you think could be encouraged more in your town? Why? What equipment or space does that sport need? What level of skill do people need to enjoy that sport? How popular is it?

7 Mind and body

WRITING

Power up

1 Work in pairs and discuss the questions.
1. Where do you eat your lunch on school days?
2. What are the advantages and disadvantages of schools providing a breakfast club for students?
3. Does your school have a canteen that provides lunch? What do you like about it? What are the problems?

Plan on

2 Read the task. What do you have to write? What do you have to include? What ideas do you have on the topic? Make notes below.

> Your school wants to make the food choices on offer in its canteen healthier.
>
> > The principal wants students to send in a proposal outlining the three main problems, suggesting changes and explaining how these changes would benefit students. Decisions will then be made about a suitable course of action.
>
> Write your proposal in **220–260** words.

....
....
....
....
....
....

3 Look at your ideas from Ex 2. What are your main themes? What subheadings do you need?

4 Read the proposal. What subheadings do you need? Write your ideas in gaps A–E.

Proposal for changes to the food served at the Grange Park High School

A ....
[1]Absolutely everyone agrees that it is extremely important to promote healthy eating. The college [2]really must encourage healthy choices among staff and students alike. The aim of this proposal is to outline three key areas for change.

B ....
While currently one healthy hot food choice is provided every day, [3]all the students hate it and many prefer the fast food alternatives. In addition, [4]tonnes of cakes and biscuits are bought from vending machines around the college. [5]This means that students have no idea about the school's policy towards healthy eating.

C ....
[6]You need to offer only healthy choices Monday to Thursday, with a 'Fat Friday' policy, where students can celebrate the end of the week with their fast food favourites. [7]There will still be some rubbish food but this would be a happy compromise.

D ....
[8]I suggest that the contract with the current supplier be cancelled and machines with healthier choices be introduced. If the only option is healthy food, students will choose it.

E ....
Encouraging change in dietary habits is [9]a total nightmare, but it is the role of schools to set high standards. We propose that the three matters listed above [10]have to be sorted out right now. If we do so, it will encourage students to commit to healthier lifestyle choices.

5 Read the language box and complete the task. Then read the proposal again. Replace the highlighted strong views (1–10) with the more neutral phrases below.

explore **language**

expressing ideas in a neutral way

Even if you have strong views, it is important to express ideas in a neutral way in a formal proposal. You can do this by using set phrases.

Choose the more neutral phrase in each pair.
1 everyone hates it / it proved unpopular in our survey
2 there is little nutritional value / the food is full of fat and grease
3 I think we should / I tend to think that we should

---

a large number   always challenging   be addressed with immediate effect
has a responsibility to   in the view of many members of staff and students
it has not proved popular with students   it is our recommendation
this sends a mixed message on   we suggest the provision of
while not completely ideal

---

6 Look at the phrases (A–D). Which paragraph could each phrase help to structure in a proposal (introduction, main paragraphs, recommendations)?

A Many students feel that/have commented that …
B The aims of this proposal are …
C Implementation of the above suggestions would result in …
D Following a survey of …, we found that …

Write on

7 You are going to write a proposal. Turn to page 174 and read the task. Make notes on your suggestions.

8 Work in pairs and compare your suggestions. Are you able to give convincing reasons for each suggestion?

9 Plan your proposal. Think about:
- your audience and tone
- the headings and subheadings you need
- the recommendations you are going to give.

10 e Write your proposal in 220–260 words.

Improve it

11 Check your proposal using this checklist.
- Did you include an overall heading?
- Did you mention who asked you to write the proposal?
- Did you use neutral language?
- Did you make clear recommendations?

SWITCH ON ▶

Pepper the robot

1 Work in pairs. List some important characteristics of a best friend. Then rate them from most important to least important.

2 ▶ Watch the clip. Work in pairs.
1. What is Pepper's special ability?
2. Explain how Pepper uses this ability to support humans.

3 ▶ Watch again. List some of the software components that enable Pepper to be one of the world's most advanced artificial intelligences.

4 Work in pairs. Decide if these statements are true or false.
1. Pepper was designed to help with chores around the house.
2. Pepper has to be programmed to acquire new skills.
3. Pepper adapts his behaviour in response to humans.
4. Pepper was designed by an engineer who worked in a post office.

5 Work in pairs. Do you think it's a good idea to form a strong attachment to a robot? Why/Why not?

Project

6 Work in small groups to create a presentation about robots.
1. Research different kinds of robots that are being developed today.
2. Choose three different robots and investigate the roles they play.
3. Present your findings to the class. Include information about:
   - who your robots can help and how
   - why they are needed in the environments they work in
   - specific tasks that they can do
   - the benefits each robot offers to society (e.g. safety, happiness, medical assistance, space exploration)
4. Vote on which robot you think is best.

INDEPENDENT LEARNING

Reading and writing

1 Match the reading goals (1–4) with the problems (A–D).
1. I will read fifty words a minute and not worry too much about unknown words.
2. I will read something, choose some unknown words, work out the meaning and then check.
3. I will think about what information I need to understand before I start to read.
4. I will practise reading five minutes each day so I see plenty of examples of good sentence structure.

A not having a wide enough vocabulary
B forgetting about the specific purpose of reading
C making mistakes with grammar
D not reading fluently enough

2 Make a list of other problems you have when reading and think of possible goals for practising and improving. Then work in small groups and share your ideas.

Challenges when reading	Goals for practising and improving

3 Complete the sentences to make them true for you.
1. When reading, I have problems with ...., so I'm going to ....
2. I need to do this because I want to ....
3. When I improve, I'll feel ....!

4 How will you know if you have succeeded?

UNIT CHECK

Wordlist

Health and diet
alert (*adj*)
diet drinks (*n*)
caffeine (*n*)
calorie (*n*)
energy boost (*n*)
energy crash (*n*)
heartbeat (*n*)
high energy drinks (*n*)
knackered (*adj*)
low-fat yoghurt (*n*)
posture (*n*)
take a nap (*phr*)
weight gain (*n*)
work out (*phr v*)

Phrasal verbs of food and drink
binge out on
cut out
eat out
go easy on
peel off
wind down

Sports phrases
achieve a personal best (*phr*)
bond in a team (*phr*)
build self-esteem (*phr*)
develop fitness (*phr*)
develop strength and stamina (*phr*)
provide relaxation (*phr*)

Similar words
alternately (*adv*) / alternatively (*adv*)
beside (*prep*) / besides (*adv*)
cite (*v*) / site (*n*)
elicit (*v*) / illicit (*adj*)
eligible (*adj*) / legible (*adj*)
imply (*v*) / infer (*v*)
precede (*v*) / proceed (*v*)
convince (*v*) / persuade (*v*)

Other
an awful lot (*phr*)
a great deal (*phr*)
a number of (*phr*)
bags of (*phr*)
countless (*adj*)
heaps of (*phr*)
no end of (*phr*)
(the) majority (*n*)
the number of (*phr*)
tons of (*phr*)
upwards of (*phr*)

Vocabulary

1 🔊 **7.11 Listen to eight people. What word from the *Health and diet* section of the wordlist does the beep represent?**

1 .... 5 ....
2 .... 6 ....
3 .... 7 ....
4 .... 8 ....

2 🔊 **7.12 Listen and check your answers.**

3 Match the first half of each sentence (1–6) with the second (A–F).

1 I binged out at the weekend and
2 I cut out sugar from my diet and
3 I ate out last night and
4 I went easy on the caffeine today and
5 I peeled the skin off my apple and
6 I wind down after a gym session and

A I'm feeling a bit tired without my usual energy boost.
B stopped eating cakes, biscuits and desserts.
C put it in the compost bin.
D ate a whole birthday cake while watching an entire box set.
E do a few stretches.
F joined my family at a nice Italian restaurant.

4 Complete the article with words from the *Similar words* and *Other* sections of the wordlist.

Reasons to hate sport

Some people hate sport with a kind of passion that you rarely see against any other form of entertainment. No amount of reasoning can [1]..................... them to change their minds. Many people [2]..................... the extreme reactions some fans have as a reason to hate sport. Many fans overreact when their team loses, and go into a bad mood for days or worse. [3]....................., it's not just a problem when their team loses; whole cities have experienced violence even when their local team wins. Another reason often given is that sports stars are everywhere. There is [4]..................... football stars advertising everything from food to perfume and they earn a [5]..................... money doing so. Others might object to the use of [6]..................... drugs in sport to gain an unfair advantage. A final reason is that some American television shows and films [7]..................... that being good at sport is the only way to become popular at school, ignoring the wide spectrum of qualities children have.

It's no wonder the topic divides people.

UNIT CHECK

Review

1 Complete the extract from a blog with these words.

> all the   both   either   the whole   neither

Whether you do five exercise sessions a week or none at all, the chances are you still wear the gear. Sales of 'athleisure' clothes have been rising and ¹........................... of the jeans industry has taken a huge hit. ² .... the sports and general leisure wear industries are being driven by fitness-inspired clothing. ³ .... main reasons why any fashion takes off – comfortable, affordable, versatile and increasingly stylish – apply to athleisure clothing. You need to be ⁴ .... sporty nor stylish to pull this trend off! The good news is, ⁵ .... way gives you the sensation of being sporty, even if you're not. It's like buying an exercise bike: even if it gets no use at all, you'll feel better about yourself for owning one!

2 🔊 **7.13** Choose the correct verb forms to complete the text about governing sports. Then listen to a woman talking on this topic to check your answers. Which verb forms could both be correct?

Almost any sport you do probably ¹**has / have** a national governing body. The national political government often ²**has / have** very little control over these organisations. They often represent people who enjoy the sport when the media ³**needs / need** to ask questions. A number of governing bodies ⁴**is / are** influential enough to be able to decide rules for the sport or organise competitions. The majority ⁵**is / are** very small organisations. If a club ⁶**wants / want** to apply for membership, they pay a small annual fee to meet administration costs. Staff who ⁷**works / work** for these organisations usually ⁸**has / have** some historical connection with the sport, but not always. Governing bodies are becoming more numerous. The number of countries with an Olympic Committee, for example, ⁹**has / have** gone up to 193 nations – in other words, 100 percent of the member states in the UN ¹⁰**participates / participate**.

3 Choose the correct option to complete the sentences.

1 We've got bags of
   A time, so we don't have to hurry to the gym.
   B hours, so let's watch the match.
2 There are no end of
   A advice for people who want to get fit.
   B opportunities to take part in sport.
3 I swear the whole town
   A was watching the team that day!
   B were cheering for the team!
4 There were countless
   A crowd waiting to get in.
   B people outside the stadium.
5 The number of sports shirts
   A he owns is crazy!
   B they sell are incredible!

4 Read the article and complete the gaps with one word only.

How do **modern** sports stars compare with sporting heroes of the **past**?

Here are two all-time greats.

Jackie Joyner-Kersee was born in the US in 1962. Being one of a handful of athletes who ¹........................... managed to overcome severe asthma, she won a national silver medal in basketball at a young age. She achieved a personal best in the Olympics in 1988, picking ²........................... gold Olympic medals in the heptathlon and the long jump, ³........................... of which are demanding events. In fact, after seven Olympic medals, she finally wound ⁴........................... her career after her record fourth Olympic Games in 1996.

Max Woosnam was born in Liverpool in 1892. He played football for amateur team Chelsea when he left university. He ⁵........................... on to captain Manchester City FC and then the England national team. As ⁶........................... of these two achievements was enough to satisfy him, he then represented his country in tennis and won Olympic gold and silver. He captained the British golf team and played for the national cricket team. ⁷........................... all of this, he refused to take up any sport professionally, saying that being paid to play was 'vulgar'. One of his greatest achievements was defeating Charlie Chaplin at table tennis. He played with a butter knife ⁸........................... of a bat but still won!

5 Who do you think is the greatest sports hero of all time? Write a paragraph explaining:
- what that person has achieved
- why you think this is outstanding
- what qualities you think make this person successful.

104

> "Turn up.
> Tune in.
> Be happy."

Look at the photo and discuss the questions.
1 Read the quote. What does it mean for you?
2 What three forms of entertainment do you enjoy the most? Why?
3 What's the most entertaining day you've ever had? Why?

Entertain me

8

READING
topic: storytelling in games
skill: dealing with unknown vocabulary
task: multiple matching

GRAMMAR
the future
conditional sentences

VOCABULARY
entertainment: prepositional phrases
negative prefixes

LISTENING
topic: attracting attention
skill: following an argument
task: multiple choice: short texts

USE OF ENGLISH
key word transformation
word formation

SPEAKING
topic: a world without music
skill: talking about potential consequences
task: collaborative task and discussion

WRITING
topic: documentaries for teens
skill: paraphrasing and cohesion
task: essay

SWITCH ON ▶
video: do you think it's funny?
project: the greatest prank

105

8 Entertain me

READING

Power up

1 Work with a partner. Discuss the questions.
1. Look at the photo on this page. Do you think it tells a story?
2. Where can you find the best stories: books, films, video games, the internet or TV? Why?
3. Which do you find more exciting: films or video games? Why?

2 Read the title of the article. What's your view on this? Discuss in pairs.

Read on

3 Read the article quickly. Does the writer agree or disagree with your point of view?

4 Read section A of the article. Highlight the part which questions whether one entertainment medium deserves its status.

5 Read the exam tip. What can help you guess the part of speech and meaning of an unknown word?

> **exam tip: multiple matching**
> You don't need to understand every word in the text to complete the task. Ignore unknown words in untested sections of the text.

6 Which of the words in bold in section A of the article do you need to know in order to understand the part you highlighted in Ex 4?

7 Match the words in bold in section A of the article with their synonyms. Choose four of these words.

defended against   duty   important
is worth   leadership   profit   requires   saved from

8 e Read the article again. For questions 1–10, choose from the sections A–D. The sections may be chosen more than once.

In which section does the writer:
1. question whether one entertainment medium deserves its status?
2. suggest that some fans of a film genre are likely to become bored with it?
3. explain how one film used a game concept in its story.
4. provide evidence that one genre is more popular than another?
5. cite examples of subjects covered by games?
6. compare the different way that people follow a story in films and games?
7. give one example of how a medium fails to tell a story effectively?
8. mention the relatively fast development of one entertainment medium?
9. predict a shift in power from one storytelling medium to another?
10. describe how games-makers have adopted techniques used by another medium?

9 Find words or phrases in the article that mean the following.
1. changed gradually over time (section A)
2. unable to move (section B)
3. (an idea) used a lot so it no longer has meaning (section B)
4. great tiredness (section B)
5. real, not fake (section C)
6. become completely involved in an activity (section D)

Sum up

10 Which of these reasons does the writer give for games replacing films as a narrative medium? How persuasive are these reasons?

ability to explore different storylines   generating discussion   gripping stories
length of playing time   game sequels   varied themes

Speak up

11 Work in groups. What films and games do you know that tell a story in an exciting way? How do they do that? What films and games fail to do this well? Why?

HAVE GAMES REPLACED FILMS AS THE MODERN POPULAR METHOD OF STORYTELLING?

A Cinema has been a dominant force in the world of entertainment for over a century. In that time it has successfully **fended off** television and video and is still considered by most to be the most popular means of storytelling today. However, with changes in the industry, it is **crucial** to ask whether it **merits** this reputation or whether there is another form of narrative entertainment which is about to take over the **mantle**. While television is a possibility due to the transformation it has undergone in recent years and the innovative content the industry produces, gaming is another. In just thirty-five years, games have evolved from a dot moving across a screen to online multiplayer first person shooters with complex storylines today. While the global film industry earned $38.6 billion in 2016, the games industry generated $91 billion around the world.

B Cinema, it seems, is currently stuck in a whirlwind of big action films with scene after scene of incredible special effects that wow the audience. However, they do little to advance the telling of stories. *Captain America*, for instance, had thrilling action but so little time was spent telling the audience who the protagonists were fighting and why that viewers left the cinema feeling dazed and confused. In spite of this, film companies are continuing to invest millions into clichéd good vs bad superhero films and then their prequels or sequels because they continue to attract an audience. However, even audience members with an interest in comic books will soon be feeling superhero fatigue and viewers not interested in them at all have probably turned to other forms of entertainment in a bid to satisfy their craving for something more creative. Will the industry have realised this before it's too late and sales start to drop?

C Video games are proving to be more experimental, more sophisticated and more intelligent. In fact, I'd say they are on the verge of taking over from film as the more effective narrative form. They are no longer simple score-attack games for kids. There are now broader, open-ended narrative experiences with graphics so good they can, on occasion, look entirely authentic. These games cover themes such as the rise of technology and dehumanisation as well as morality in government and the law, and the quality of the narratives are set to improve further. Games have learnt from films, of course. Producers have begun to pay more attention to dialogue in scripted scenes so that people sound much more realistic. As a bonus the publicity is improved by the use of well-known actors.

D It is not just these aspects of a game that make it a worthy competitor to films, however. What makes them so much more exciting as a storytelling form is the fact that a player can immerse themselves in a story for hours and hours. Film-viewers passively rely on characters' lines or close-ups to highlight what is important for them to know or see. If the camera pans across to a particular object, you can be sure that the object is due to appear again later. In a game, there isn't just one story, there are hundreds. Players explore their environment and make decisions based on things that may or may not be important to the main story. Their decision may be effective or it may result in disaster. Whichever, the player has to live with that decision, which makes it more involving and exciting. Some film-makers are learning from games. When Tom Cruise's character in *Edge of Tomorrow* lives the same moment over again, it feels like a game character returning to the beginning of a level. We watch with anticipation as he tries to 'level up'. Perhaps film-makers need to do more of this to keep their position as king of entertainment as it certainly feels like the entertainment industry is on the point of change.

Did you know you can hear the same scream in over 200 films and TV shows as well as several video games?

8 Entertain me

GRAMMAR

1 Read the grammar box. What word do you think is missing in each future phrase or form in the example sentences? Check your answers in the article on page 107.

> ### explore grammar → p156
>
> **future phrases**
>
> We use the following phrases to say that something is going to happen very soon:
>
> I'd say games are on the verge ¹.................... taking over from film.
>
> It certainly feels like the entertainment industry is on/at the point ².................... change.
>
> We use the following phrase to talk formally about something that will definitely happen.
>
> There is another form of narrative entertainment which is ³.................... to take over the mantle.
>
> We use the following phrases to talk about something that is expected to happen:
>
> The quality of the narratives are set ⁴.................... improve further.
>
> If the camera pans to an object, you can be sure that object is due ⁵.................... appear again later.
>
> **future continuous and future perfect**
>
> We use the future continuous to talk about an action in progress at a specific future time and the future perfect to talk about an action that will be completed by a future time.
>
> Even audience members with an interest in comic books will soon ⁶.................... feeling superhero fatigue.
>
> Will the industry ⁷.................... realised this before it's too late?

2 🔊 8.1 Listen to how the prepositions and auxiliary verbs are pronounced in each future phrase or form. Listen again and repeat the sentences.

3 ▶️🔊 8.2 Watch or listen to seven people making predictions about the future of the entertainment industry. What prediction does each person make?

4 ▶️🔊 8.3 Match the first half of each prediction (1–7) with the second half (A–G). Watch or listen again and check your answers. Which predictions do you agree with? Why?

1. There's some obvious things that will
2. We're just at the point
3. I think that [virtual reality] is due
4. The entertainment industry, I think, is on the
5. People will be
6. I think everyone will
7. The only thing that is going to

A. experiencing entertainment a lot with virtual reality.
B. to become even bigger in the gaming world.
C. have changed in entertainment is the mediums that we watch them on.
D. have changed.
E. be using it [VR] by the time we're thirty.
F. of cutting out everyone in our vicinity.
G. verge of becoming less accessible.

5 Complete the news headlines with these words. What do you think each story is about?

China   radio   reality

① **ENTERTAINMENT AND .... ARE ON THE VERGE OF MERGING**

② **.................... IS SET TO BECOME THE BIGGEST MOVIE MARKET IN THE WORLD**

③ **.................... IS TO GET MORE PERSONAL**

6 Work in groups of three. Share your ideas from Ex 5. Then turn to page 175 and follow the instructions.

Speak up

7 What innovations in entertainment would you like to see? Why? How likely are they?

VOCABULARY
entertainment

1. Work in pairs. What TV shows do you enjoy? Do you usually watch them on TV or online? Why?

2. Put these words into three categories: film, TV or music. Some words can go into more than one category.

> beat (n) blockbuster broadcast (n/v) catchy
> crowdfund (v) flop (n/v) genre gig primetime
> ratings record label remake screenplay
> televise

3. Read the blog posts about the future of TV. Complete the gaps with the correct form of words from Ex 2.

Buster3   Add message | Report
Today, channels ¹_____ their best shows in the early evening but in future everyone will watch what they want when they want. A ²_____ show will be an out-of-date concept.

GazzaG   Add message | Report
On-demand channels make money through subscriptions, not advertising, so they care less about ³_____. They'll continue to create programmes that cover different ⁴_____, even if they're unsuccessful and they ⁵_____.

Caitlin99   Add message | Report
People already prefer to watch an epic TV series to the latest ⁶_____ film these days. I think in future we'll see more old films ⁷_____ into amazing TV series.

BigDog   Add message | Report
I reckon more TV will be ⁸_____. It's a great way to get money and find out if people like your idea.

4. Work in pairs. Which predictions in Ex 3 do you agree with? What other predictions can you make about TV, film or music? Try to use vocabulary from Ex 2.

prepositional phrases

5. Read the language box. Choose the correct prepositions in the examples.

explore language ➡ p161

prepositional phrases

A prepositional phrase is a phrase that starts with a preposition and is followed by a noun or noun phrase.
The camera isn't ¹**at / in** focus. It's all blurry.
That singer's really ²**in / out of** tune. She sounds awful.
Have you seen that new sci-fi film ³**by / from** any chance?

6. Read the article. What problem and solution does the writer describe?

If you want something done well, ...

We've all shouted ¹_____ loud when we've binge-watched our favourite TV shows and there's nothing else good to see. TV ²_____ demand means having series after series ³_____ our fingertips and yet for the telly addict, it's still not enough. But next time this happens, don't sit around at home ⁴_____ a mood; get out and make your own show.

⁵_____ the face of it this might seem like an impossible challenge, but pick one of the hundreds of web series online ⁶_____ random and you'll see that ⁷_____ reality, it's not. ⁸_____ the whole, web series are going ⁹_____ strength to strength and yet they're made with little to no money. Having said that, you can't just go out and film something ¹⁰_____ the top of your head. Making something good takes a lot of hard work. ¹¹_____ brief, create a simple story that shows the world ¹²_____ your perspective; film short episodes and borrow props from friends and family to keep costs low.

7. Complete the article in Ex 6 with prepositions.

Speak up

8. Work in pairs and discuss the questions.
   1. Have you seen any web series? Did you enjoy them? Why/Why not?
   2. In reality, how easy do you think it would be to create your own web series?

20th Century Fox's Darryl Zanuch once said, 'People will soon get tired of staring at a box every night.'

8 Entertain me

LISTENING

Power up

1 Work in pairs. How might the photo below catch your attention? Think of some examples of how these people and things might catch your attention.

a comedian   a new film   a newspaper or magazine
a clothing brand   a musician

Listen up

2 Read the exam tip. Identify the two different points of view and the conclusion in the example.

exam tip: multiple choice: short texts

Speakers don't always present a clear argument, and often discuss different points of view before coming to a conclusion. To fully understand their view, make sure you listen to the end of what the person says. For example:

'Never tell a joke unless you know it's a good one or you'll embarrass yourself. Having said that, you have to test it out somewhere. I guess, in the end it's about choosing the right listener to try it out on first.'

3 🔊 8.4 Listen to two friends talking about the art of storytelling. What three things does the boy say are important when telling a story? Which does he conclude is the most important?

4 Look at question 1 in Ex 5. Which option best fits what you heard?

5 🔊 8.5 Listen to three conversations about different forms of media and choose the answer (A, B or C) which fits best according to what you hear.

Extract 1

You hear two friends talking about the art of storytelling.

1 The boy thinks that the most important thing for a storyteller to focus on is
  A attracting the listeners' attention.
  B building up to an exciting finish.
  C using a variety of voices.

2 The girl believes she benefited from a storytelling event by
  A experiencing more emotions than when reading silently.
  B hearing how the words sound when said aloud.
  C visualising the same images as other listeners.

Extract 2

You hear two classmates talking about launching a school newspaper.

3 What do the boy and girl agree is a good way to attract readers?
  A Build a sense of community at the school.
  B Include content with a universal appeal.
  C Focus mainly on humorous stories.

4 What does the boy say is the main reason articles fail?
  A an ineffective writing style
  B inappropriate visual support
  C too many lightweight topics

Extract 3

You hear two colleagues talking about attracting younger consumers.

5 What does the man think is the best approach for their business?
  A using authentic images
  B exploiting the company's history
  C focussing on current principles

6 How does the woman feel about another company's brand campaign?
  A envious of the unique idea
  B cautious about its transferability
  C surprised by its success

Speak up

6 Work in pairs and discuss the questions.

1 Would you say you're good at telling stories or anecdotes? Is it a useful skill to have?
2 Think of a brand you like. Why do you like it? How does the company attract your custom?

USE OF ENGLISH 1

1 Read the language box. Complete the rules with words from the example sentences. Then find more examples of this language in audioscript 8.5.

explore language ➙ p156

conditional sentences

We can use *provided/providing that*, ¹............................ and *on condition that* (more formal) to say that one thing has to happen in order for another thing to happen.

As long as you can practise first, you'll be OK.

We can use *suppose/supposing that*, ²............................ *if/that* and *what if* to ask the listener to imagine a situation and its hypothetical result.

Imagine if we overused them – they'd detract from the writing.

Note: We can mix conditional forms, e.g. to talk about a past situation with a present result.

Supposing I'd paid more attention to the storytellers, I'd know what to do now.

2 Read the article. Why are the writer's stories unusual?

What if? stories

Imagine that *Twilight's* Bella Swann had decided not to hang around with Edward in Forks but ¹............................ (go) to the Capitol to take part in *The Hunger Games* instead. ²............................ she .... (beat) Katniss Everdeen? ³............................ we .... (view) Katniss differently today? **Supposing** Harry Potter was actually the half brother of Luke Skywalker. Who ⁴............................ (feel) the force the strongest? And what ⁵............................ (happen) if Tony Stark, aka Ironman, fell through a portal and found himself in Tolkien's Middle-earth? Would his arrogance lead him to fight with the hobbits or ⁶............................ he .... (be) pulled towards the evil of Sauron? Imagine these ⁷............................ (can) come true. They'd attract new readers from all over the world!

There are thousands of stories we know and love but **what if** we ⁸............................ (play) around with them a bit? Stories with alternative versions exist in all kinds of genres. **Provided that** the reader ⁹............................ (recognise) the original stories, putting two characters from different places and times together can be fun. So, take your two favourite characters and have them meet. **As long as** you stay true to both characters, the outcome ¹⁰............................ (be) pretty interesting.

3 Complete the article with the correct form of the verbs in brackets. More than one answer might be possible.

4 Read the exam tip and complete the task.

exam tip: key word transformation

Read the first and second sentences carefully to identify which information in the first sentence is missing from the second.

Read the key word transformations in Ex 5 and identify the missing information.

5 e Complete the second sentence so that it has a similar meaning to the first sentence using the word given. Do not change the word given. Use between three and six words.

1 Accept our user policy and you can get access to our online library.
   CONDITION
   Access to our online library is provided to people ....
   to our user policy.

2 I became a writer because you helped me.
   NEVER
   Supposing you hadn't helped me, I .... into a writer.

3 If the judges award your book the top prize, how would you feel?
   SUPPOSING
   How would you feel .... the top prize by the judges?

4 Story books only exist because large numbers of people read them.
   LONG
   Story books will exist .... read by large numbers of people.

5 If a writer has patience, creating a story can be very rewarding.
   PROVIDED
   Creating a story can be very rewarding .... patient.

Speak up

6 Work in pairs. Choose two of your favourite characters and put them in the situation of a completely different story. What happens? Tell the story to another pair.

What does a superhero put in his or her drink? Just ice!

8 Entertain me

USE OF ENGLISH 2

1 Read part of an article on music videos. Do you agree with it? Why/Why not?

> With so many **regular** views online, music videos are clearly a **significant** part of the music industry. They help listeners to **understand** a song's meaning and **connect** to it better, even if the videos are sometimes a little **predictable**. They're also **perfect** for a bit of escapism.

2 Complete the language box with the words in bold in the article in Ex 1 and an appropriate prefix.

explore language → p161

negative prefixes

We can make words negative by adding prefixes.

un-	unrelated, unintelligible, ¹...............
dis-	disrespectful, discomfort, ²..............
in-	incorrectly, indirectly, ³...............
mis-	misuse, mislead, ⁴...............

The less common prefixes *il-*, *ir-* and *im-* often come before words beginning with *l*, *r* and *m* or *p* respectively, although not always.

il-	illiterate, illegitimate, illegally
ir-	irrelevant, irrational, ⁵...............
im-	impatient, impossible, ⁶...............

3 Complete the words in the sentences with the correct negative prefixes.

1. There's a lot of ....certainty in the music industry these days.
2. Some people ....correctly believe they can download all music for free.
3. Musicians want to sound unique and not be ....taken for another artist.
4. Bands that release records at ....regular intervals may lose fans.
5. If a musician doesn't release videos, they can become ....connected from their fans.
6. Some music videos might be considered ....moral by some people.

4 Work in pairs. Do you agree with the sentences in Ex 3? Why/Why not?

5 Read the article. What is the writer's main point?

Why MUSIC VIDEOS are still so important

Music videos are everywhere, which makes them ¹............... easy to discover. However, because the internet is ²............... to anyone with a camera, there is an abundance of music videos at any one given time – both professional and amateur. This means that most videos are watched and ³............... in the space of a few minutes. A musician, therefore, needs to ensure that a video is as ⁴............... as possible to avoid this. Artists without a good video are at a major ⁵............... as they are unable to stand out from the crowd.

Music videos are so vital to the industry that they have become ⁶..............., in my view. Their ⁷............... will mean we start seeing shorter videos to suit different mediums. Of course, this means there'll be even more content online to add to what's already overwhelming to an audience, but music ⁸............... sites will become much better at making the right recommendations to help their customers.

| DENY |
| ACCESS |
| |
| |
| FORGET |
| |
| MEMORY |
| ADVANTAGE |
| |
| REPLACE |
| EVOLVE |
| |
| |
| SUBSCRIBE |

6 e Read the article in Ex 5 again. Use the word given at the end of some of the lines to form a word that fits in the gap in the same line.

game on

Work in groups. Think of three words each using different prefixes from the language box. Take turns to describe the word to your group. The person who guesses it correctly gets one point. The person with the most points at the end wins!

Speak up

7 Work in pairs and discuss the questions.
1. What are some of your favourite music videos? Why?
2. What kind of music videos do you dislike? Why?
3. How important do you think videos are for the music industry?

The first video ever played by MTV was 'Video Killed the Radio Star' by The Buggles in 1981.

SPEAKING

Power up

1 Work in pairs. In what ways is music important to you? Why?

2 Look at the diagram on the right. What could you say about each thing? Note down some ideas.

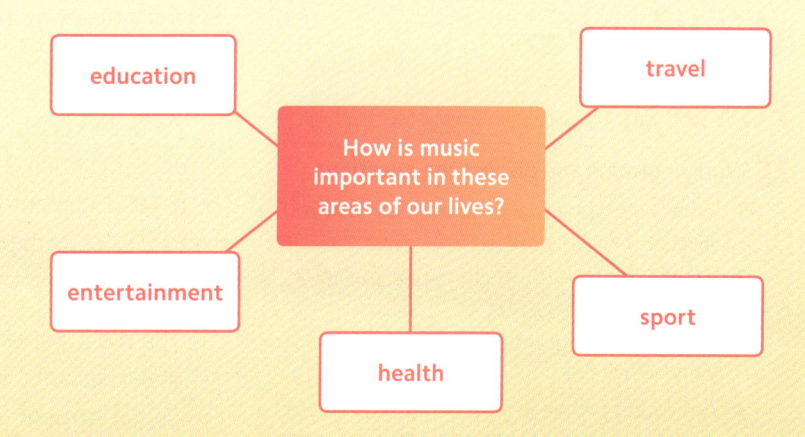

3 🇪 Work in pairs. Discuss the question in the diagram for two minutes. Then take one minute to decide in which two areas of our lives music is most important. Use these words and phrases to help you.

> destress   develop creativity   go to a gig
> give you a boost   pass the time

4 🔊 8.6 Listen to two students answering the discussion question below. Do they agree or disagree with each other?

Is it acceptable to download any music for free?

5 🔊 8.7 Read the language box. Listen again and complete the examples with one or two words.

explore language

expressing potential consequences

To talk about the potential consequences of an action or event, we can use:

Conditional sentences

¹............................ everyone downloaded everything for free all the time.

Modal verbs

Bringing the price down ²............................ make a difference.

Language of cause and effect

This could ³............................ more people paying for the songs.

6 Read the question and complete the answers with your own ideas. Then work in pairs and discuss your ideas. Give reasons.

What would the world be like without music?

1 There'd be no …
2 It would affect …
3 As an alternative, people might …

[Diagram: How is music important in these areas of our lives? — education, travel, entertainment, sport, health]

Speak up

7 Work in pairs and discuss the questions. Extend your answers, and take turns to speak and respond to each other's points. Use these words and phrases to help you.

> adapt to   as long as   have a significant impact   may/might lead to
> provided that   result in   traditions   a necessary feature of

1 Why do you think music is important in many cultures?
2 What impact does music have in films?
3 How do you think a band or musician can stay popular for a long time?
4 Do you think our tastes in music change as we get older? Why/Why not?

game on

Work in groups of two pairs each. Pair A starts by discussing a question from Ex 7. Each time the teacher shouts 'Change!', Pair B must continue the conversation. If you can continue the conversation, you get one point. If not, you must start discussing another question. Which pair can get the most points?

Speaking extra

8 Work in pairs. What would be the consequences of these events on your life and other people's lives?

- Your favourite musician or band have stopped making music.
- Cinemas have gone out of business.
- Nightclubs have closed down.
- Music streaming sites have tripled their prices.

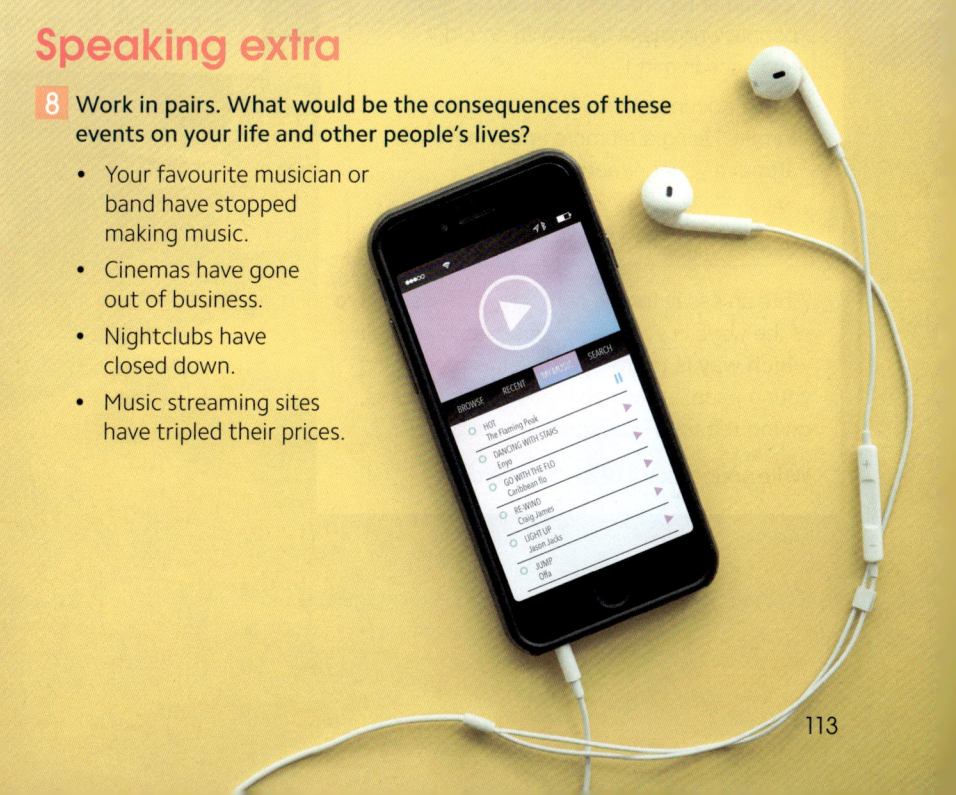

8 Entertain me

WRITING

Power up

1 Work in groups and discuss the questions.

1. What kind of factual programmes have you seen on TV or online?
2. What's the most interesting one you've seen? Why?
3. Are factual programmes important? Why/Why not?
4. Are young people in your country interested in documentaries? How could they be more appealing?

Plan on

2 Work in pairs. Read the task and add one more idea to each of the three prompts, in addition to those in the notes.

> You watched a television debate where young people were asked how TV companies could make documentary programmes more appealing to them. You have made the notes below:
>
> > Ways of making TV documentaries more interesting to young people:
> > - choice of topic
> > - creativity
> > - length of programme
> >
> > Some opinions expressed in the debate:
> >
> > 'Documentary makers tend to be older people who make them with an older audience in mind.'
> >
> > 'Most documentaries follow a similar format. Being a bit more imaginative will attract a younger audience.'
> >
> > 'Young people prefer not to spend a long time on one programme.'
>
> Write an essay for the company discussing **two** of the ways in your notes. You should **explain which way is more effective** in encouraging young people to watch more documentaries, **giving reasons** in support of your answer.
>
> Write your essay in **220–260** words.

3 Read the essay. Do you agree with the writer's point of view? Why/Why not?

> TV documentaries are a popular form of both entertainment and education. However, young people are less likely to watch a TV documentary than other types of **programmes** such as reality or comedy shows. The main reasons for this are the topics chosen and the length of a typical documentary.
>
> The most popular documentaries on TV in my country are those about animals. While some **young people** will watch them, they do not **appeal** to all due to the fact that topics are chosen for a wide audience. Offering programmes on subjects that are more of interest to teenagers and those in their early twenties is likely to result in more of these people watching them.
>
> In addition to this, a change in the length of the documentaries will help to persuade more young people to **watch** them. Currently, programmes of this **kind** are sixty minutes **long** when many younger people prefer videos with a length of thirty minutes or less. TV companies should create shorter documentaries since this will lead to a larger teen audience. Creative three-minute programmes might be successful as young people are used to viewing videos of this type.
>
> In conclusion, current documentaries could be considered to be too long and **concentrate** on topics not always of interest to teens. As a result, TV production companies should make shorter documentaries focussing on more teen-friendly topics. In my view, shortening the length of the documentary would be the most successful course of action as it will make them more accessible to younger people.

4 Read the language box. Complete the examples with synonyms, paraphrases or words formed from the words in bold.

explore language

paraphrasing and cohesion

To avoid repetition, create cohesion in a text and demonstrate a wider range of language, you can use synonyms or paraphrases. A paraphrase could be a different word or phrase, or the same word in a different form (e.g. *repeat/repetition, avoid/avoidance*).

Documentaries are **well-received** by older adults but less [1]............... with younger adults.

There has been a **growth** in on-demand viewing. Sharing videos online has also [2]............... in popularity.

Documentaries **explore** different areas of life. This [3]............... can often be fascinating for viewers.

5 Look at the words in bold in the essay. Find a synonym or paraphrase in the same paragraph for each one.

6 Write the highlighted linkers of cause and effect in the essay in the correct column.

cause		effect	
because (of)	[2]...............	as a consequence	[5]...............
[1]...............	[3]...............	[4]...............	[6]...............

7 Complete the sentences with linkers from Ex 6. More than one answer might be possible, but choose a different one for each gap.

1 There are many TV channels these days. ...., viewers have a lot of choice.
2 .... you can stream documentaries online, you no longer need a TV.
3 Viewers can always find a documentary of interest .... so many are made.
4 Some documentaries are so important that they .... a change in society.
5 .... documentaries sometimes sound dull, not everyone gives them a chance.
6 Documentary making occasionally .... big blockbuster films for the director.

8 Improve the paragraph by making four or five changes. Use synonyms and paraphrases to replace repeated words, and add linkers of cause and effect.

Documentaries are sometimes traditional in the way they are made. They are not attractive to younger people, who are looking for something different and more attractive. Rather than simply tell a story through a narrator with some interviews, documentary makers should think of new and original ways to tell the story such as through imagery. People will watch the documentary, talking about it online and then other people watching it.

Write on

9 Work in groups. Turn to page 175 and read the task. Discuss which two ideas you could write about.

game on

Play in pairs. Individually, note down words and phrases that you can include in this essay. You have two minutes. Can you note down more than your partner?

10 Prepare to write your essay. Create a paragraph plan with key words.

11 Work in pairs and compare your plans. Explain your ideas to your partner.

12 **e** Read the exam tip and complete the task. Then write your essay in 220–260 words.

exam tip: essay

If you write less than 220 words or more than 260 words, you might lose marks for not including enough relevant information or writing too much irrelevant information.

Count the number of words you usually write in a paragraph and work out how many you write on a page. Then work in pairs and compare your answers.

Improve it

13 Swap essays with your partner from Ex 11. Read his/her essay and discuss the questions.

1 Does the essay match the plan?
2 Is the essay content appropriate?
3 Does the writer use synonyms or paraphrases? What is the effect of this?
4 Does the writer use linkers of cause and effect appropriately?

14 Think about your discussion in Ex 13 and edit your essay. Then read it through and check for errors, especially those you often make.

If you watch a whole TV series in a few hours or days, it's called 'binge-watching'.

SWITCH ON

Do you think it's funny?

1 Work in pairs. Discuss what kinds of things make you laugh.

2 ▶ Watch the clip. This episode was voted the most 'epic' in the series. List as many synonyms as you can for 'epic' in this context.

3 ▶ Watch again. Work in pairs. List the three things that happened which enabled Ben to get Simon away from his bandmates and into the caravan.

4 Work in pairs. Did you enjoy watching this prank? Why/Why not?

5 Work in small groups. You are going to play a prank on somebody you know. Follow these steps.
   1 Think about who you will choose and why, what the prank will be and what you hope the outcome will be.
   2 Share your ideas with another group. Which group has the best idea?

Project

6 Work in groups to research history's greatest pranks and hoaxes.
   1 Research a prank or hoax that you think was very successful or that you like.
   3 Present your findings to the class. Include information about:
      - the original intention of the prank/hoax
      - how the prank/hoax unfolded
      - the result and repercussions of the prank/hoax

INDEPENDENT LEARNING

Speaking and writing

1 Work in pairs. Think about your listening skills. Which of these things make listening difficult for you? Can you think of anything else? How could you overcome these difficulties?

accent   illogical flow of ideas   intonation
lack of vocabulary   pronunciation
repetition and corrections   speed of delivery   stress

2 Read the exam goals for speaking. How confident do you feel about them? Rate them 1–5 (1 = not confident, 5 = very confident).

I can use a wide range of simple and some more advanced grammar accurately. ....

I can use a range of vocabulary appropriately to talk about familiar and unfamiliar subjects. ....

I can speak with a few pauses and organise my ideas well with a range of discourse markers. ....

I can pronounce sounds clearly and use appropriate intonation and stress. ....

I can initiate a conversation, respond to others and maintain interaction. ....

3 Work in pairs and discuss your answers to Ex 2. Share tips on how you can improve in the areas you find challenging.

4 Look ahead to Unit 9. Look at the focus of the Listening and Speaking lessons on page 119. What is the main goal of each one?
   1 Listening: ....
      ....
   2 Speaking: ....
      ....

5 Write down two tips you will use to help you reach your goals at the end of unit 9.

1
2

UNIT CHECK

Wordlist

Entertainment
adapt (v)
applaud (v)
beat (n)
blockbuster (n)
broadcast (v)
catchy (adj)
crowdfund (v)
depict (v)
dub (v)
flop (n/v)
genre (n)
gig (n)
portray (v)
primetime (n)
ratings (n)
record label (n)
rehearse (v)
remake (v)
screenplay (n)
stream (v)
televise (v)

Prepositional phrases
at our fingertips
at random
from strength to strength
from your perspective
in focus
in a mood
in reality
in tune
off the top of your head
on demand
on the face of it
on the whole
out of tune
out loud

Negative prefixes
disadvantage (n)
disconnected (adj)
discontinue (v)
immoral (adj)
imperfect (adj)
incorrectly (adv)
insignificant (adj)
irregular (adj)
irrelevant (adj)
irreplaceable (adj)
mistaken (adj)
misunderstand (v)
uncertainty (n)
undeniably (adv)
unimportant (adj)

Other
anticipation (n)
clinical (adj)
convincing (adj)
dehumanisation (n)
dominance (n)
ensuing (adj)
evolution (n)
fend off (phr v)
grab (v)
rivalry (n)
primitive (adj)

Vocabulary

1 🔊 **8.8** Listen to eight people talking about entertainment. What word from the *Entertainment* and *Prepositional phrases* sections of the wordlist does the beep represent?

1 .... 4 .... 7 ....
2 .... 5 .... 8 ....
3 .... 6 ....

2 🔊 **8.9** Listen and check your answers.

3 Use the word given in brackets to form a word that fits the gap in each sentence. Check your answers in the *Negative prefixes* section of the wordlist.

1 A stranger .... (correct) believed my friend was a famous singer but she's not!
2 Few musicians are .... (place) these days. Most disappear after a few years.
3 Jazz music is usually .... (important) to people my age as they prefer pop or R&B.
4 There might have been some good 90s bands but their music is .... (relevant) today.
5 The cover made it look like a heavy rock album but I was .... (take).
6 I think it's a real .... (advantage) when you can't hear the words a singer is singing.
7 Most albums are .... (perfect) in some way but this one's just wonderful.
8 Selling a few hundred thousand records is not .... (significant). It's actually quite a lot.

4 Complete the text with the correct form of words from the *Other* section of the wordlist.

I saw my favourite band play last night. I've watched their ¹.......................... from a local band to a stadium rock band and I've followed them every step of the way. I was full of ².......................... leading up to the gig but it was a bit of a letdown. They played OK but they didn't put any feeling into it, so it all felt a bit ³.......................... . Their performance just didn't ⁴.......................... people's attention at all. I have a feeling they might struggle to maintain their ⁵.......................... over the rock charts over the next few months. There's a lot of ⁶.......................... between them and newer bands who want to take over.

UNIT CHECK

Review

1 Complete the sentences with the correct form of the verbs in brackets. Use the time expressions to help you.

1. Over the last decade, scientists .... (work) on the development of social robots.
2. By the middle of the century, most of us .... (buy) at least one social robot.
3. Already, social robots .... (use) by elderly people living on their own.
4. These days, children with learning difficulties .... (help) by social robots.
5. Soon, we .... (all / have) conversations with our phone as if it's a real person.
6. By 2030, voice activation .... (completely / change) the internet.
7. By the time we reach 2070, we .... (might / all / ask) a robot to do housework.
8. It's possible that when the century ends, robots .... (live) with us like friends.

2 Use the prompts to make predictions. Make any changes necessary.

1. machines / set / take over / more jobs / humans
2. some machines / verge of / perform / intellectual tasks
3. by the middle / century / we / may / create / intelligent machines that make us redundant
4. as a result / people around the world / look for / new forms / employment
5. musicians / point of / be / replaced / today?
6. machines / due / have / a bigger role / production of music

3 🔊 8.10 Listen and check your answers to Ex 2.

4 Read the text and complete the gaps with one word only.

Streaming any time, any place

Many experts predict that in just a few decades' time, scientists ¹........................ have sorted out the problem of connectivity. In the future, we'll no longer struggle to get online ²........................ internet connections will be accessible everywhere. This means we're all set ³........................ stream music, films or games wherever we are without being restricted by data limits, a lack of wi-fi or cost. Yay!

Because we'll have the virtual world ⁴........................ our fingertips wherever we go, we'll also be able to enhance real life through the application of augmented reality apps. In future, more of us will ⁵........................ wandering around playing games like *Pokémon Go* (but probably more advanced) or finding out about the history of a building simply ⁶........................ pointing our phones at it. Of course, if permanent and universal connectivity ⁷........................ to happen, we will have to overcome some major privacy issues. However, by the time our children are born, our definition of privacy may ⁸........................ become very different anyway.

5 Complete the blog post and comments with the correct form of these verbs.

be   carry on   hold out   keep   like   not be   scream   see

I wish I ¹........................ so obsessed with a boy band when I was younger. I spent hours, days, staring at photos and videos, dreaming of the time I'd meet them. As if! So, what past music regrets do you have?

MavisP The first song I ever downloaded was one from a kids' TV show. I wish I ²........................ for something a bit cooler.

Tricky99 Imagine that the first band you ³........................ was with your mum and she ⁴........................ louder than you. Yes, that happened to me and I still cringe when I think about it now.

Youknowmyname I gave up the piano six years ago. If only I ⁵........................ , I ⁶........................ brilliant by now.

Redgirl I don't really have regrets because our tastes are bound to change. As long as what I ⁷........................ now is cool, then I'm happy.

Mickey104 Last year my parents let me go to a music festival on condition that I ⁸........................ my room tidy for the next year. The festival was rubbish and I immediately regretted agreeing to the deal.

6 Write two or three sentences about a regret you have related to music. Share your sentences with the class. Use at least one conditional form.

"I don't like being the centre of attention."

Look at the photo and discuss the questions.
1 Do you think it's wrong to disturb wild animals by watching or photographing them?
2 Why do you think some people choose to have wild animals as pets?
3 What natural environment would you most like to visit (e.g. a desert, a high mountain, a rainforest)? Why?

9

It's a wild world

READING
topic: why humans are interested in wild animals
skill: understanding inferred meaning
task: cross-text multiple matching

GRAMMAR
verb + -ing form or infinitive
reported speech

VOCABULARY
compound nouns on the environment
adjective + noun collocations

LISTENING
topic: funny things pets do
skill: following contrasting ideas and corrections to opinions
task: multiple matching

USE OF ENGLISH
key word transformation
multiple-choice cloze

SPEAKING
topic: working at night
skill: using a variety of phrases
task: long turn

WRITING
topic: outdoor activities
skill: effective introductions and conclusions
task: informal email

SWITCH ON ▶
video: turtle survival
project: environmental protection

9 It's a wild world

READING

Power up

1 Work in pairs and discuss the questions.
1 What animals live wild in your country?
2 What is the relationship like between the wild animals and human populations in your country?
3 What conservation projects do you know in your country or other countries? Do you think they're effective? Why/Why not?

Read on

2 Read the texts by four wildlife conservationists. What are they about? Can you see any immediate similarities or differences in the writers' opinions?

3 What is wildlife tourism? Does it exist in your country?

4 Read the exam tip. Then look at the highlighted section of text A. If the section were followed by the words 'and so … ,' what idea would logically follow it?

> **exam tip: cross-text multiple matching**
>
> Thinking about the implication of a statement often helps you to understand it. It can be useful when you read a statement to think: 'What would come next if the statement was followed by 'and so… ?''
>
> Read the sentence beginning and choose the logical continuation.
>
> The existing conservation projects have been ineffective and so
> A we should continue using the same methods.
> B we should consider an alternative approach.

5 Find the sentences in texts B–D about the impact of human contact on animals' way of life. Which text also implies we should stop contact with animals?

6 e Read the texts again. For questions 1–4, choose from the texts (A–D).
Which writer:
1 has the same opinion as writer A on the impact of human-animal contact on animals' way of life?
2 shares the same views as writer D on wildlife experts in the media and conservation?
3 has a different opinion to the other three writers on why people want to interact with wild animals?
4 expresses a similar opinion to writer B on the impact of wildlife tourism on the animals?

7 What ideas do the highlighted words from the texts refer back to? What is the implication of these statements?
1 Its impact on animal health is a concern. (text A)
2 Such images can draw attention away from the fact that mass extinction is threatening all life. (text B)
3 It's controversial but often it may be the only way of making them safe. (text C)
4 This is not necessarily so. (text D)

Sum up

8 What were the main points that the writers highlighted? Whose views did you find the most persuasive? Why?

Speak up

9 Work in pairs and discuss the questions.
1 Do you think that the benefits of wildlife tourism outweigh the downsides?
2 Do you enjoy wildlife programmes on television? Has this article changed your opinion of them? Why/Why not?

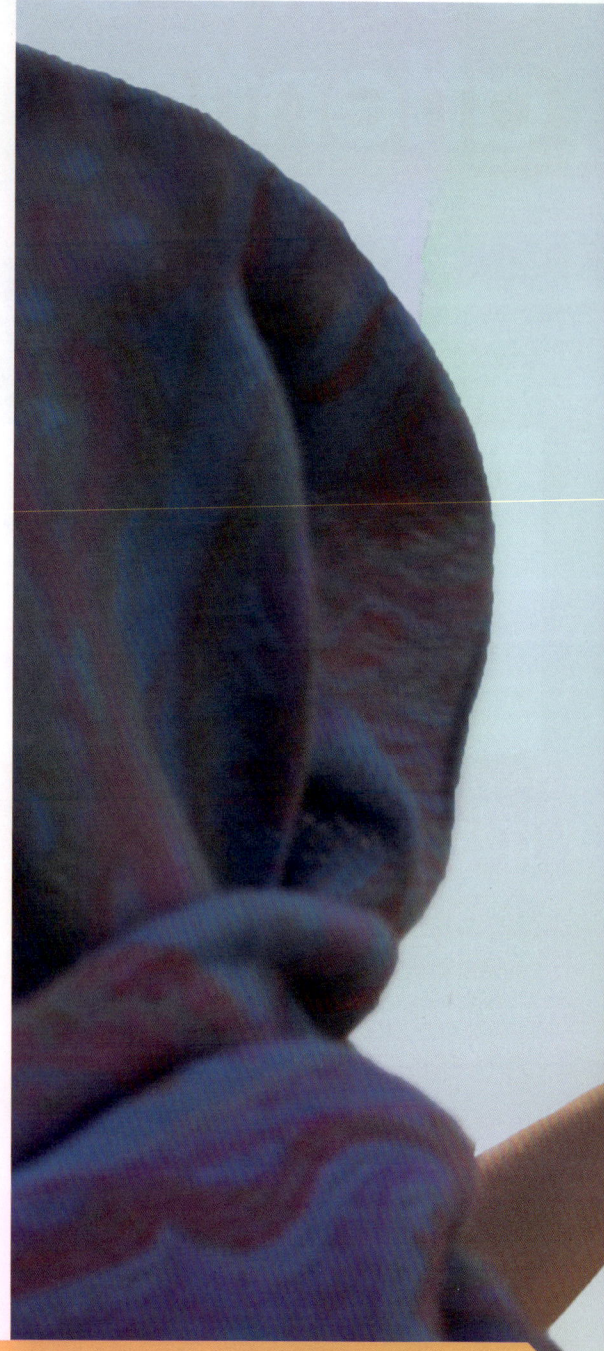

Why are humans drawn to wild animals

A Do we need to get close to animals to value and protect them? One viral video recently showed the conservationist Kevin Richardson hugging lions that he'd helped raise and then released into the wild. It showed these killer animals in a positive light, as emotional beings, with the capacity to remember kindness. This emotional connection draws many of us to form bonds with animals, especially now we've swapped farm life for office cubicles and concrete jungles. The appeal of wild animals is strong, and as a result, wildlife tourism is growing in popularity. However, we know that getting close to wild animals will inevitably be intrusive. It interferes negatively with the animals' natural behaviour, and in the worst case, may be catastrophic, no matter how much we want to do it. Mass wildlife tourism does just that. Its impact on animal health is a concern and there's already a wide body of evidence to support this view. Therefore, tourism isn't the way forward.

B Many people desire to be close to nature. There's a spirit of joy and happiness in the natural world that we're losing now we live in cities. Television documentaries serve to remind us of this. Presenters encourage us to share their appreciation and love for the animals they work with, and we do, but the world isn't like that anymore. Such images can draw attention away from the fact that mass extinction is threatening all life on our planet. They encourage contact between humans and wild animals, with wildlife tourism on the rise, and it's taking a tragic toll on the creatures it's meant to protect. For example, in one study, stingrays that lived around a tourist beach had weak immune systems due to contact with humans. However, while allowing tourism isn't the perfect solution, it may be the only hope for survival for many creatures. Alternative approaches to guaranteeing their habitats for the future are few and ineffective.

C Humans increasingly live their lives inside buildings. Although we often have little direct experience of animals, we've been encouraged to expect that contact with them will provide opportunities for photographs and a transitory feeling of well-being. Television shows often reinforce these false impressions. Recently, one six-year-old child ended up bitten after trying to approach a rattlesnake. The child cited a TV presenter's actions as proof that it was safe to do so. When wild animals and humans meet even today humans can come to harm. Governments have a difficult decision to make when deciding whether to allow extensive tourism in wildlife areas. It's controversial but often it may be the only way of making them safe. Alternative types of land use would almost guarantee the animal's death. Providing food for the animals often means allowing certain levels of tourism. And demand for such tourism is booming.

D You would hope that any contact between humans and animals would remind us of the value of the world around us and make us do more to save it. This is not necessarily so. Historically, people feared wild animals, and part of our fascination today is the natural draw to overcome those fears. Contact with wild animals can make you feel stronger and more powerful. Promoting tourism in wildlife conservation areas attempts to exploit these primal needs. Our desire to travel to see wild animals in their natural habitat is also stoked by the increasing sophistication of TV wildlife documentaries. But even the best documentaries give the wrong impression. By focussing on nature reserves where wildlife is flourishing, they also draw attention away from the reality that much of the countryside is now sterile and overfarmed. And while green tourism brings income into an area in need, only a tiny fraction of that money goes directly to conserving the land. The majority is taken as profit and is often used to promote more tourism. This, in turn, leaves animals with new threats to their well-being and new problems to solve, which is not a solution.

9 It's a wild world

GRAMMAR

1 What two verb patterns are used with the verb 'mean' in these sentences? What is the difference in meaning between the two uses?

1 Contact is taking its toll on the very creatures it's meant to protect.
2 Providing food for the animals often means allowing certain levels of tourism.

2 Read the grammar box and check your answers to Ex 1.

explore grammar → p158

verb + -ing form or infinitive

Some verbs are followed by an -ing form or a to-infinitive with no change in meaning.

I **can't bear seeing/to see** him like this.

Some verbs are followed by an -ing form or a to-infinitive but there is a change in meaning.

We **mean to protect** animals. (mean = intend to)

Protecting animals **means allowing** tourism. (means = involves)

With sense verbs (e.g. feel, hear, notice, see, smell, taste, watch), we can use an -ing form or an infinitive without to, but there is a slight change in meaning.

I **heard** her **singing**. (The action was in progress.)
I **heard** her **sing**. (The action is completed.)

3 🔊 9.1 Listen to part of a talk about the next steps for environmentalists. What does it say about people's attitudes to environmentalism?

4 🔊 9.2 Complete the sentences with the correct form of the verbs. Then listen again and check your answers. Which piece of information did you find surprising?

1 If we intend .... (move) things forward, we need to consider our message.
2 People will soon resent .... (waste) their time listening to the same old complaints.
3 We cannot risk .... (harm) important natural habitats any longer.
4 I increasingly overhear .... (audiences / say) that the message has become repetitive.
5 We need to make .... (people / reconsider) the environmentalist movement.
6 They had noticed .... (soap suds / pour) out of taps.
7 Housewives initially obliged .... (governments / take) action.
8 Our ancestors permitted .... (whole populations / destroy) forests.

5 Read the article. Where do polar bears normally live? What do some biologists propose doing to save them?

Let's FedEx polar bears to the South Pole

The climate is heating up faster than we can react, and few have stopped ¹**to think / thinking** about the consequences. Some biologists are coming round to the view that if we seriously mean ²**to save / saving** certain animals, then it's time to take drastic action – even if this means ³**to transplant / transplanting** creatures around the planet. Is it time to FedEx polar bears to Antarctica? It may seem unthinkable, but a few scientists are starting to consider relocating animals in this way. Many biologists have tried everything ⁴**to save / saving** the habitats where these animals live, with no notable success. We can't go on ⁵**to create / creating** barriers of urban and agricultural land across their natural environment and expect them to survive. And so for some, it's now time to forget ⁶**to leave / leaving** nature to sort the problem out, and look at all possible solutions.

6 Read the article again and choose the correct verbs. Explain your aswers.

Speak up

7 Work in pairs. Think of three other endangered animals and discuss what can be done to protect them.

VOCABULARY
compound nouns on the environment

1 Work in pairs. What do you think are the most persuasive reasons to look after the environment? Rank these ideas 1–6, (1 = most persuasive, 6 = least persuasive).

caring about future generations   feeling good about yourself
good for the national economy   having nice countryside to enjoy
personal health reasons   saving money personally

2 Read the article. What is the dangerous realisation?

A dangerous realisation

Much has been written about the hole in the **ozone layer**. Various scientists had speculated about the role that ozone played in regulating our atmosphere, but by the 1990s, it became inescapable that the delicate balance of chemicals was changing and dangerous rays from the sun were coming through the ozone towards the surface of the Earth. At the same time, other changes were taking place. Burning **fossil fuels**, such as oil and coal, were producing carbon dioxide and **carbon monoxide**, both of which are **greenhouse gases**. These gases created a layer around the planet that stopped heat being reflected back into space. These gases became even more common with intensive farming methods and increased numbers of **landfill sites**, where huge amounts of rubbish were dumped. The whole process became known as the **greenhouse effect**. Thanks to global efforts to control these problems, the hole in the ozone is beginning to repair itself again, but more work is needed to reduce the greenhouse effect.

3 Read the article again. Complete the sentences with the compound nouns in bold from the text.

1 The .... is the gradual warming of the air around the planet.
2 .... are places where waste is buried under the ground.
3 .... are produced over millions of years from decayed animals and plants.
4 .... are thought to trap heat above the Earth.
5 The .... prevents harmful radiation from the sun reaching the Earth.
6 .... is a poisonous gas that is produced when things burn in too little air.

4 Work in pairs. Cover the article and try to explain the causes and effects of damage to the ozone layer and the greenhouse effect.

5 🔊 9.3 Listen to a man talking about changes in the way we now look at the environment. What main change does he mention?

6 🔊 9.4 Match a word from each group to form compound nouns. Listen again and check. Can you explain what the words mean?

acid   carbon   climate   conservation   emissions   green
nature   ~~rain~~   sustainable

area   audit   change   development   ~~forest~~
rain   reserve   trading (x2)

7 Complete the questions with compound nouns from this page.

1 Would you buy from a company that has had a very poor .... ? Why/Why not?
2 Do you think rich governments should be allowed to practise .... ? Why/Why not?
3 Do you think tax breaks for good behaviour are the only way to reduce .... ? Why/Why not?
4 Do you think that .... such as forests can only be protected by laws? Why/Why not?
5 Is .... economic .... possible without lowering living standards?

8 Work in pairs and discuss the questions in Ex 7. Use at least one different compound noun from this page in each answer.

Speak up

9 Do you think countries that produce consumer goods such as cars and mobile phones should be responsible for their carbon emissions? Or should the countries where these goods are consumed take responsibility? Why?

9 It's a wild world

LISTENING

Power up

1 Work in pairs and discuss the questions.
1. Do you have a pet? If so, how did you end up with that particular pet? If not, what kind of pet would you like? Why?
2. Do you think that pets can have their own personality? Why/Why not?

Listen up

2 9.5 Listen to a man talking about his cat. You will hear a gap with a beep. Choose the best phrase to complete the gap. Why are the other two phrases wrong?
1. she's lazy
2. she loves her toy
3. nothing happened

3 9.6 Listen again and answer the questions.
1. What does the man first say about his cat?
2. What topic does he move on to?
3. Which option (A–C) best summarises how he feels about his cat?
   A impressed how proud his cat can be
   B amused by how excited certain objects make his cat
   C entertained by the cat's attempts to hide its behaviour

4 Read the exam tip and complete the task.

> **exam** tip: multiple matching
>
> People often clarify ideas after they've said them. Don't worry if you don't understand something as it might be explained immediately after.
>
> Listen again. What do these phrases mean? Which words helped you?
>
> little more than a lazy ball of fur
> take a nap

5 9.7 You are going to hear five people talking about their pets. Listen and complete the tasks.

Task 1

For questions 1–5, choose from the list (A–H) what made each speaker choose to get their pet from a specific place.

A the type of organisations involved
B the attractiveness of the website
C the involvement with charities
D the accuracy of information provided
E the ease of communication
F the speed of the service
G the availability of advice
H the use of social media

Speaker 1 1 ☐
Speaker 2 2 ☐
Speaker 3 3 ☐
Speaker 4 4 ☐
Speaker 5 5 ☐

Task 2

For questions 6–10, choose from the list (A–H) how each speaker feels about their pet.

A entertained by its attempts to hide its behaviour
B taken aback by how scared other people make it
C touched by the way it copies its owners
D amused by its enjoyment of television
E curious about its attitude to a partner
F amazed that it can't recognise itself
G impressed how proud it can get
H surprised that it dislikes change

Speaker 1 6 ☐
Speaker 2 7 ☐
Speaker 3 8 ☐
Speaker 4 9 ☐
Speaker 5 10 ☐

6 How did the speakers use these phrases? What did they say about them?

the right priorities   easily distracted
make the transition easier
I love my dog to bits!

Speak up

7 Work in pairs. What kind of things should you consider before choosing a pet? Think about size, cost, the pet's needs and the time you can invest. What pet might suit your partner?

Did you know a cat will almost never meow at another cat? It's a sound they reserve for humans!

USE OF ENGLISH 1

1 🔊 **9.8 Listen to people talking about odd pets. Which speaker (1–6):**
- **A** denied doing anything wrong?
- **B** refused to let the animal do something?
- **C** admitted to giving the animal what it wanted?
- **D** confessed to doing something the pet didn't like?
- **E** blamed a very small pet for something wrong?
- **F** regretted making a mistake?

2 Read the grammar box. Which patterns are used with the reporting verbs in Ex 1? Complete the examples.

explore grammar → p158

reported speech

A lot of reporting verbs can be followed by a *that* clause or another verb pattern (e.g. *to*-infinitive, *-ing* form, preposition + *-ing* form).

The man denied that he had done anything wrong.
The man denied ¹............................ anything wrong.

The woman confessed that she'd put her dog in a ballerina costume.
The woman confessed ²............................ her dog in a ballerina costume.

3 Complete the article with the correct form of the verbs in brackets. Add a preposition if necessary.

Find your **perfect pet** through an algorithm

Few would deny ¹............................ (feel) concerned about the problem of pets that are abandoned because their owners can't look after them. However, a new service claims ²............................ (ease) the process of rehousing them for everyone involved.

Pet-matching company Pawslikeme have boasted ³............................ (use) an algorithm that will help match potential dog owners with their perfect pet with astonishing accuracy. Founder Elizabeth Holmes insists ⁴............................ (it / be) possible to achieve a ninety percent accuracy rate with their search engine algorithm.

Existing pet owners are advised ⁵............................ (complete) a personality assessment for their furry friends. Then new owners agree ⁶............................ (meet) certain criteria for the pet, such as the size of the garden, the ages of the other members of the household and any pre-existing pets. New owners are urged ⁷............................ (consider) their human lifestyle considerations very carefully before being matched with unique canine qualities, such as energy levels, independence and the need for affection. The company admits ⁸............................ (adapt) their assessment from work in the fields of animal behaviour and veterinary psychology.

4 Read the exam tip and complete the task.

exam tip: key word transformation

In reported speech, don't forget to change pronouns and adverbs where necessary.

What do these words change to in reported speech?

I – ....
tonight – ....
here – ....

5 🅔 Complete the second sentence so that it has a similar meaning to the first sentence using the word given. Do not change the word given. Use between three and six words.

1 Olivia said that hurting John's feelings wasn't intentional.
MEAN
Olivia said that she .... John's feelings.

2 Emily said I'd done something wrong.
BLAMED
Emily .... something wrong.

3 The man said, 'It was me that let the dog out.'
CONFESSED
The man .... the dog out.

4 'I'm going to have to say that I made this mistake,' said Diana.
ADMIT
Diana said she was going to have to .... mistake.

5 Max said, 'I won't go with you tonight, Susie'.
REFUSED
Max .... Susie that night.

6 Jack said he shouldn't have kept so many animals in his flat.
REGRETTED
Jack .... a lot of animals in his flat.

Speak up

6 Do you think the algorithm used in Ex 3 is a good method of matching pets to owners? What is the best way to choose a pet?

9 It's a wild world

USE OF ENGLISH 2

1 Work in pairs and discuss the questions.

1. Does your culture have myths about the moon?
2. Why do you think many cultures see moonlight as romantic?
3. How might life on our planet be different if the moon weren't there?

2 🔊 9.9 Read the language box below and complete the task. Then read these statements. Look at the highlighted nouns and choose the best adjectives to complete the collocations. Listen and check your answers.

1. This **up-to-date / groundbreaking** project was little more than some **elaborate / complicated** hoax.
2. The lunar cycle has a **direct / straight** impact on the **environmental / natural** development of plants.
3. The moon has such a **heavy / strong** influence on the planet that without it, an earth day would last a **simple / mere** six to eight hours.
4. When a full moon fell on a Sunday, it was considered a **warning / risky** sign, but it was thought to have the **opposite / contrasting** effect on a Monday.
5. People develop **annoyed / aggressive** behaviour around a full moon or are less likely to fall into a **rich / sound** sleep.

explore language → p161

adjective + noun collocations

The best way to learn collocations is by reading and noticing them in context.

Find three adjective + noun collocations in these sentences.

The earliest forms of space travel involved sending animals rather than highly-trained astronauts into space. The moon landings represented a major breakthrough at that time.

3 🔊 9.10 Listen again. Which ideas do the speakers think are myth? Which do they think are real?

4 Read the article. What is daylight saving? Does it happen in your country?

What a difference an hour makes!

In many countries, every spring and autumn, they move the clocks backwards or forwards one hour while the population is **1**........ asleep. Benjamin Franklin takes the honour, or the **2**........, depending on how you see it, for resetting clocks in this way. He **3**........ people to take advantage of the extra evening light in summer to do worthwhile activities, and he highlighted the obvious savings on lighting their homes. **4**........, it was over a century before his plans were introduced into the US. Spare a thought for the people living there when it first came in. The government **5**........ it up to individual towns to decide if they wanted to **6**........ the proposal, and chaos followed.

Russia introduced year-round daylight saving time in 2011, to take advantage of the sunlight, but it had the **7**........ effect. In the depths of winter, sunrise wasn't until 11 a.m., and the plan was abolished. With modern lighting and over half the planet refusing to join in, it might all seem a bit **8**........ continuing with the idea.

1	**A** hard	**B** light	**C** shallow	**D** sound
2	**A** blame	**B** guilt	**C** complaint	**D** duty
3	**A** complained	**B** urged	**C** commented	**D** confessed
4	**A** Indeed	**B** However	**C** Likewise	**D** Otherwise
5	**A** brought	**B** took	**C** made	**D** left
6	**A** obey	**B** implement	**C** stick	**D** observe
7	**A** differing	**B** contrasting	**C** opposite	**D** competing
8	**A** pointless	**B** aimless	**C** directionless	**D** goalless

5 e Read the article again and decide which answer (A, B, C or D) best fits each gap.

Speak up

6 Do you think it's better to live in a country where the sun comes up and sets at the same time all year round? Why/Why not?

SPEAKING

Power up

1 Work in pairs and discuss the questions.
1 What time of day do you work best? Why?
2 Which of these activities do you enjoy doing when it's sunny outside? Which do you prefer to do after dark? Why?

a barbecue   a beach party   bowling   the cinema   a pool party

2 Work in pairs. Look at photos A and C. What do they show? What do the jobs have in common? How are they different? How do you think the people feel doing their job?

3 Work in pairs. How could you complete the sentences for picture A?
1 On the one hand, it must feel good to know that you're offering an important service, but on the other hand, …
2 I'm sure he meets a lot of nice people in his work, but …
3 The roads should be much quieter as …
4 All in all, I think he probably feels …

4 9.11 Listen to a student comparing photos A and B. How could she expand her answer?

5 9.12 Listen to another student comparing the same photos. Why is his answer better?

exam tip: long turn

Listen to what your partner says and look at all three photos. Be ready to answer a follow-up question.

Complete the phrases with these words.

coming from   point

1 I see Yerhan's ………………… about the two jobs, but …
2 I see where Yerhan's ………………… , but I think any successful DJ probably loves their job.

6 9.13 Read the exam tip and complete the task. Listen to how another student answers a follow-up question on which job is preferable. Do you agree with him? Why/Why not?

7 Repeat the activity in Ex 2 comparing one of the photos with photo C.

8 e Work in pairs. Turn to page 177 and complete the task.

Speak up

9 At what age do you think people should be allowed to work after dark? Why? What are some of the problems of working in the late evening?

Did you know that in Reykjavik, in June, the night only lasts an hour and a half?

9 It's a wild world

WRITING

Power up

1 Work in pairs. Compare the two sports in the photos. What do they have in common? What differences are there? What benefits do they have? What problems do you associate with them?

2 Match these words with the categories below. Which activity might you need these things for?

helmet   life jacket   open water   paddle   perseverance   plenty of layers
rapids   ropes   strong swimmer   upper body strength   wetsuit

clothing	equipment	places	qualities

Plan on

3 Read an extract from an email. What do you need to bear in mind when you write your reply?

Hi!
Can you help me find a new sport to do? I'm bored with badminton and I want something that will do me good without costing a fortune! I don't really have any restrictions, except that it must be an activity I can do outdoors, and I don't have a big budget for this. I want to get away from my desk and get out in the open air. What do you suggest?

---

4 Work in pairs and discuss one activity that you would each recommend. Consider these points.
- the benefits of the activity
- the ease/cost of the activity
- ways to get started in the activity
- how it gets you into the fresh air/natural environment
- any disadvantages of the activity

5 Read a reply to the email in Ex 3. Choose the most suitable phrases to complete it. Why are they suitable?

👤 To: **Jemma**   👤 From: **Clare**

Hi Jemma,

¹**It's so lovely to hear from you!** / I'm writing in response to your request for activity ideas. It's been ages. I'm really pleased to hear that you're finally getting a bit of time to yourself after all that studying!

Well, you know I'm a bit of an outdoor activity fan, so you've come to the right person. Without a doubt, the best activity I can recommend is kayaking. Provided you stick to calm water on a clear day, it's easier than it sounds and ²**I think it would be beneficial to you.** / I'm sure you'd get so much out of it! It's so relaxing, plus you get to see the landscape from a completely new perspective. ³**I have to admit to feeling a bit envious of you, with all those gorgeous mountains!** / I feel confident that the mountain air will be suitable. Just a word of warning, ⁴**I must insist on you sharing information on your whereabouts with others.** / Whatever you do, make sure you let someone know where you're going.

The downside of kayaking is that you do need transport and you need to spend a bit of money, although you can get a second-hand kayak online these days. Have you thought about gardening? You can do it in our local neighbourhood. There's a charity near you that arranges to send volunteers to tidy up gardens for elderly people who can't manage it any more. You'll feel good inside and out! I can send you their details if you want!

Anyway, ⁵**I look forward to hearing from you shortly.** / I'll finish up now because I have to run to the shops before closing.

Lots of love to you and your family!

Clare

6 Match the phrases (1–5) in the email in Ex 5 with the functions (A–E).
   A describing something positively
   B warning someone
   C closing an email
   D greeting someone
   E persuading someone

7 Read the language box and complete the task.

explore language

using a consistent style

Remember that you need to show a consistently appropriate style, even in your choice of linkers.

What is wrong with this sentence? Which of the phrases below could you use to make the style consistent?

In addition, just imagine all that amazing scenery around you!

1 Oh, by the way, …
2 On top of all that, …

8 Read the extract from another email. Which five highlighted words or phrases are too formal? How could you express the ideas in more informal language?

---

¹I just know you'll love open water paddle boarding. I know that buying a paddle board ²might be inadvisable, but you don't have to ³resort to buying your own. ⁴There are opportunities to rent rather than ⁵purchase one. ⁶In the case of any problems obtaining the equipment, just drop me a line and ⁷I'll see if I can help out. Oh, and another thing – ⁸please let me assure you that ⁹I'm always up for a weekend trip with you if you want ¹⁰a bit of company.

Write on

9 Look at the email in Ex 3 again and think about your reply. Choose a different activity, NOT kayaking. Think about how to recommend the activity and make a paragraph plan.

Paragraph 1: greeting ....
Paragraph 2: ....
Paragraph 3: ....
Paragraph 4: closing comments ....

10 Now plan your reply. Think about:
   • a friendly greeting
   • your audience and tone
   • persuasive language
   • informal connectors
   • some friendly closing remarks.

11 e Write your email in 220–260 words.

Improve it

12 Read your email again. Highlight any examples of vocabulary or grammar that you have learnt in the last year. Are you using the full range of language available to you?

13 Work in pairs. Read your partner's email. Is there anywhere they could add some higher level language?

129

SWITCH ON

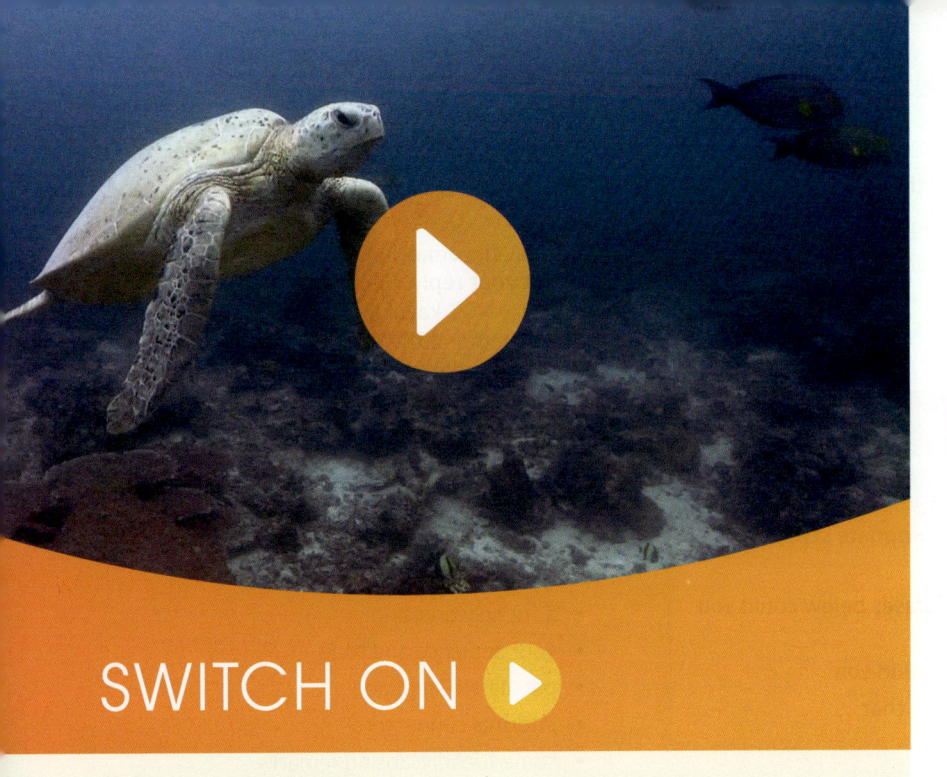

Turtle survival

1. Work in pairs. In five minutes, list as many animals as you can in three categories: Endangered, Vulnerable and Least concern. Check your answers online.

2. ▶ Watch the clip. List the ways in which humans intervene to boost turtle numbers.

3. ▶ Watch again. Work in pairs.
   1. How do we know the gender of the turtles without checking? Explain in one sentence.
   2. How many green turtles survive into adulthood in the wild and why? How do we know?

4. Work in pairs. What was the purpose of filming and broadcasting this project?

5. As a class, debate this statement.
   'It is inappropriate for humans to intervene when a species is not surviving in the wild.'

Project

6. Work in small groups to research the impact of humans on an endangered species.
   1. Research information about its natural environment and the impact of humans on the species.
   2. Choose a particular conservation project or initiative connected to this species. Explain why you think it has been a success or a failure.
   3. Convert your findings into graphics with statistical information.
   4. Present and explain it to the class.

INDEPENDENT LEARNING

Skill review

1. Thinking about your progress over the course so far, what skill areas have you improved? Use the independent learning goals from Units 1–8 if you need a reminder. How have you improved? Write two tips for another student on how to improve in that skill.

   1 ....

   2 ....

2. Work in groups. Share your ideas and notes on the tips that other students have written. Find two that you would like to try in the future. Write them here.

   1 ....

   2 ....

3. Was there one goal that you feel you didn't achieve? What can you do in the next few weeks to make a difference in that area?

   ....

4. How would you like to use English in the future? Which skills (reading, writing, listening or speaking) do you think you will need? How would you use them?

   ....

130

UNIT CHECK

Wordlist

The environment
acid rain (n)
carbon monoxide (n)
carbon trading (n)
climate change (n)
conservation area (n)
emissions trading (n)
fossil fuels (n)
green audit (n)
greenhouse effect (n)
greenhouse gases (n)
landfill site (n)
nature reserve (n)
ozone layer (n)
rain forest (n)
sustainable development (n)

Reporting verbs
admit to (doing smth)
advise (doing smth)
advise (sb to do smth)
agree (to do smth)
blame (sb for doing smth)
boast (about doing smth)
claim (to do smth)
confess (to doing smth)
deny (doing smth)
insist on (doing smth)
recommend (doing smth)
refuse (to do smth)
regret (doing smth)
urge (sb to do smth)

Adjective + noun collocations
aggressive behaviour
a mere (six hours/four days/etc.)
elaborate hoax
groundbreaking project
have a direct impact (on smth)
have a strong influence (on smth)
have the opposite effect
natural development
sound sleep
warning sign

Sports clothing, equipment, places and qualities
buoyancy aid (n)
cliff (n)
helmet (n)
open water (n)
paddle (n)
perseverance (n)
plenty of layers (phr)
rapids (n)
ropes (n)
strong swimmer (phr)
training wall (n)
upper-body strength (n)
wetsuit (n)

Other
donate money (phr)
easily distracted (phr)
faceless (adj)
lazy ball of fur (phr)
love (sb/smth) to bits (phr)
the right priorities (phr)

Vocabulary

1 Complete the article with compound nouns from the *Environment* section of the wordlist.

The blame game

Every organism on Earth is affected by others around it. When temperatures rise as a result of ¹..................., plants begin to die out and even former safe zones, such as ²..................., can become hostile places. The environment crosses international borders. When harmful ³................... are burned in one country, winds carry the resulting ⁴................... far beyond national borders. For centuries, the forests in Northern Sweden were a ⁵................... where the natural environment was protected, but then the trees started dying off. The cause was a mixture of chemicals produced by early industrialisation. Those chemicals mixed with water in the air and fell back down over Sweden as ⁶.................... This pollution was beyond the control of the Swedish government. Similar problems have affected the Southern Hemisphere. For economic reasons, some nations have sold off their natural resources, such as trees or minerals, but this is not ⁷.................... So, which nation should take the blame?

2 🔊 9.14 Listen to six people. What collocation from the *Adjective + noun collocations* section of the wordlist does the beep represent?

1 ....   3 ....   5 ....
2 ....   4 ....   6 ....

3 🔊 9.15 Listen and check your answers.

4 Complete the ads with vocabulary for sports clothing, equipment, places and qualities.

Try out a new SPORT TODAY!

Abseiling
Join our team as they descend down a ¹................... attached to ropes. Our experts will be on hand to keep you safe. You'll need a ²................... to protect your head, which you can hire from our office, and if you're abseiling around water, you'll also need a ³..................., in case you fall in.

Paddleboarding
This popular California sport is suitable for all comers. Unlike kayaking, which often takes place in ⁴..................., paddleboarding is a much gentler sport, taking place in the calm ⁵................... of the bay. You'll need a board and a ⁶................... to move about but otherwise, just come ready to have fun!

UNIT CHECK

Review

1 Complete the sentences with the correct form of the verbs in brackets.

1. I felt obliged .... (take) my neighbour's dog for a walk when he was sick.
2. My dad resents .... (have to) feed the cat.
3. My friend neglected .... (tell) me that her dog was afraid of loud noises.
4. My sister vowed .... (get) a cat as soon as she has her own place.
5. Next door's cat quit .... (try) to get into our garden when we got a dog.

2 Complete the article with the correct form of the verbs in brackets.

Few people can deny ¹.................... (feel) uncomfortable when the question of research on animals arises. The topic has proven ².................... (be) a divisive issue. Companies that continue to test cosmetics on animals deserve ³.................... (receive) angry criticism but at the same time, not many people want to stop ⁴.................... (test) new, experimental medicines on animals. In fact, no drugs companies can neglect ⁵.................... (go through) this stage of testing by law. On the surface, the idea of testing new drugs on animals makes sense. However, there are problems with it. Many experts refuse ⁶.................... (accept) that the physiology of an animal is the same as a human's, so they argue that testing on animals is not useful. Furthermore, children do not respond in the same way as adults to medicines, so prescribing medicines to children involves ⁷.................... (apply) a different set of rules. For these reasons, many believe that animal testing requires ⁸.................... (rethink), and new guidelines are needed.

3 Match the first half of each sentence (1–6) with the second half (A–F).

Principles of animal research

1. Our legal system recommends
2. In the future, technological advances could mean
3. Internationally, governments encourage
4. Anyone carrying out experiments on animals should stop
5. International governments recommend animals
6. According to the rules on animal testing, drugs require

A. be treated humanely, with appropriate housing.
B. researchers to check if data they could use already exists somewhere else in the world.
C. administering in such a way as to ensure that the animal feels no pain.
D. replacing the use of animals with other techniques where possible.
E. to consider whether their experiment is necessary or not.
F. using computer modelling rather than live animals.

> "I always get **my own way**."

Look at the photo and discuss the questions.
1. What's the best way to get your point across? Which ways are not effective?
2. How good are you at getting your point across when you need to?
3. Which is more important in communication? Being a good speaker or a good listener? Why?

10 Speak to me

READING
topic: communicating in different cultures
task: multiple matching

LISTENING
topic: attracting attention
task: multiple choice: short extracts

USE OF ENGLISH
multiple-choice cloze
open cloze
word formation
key word transformation

SPEAKING
topic: how we communicate
tasks: interview; long turn; collaborative task; discussion

WRITING
topics: work experience; a talent show; a summer festival
task: Part 2 choices

10 Speak to me

READING

Power up

1 Work in pairs. What would you say to a friend in these situations?
1. He/She has had a terrible haircut and asks you to give an honest opinion.
2. He/She keeps talking non-stop when you're trying to study.
3. He/She has asked for feedback on an essay which you think is not very good.

2 Work in pairs. Read the definition and discuss the questions below.

> **intercultural communication skills** (*phr*): the ability to communicate with different people who speak different languages or live in different cultures

1. Why is it important to know about intercultural communication?
2. Do you think it relates only to language? Why/Why not?
3. Do you think you might deal with the situations in Ex 1 differently if your friend was from a different country or culture? Why/Why not?

Read on

3 e Read the article and choose from the paragraphs (A–G) the one which best fits each gap (1–6). There is one extra paragraph which you do not need to use.

4 Find words or phrases in the article that mean the following.
1. people the same age as you with the same job, etc. (para i)
2. difficult to deal with (para i)
3. suddenly surprised or shocked (para ii)
4. coming before something in time and order (para iii)
5. something you think is true but have no proof (para v)
6. be noticed or understood (para v)
7. explain or decide what something means (para D)
8. funny (para B)

Sum up

5 Work in pairs. Discuss how you could summarise the article, then write one sentence to summarise it. Compare your sentence with another pair. Which one is more accurate?

Speak up

6 Work in pairs and discuss the questions.
1. How direct or indirect are people when giving criticism in your culture?
2. What advice would you give someone who wants to complain or criticise someone in your culture?
3. How important is it for you to learn how to communicate with people from different cultures? Why?

A During a one-to-one meeting with a British professor, he was given the 'suggestion' to approach his dissertation differently. He considered the suggestion and decided not to use it. Little did he know that the 'suggestion' actually meant 'change your approach right away' so he was surprised when he got a low grade.

B In light of this, Markus now softens what he says to people from less direct cultures. If giving negative feedback, he starts with a few positive comments before easing into the feedback with 'a few small suggestions'. He ends by stating, 'This is just my opinion.' This process is quite humorous from Markus' point of view … but he says it works.

C On hearing those words, I thought to myself, 'This culture is … well, *different* from my own.' People in different parts of the world are conditioned to give feedback in drastically different ways. As seen, some people learn always to be honest whereas others learn never to criticise someone openly or are conditioned to wrap positive messages around negative ones.

D As a result of his newly found awareness, Markus learned to ignore all the soft words surrounding a message from his British professors. Of course, the other lesson was to consider how they might interpret his messages. He realised that when he gave feedback in the way typical of his culture, he used words that made the message sound as strong as possible without thinking much about it.

E One issue he had was being able to start a discussion in the first place. He found it easier to subtly encourage the listener to bring up the topic rather than introduce it himself. It wasn't what he was used to, but it seemed effective. He had to learn to be tentative in his approach and to expect very different things from his own cultural context.

F It was Willem's turn, one of the participants, who described a falling out with his university head. 'How can I fix this relationship?' he asked. Sophie, a fellow countrywoman, knew Willem well and offered her view. 'You're socially awkward, so you don't communicate very well.' As Willem listened, his ears turning red, everyone else stared uncomfortably at their feet.

G By contrast, other cultures use words that soften the criticism, such as 'kind of' and 'a bit'. They may also use an understatement, such as 'We're not quite there yet' when they mean 'We're nowhere close to finishing.' That's why you see humorous online translation guides such as 'What the British say and what they really mean.'

In Indian and Bulgarian cultures people move their head right and left to mean 'yes' rather than 'no'.

How to say, 'This is rubbish!' in different cultures

Read Kate's discovery of the importance of intercultural communication.

i I was in Brussels with a group of international student union leaders. We were meeting to discuss issues in our universities and ways we could solve them. We each had twenty minutes to describe in detail a challenge we were experiencing and get feedback and suggestions from our peers. There was a rather awkward interaction between one pair.

1

ii That evening at dinner, I was startled to see the two of them sitting together and laughing. 'I'm glad to see you together,' I said. 'I was afraid you might not be speaking to each other after the discussion this afternoon.' 'Sure, I didn't want to hear about my weaknesses,' came the reply, 'but I appreciated the honesty.'

> 'Sure, I didn't want to hear about my weaknesses,' came the reply, 'but I appreciated the honesty.'

2

iii One way to work out how these different nationalities handle negative feedback is by listening to the types of words they use. More direct cultures tend to use what linguists call 'upgraders', words preceding or following negative feedback that make it stronger, such as absolutely or totally: 'This is totally inappropriate.'

3

iv So why is such familiarity with a culture's way of saying things desirable? Well, globalisation means that universities and companies are international and we now study and work with people from diverse cultures. Markus, a friend from a more direct culture studying at a British university, told me how a misunderstanding almost cost him his degree.

4

v Making the assumption that the message he received was communicated in the same way he communicates himself was my friend's big error. In his culture, people typically use strong words when complaining or criticising in order to make sure the message registers clearly, whereas in Britain people are less direct. Markus soon realised this.

5

vi Self-discoveries like this can be interesting, surprising and sometimes downright painful. As you speak to people in different cultures, your words will be magnified or minimised significantly based on your listener's cultural context. So you have to work to understand how your own way of speaking is viewed in other cultures and make necessary adjustments.

6

vii So what about you? If I had to tell you that your work was rubbish, would I have to take care with my words like Markus or could I simply tell you directly? Where do you think your own culture stands in this regard? It's important to know so it doesn't impact on the success of your studies or career.

10 Speak to me

LISTENING

Power up

1 Work in pairs and discuss the questions.
1 Why do you think some people collect autographs?
2 In what situations do ordinary people need to sign their name?
3 Do you think we will continue to use handwritten signatures in the future? What might replace them?
4 Why do you think some people write their names in public places?

2 🔊 10.1 You are going to listen to a man, Nick, talking about signatures. Listen and complete each gap with a word or short phrase.

The importance of *signatures*

Nick was surprised to learn that pens used to sign important documents are often used as ¹............................ after the event.

Nick doubts that a ²............................ will continue to be used much longer for identification purposes.

Nick thinks the main problem with pen signatures is that they don't show what's called ³............................ .

Nick argues that changes to ⁴............................ have allowed computer signatures to become more accepted.

Nick prefers the words '⁵............................ signatures' to describe signatures written in pen.

Nick is convinced that ⁶............................ offer the best form of security.

According to Nick, people expect to see ⁷............................ of people signing an important document.

Nick feels that few people will be prepared to sign a ⁸............................ electronically.

3 🔊 10.2 You are going to listen to an interview with two historians about ancient graffiti. For questions 1–6, choose the answer (A, B, C or D) which fits best according to what you hear.

1 How does Jenny feel about her work?
   A She's worried about the stability of the buildings on archaeological sites.
   B She's often concerned about being locked in overnight.
   C It's unpleasant because of the difficult conditions.
   D It's risky because of the resident animals.

2 According to Mark, studying ancient graffiti
   A was more interesting than he expected.
   B became more urgent during his career.
   C proved more challenging in the past.
   D took longer than he'd expected.

3 Jenny believes that in Roman times, graffiti was
   A considered by artists to be worth risking their safety for.
   B seen as a way of sharing positive messages.
   C manipulated to communicate leaders' views.
   D used as a method of showing social status.

4 What does Mark say is the most important academic value of graffiti?
   A It gives opposing opinions to those expressed elsewhere.
   B It allows us to change the way we see historical events.
   C It contains attractive examples of literature and art.
   D It shows the views of ordinary people at the time.

5 Jenny thinks ancient graffiti is distinct from modern graffiti because people
   A were less open about their emotions in the past.
   B felt more able to be critical of the local government.
   C felt more at ease expressing intellectual ideas that way.
   D were less tolerant of the mistakes of famous individuals.

6 What do both speakers think about the international historical graffiti conferences?
   A They reveal an interest in securing important archaeological sites for future generations.
   B They show the current lack of academic interest in ancient graffiti.
   C They demonstrate the public enthusiasm to learn more about graffiti.
   D They clarify the growing number of people working in the field.

Speak up

4 Which aspects of life today do you think future historians will find the most interesting and the most strange?

USE OF ENGLISH 1

1 Work in pairs and discuss the questions.
1. How much do you use emojis to communicate? When?
2. How effective are they for communication? Why?

2 Read the article and decide which answer (A, B, C or D) best fits each gap.

The birth of a new type of language

Ninety-two percent of people online use emojis now, and one-third of them do so daily. On Instagram, **¹**....... half of the posts contain emojis, a trend that began when iOS added an emoji keyboard. Rates **²**....... higher when Android followed suit. Emojis are so popular they're **³**....... a threat to textspeak. The more emojis we use, the less we use 'LOL' and 'OMG'.

In **⁴**......., we're watching the birth of a new type of language. Emojis assist in a peculiarly modern task: **⁵**....... our emotions in short online messages. As linguist Gretchen McCulloch says, they help add tone of voice, something which is **⁶**....... when you're writing online. Some purists hate emojis and think they've **⁷**....... us into kids with crayons. Surely, words alone are enough? Maybe, but according to McCulloch, only if you're a novelist who's gained years of **⁸**....... in creating texts. We normal people tend to write speedily and conversationally, in bursts on SMS or Facebook, and emojis provide a useful shorthand for our feelings.

1	A closely	B practically	C totally	D hardly
2	A soared	B raised	C heightened	D elevated
3	A making	B posing	C giving	D placing
4	A small	B total	C balance	D short
5	A conveying	B implying	C portraying	D remarking
6	A harmful	B coordinated	C problematic	D adverse
7	A turned	B diversified	C altered	D developed
8	A intelligence	B experience	C vision	D judgement

3 Work in pairs and discuss the questions.
1. Do you agree that emojis are a new language? Why/Why not?
2. Do you think they are used too much? Why/Why not?
3. Some people think that our existing language will be negatively affected by emojis. Do you agree? Why/Why not?

4 Read the article. Then work in pairs. Do you agree with the research? Why/Why not? How do you use full stops in text messages?

Ending your messages with a **full stop** is heartless!

Everyone knows that using a full stop to end a text message is unnecessarily harsh, and research now confirms it. Psychologists have found that texts that end **¹**.......................... full stops were perceived to be insincere or fake by the 126 undergraduates they tested. This is probably because the full stop's modern usage is restricted **²**.......................... conveying annoyance.

The study **³**.......................... undertaken when the psychologists spotted a story by a journalist published online in 2013. The journalist **⁴**.......................... written that 'No' with a full stop ends a conversation, but 'No' without a full stop **⁵**..........................the conversation continue. The psychologists decided to investigate this claim and concluded that the journalist was probably right – the full stop makes you **⁶**.......................... across as insincere.

Interestingly, follow-up research by the same team found that an exclamation mark, something **⁷**.......................... used to be considered old-fashioned, is actually friendlier and more sincere than **⁸**.......................... punctuation at all.

> Let's meet at 4.
> OK, great. I'll see you there.
> Please bring cake.

5 Read the article again and complete the gaps with one word only.

Speak up

6 Work in pairs and follow these steps.
1. Think of a well-known film. Use up to eight emojis to summarise the plot.
2. Swap emoji film plots with another pair. Translate their plot summary into English and then tell the other pair what you think happens in the story. Can you guess the film?

One dictionary's Word of the Year in 2015 was the emoji 'face with tears of joy'.

10 Speak to me

USE OF ENGLISH 2

1 Work in pairs and discuss the questions.
1. What is a meme?
2. Who produces memes?
3. What kind of pictures do they use?

2 e Read the article. Use the word given at the end of some of the lines to form a word that fits in the gap in the same line.

The lifespan of a **meme**

A great meme expresses an idea ¹............................ with just a few words and an image. We know people have a poor ²............................ span and so a photo and caption can have a huge advantage over text. ³............................ have calculated that a goldfish loses ⁴............................ after nine seconds. That's one second longer than the average internet user. Memes spread quickly. The joy of finding a new one is quickly replaced with ⁵............................ when someone forwards it to you for the 100th time. The web may seem overcrowded with memes — too many grumpy looking animals — but as the ⁶............................ of an effective one can reach a wide audience with minimal ⁷............................ , memes are becoming an attractive option for marketing companies who are under constant ⁸............................ to find fresh new ways of promoting products. Internet memes are unlikely to go away any time soon.

EFFECT

ATTEND

RESEARCH
CONCENTRATE

ANNOY

POPULAR
INVEST

PRESS

Oh no ...

Here comes Monday!

3 Work in pairs. Can you summarise the information from the article? What good memes have you seen recently? Why did you like them?

4 e Complete the second sentence so that it has a similar meaning to the first sentence using the word given. Do not change the word given. Use between three and six words.

1. People say that the word 'meme' dates back to the 1970s.
   BELIEVED
   The word 'meme' ....
   .... back to the late 1970s.

2. The word 'meme' was less popular in the early days.
   NOTHING
   In the early days, the word 'meme' was .... it is today.

3. It was wrong of her to use a photo of her neighbour in a meme without his consent.
   SHOULD
   She .... of her neighbour in a meme without his consent.

4. 'Tom, you have no gift for creating good memes,' said meme artist Sean.
   ACCUSED
   Meme artist Sean .... no gift for creating good memes.

5. Most people see a new meme within a few months of its creation.
   WILL
   A new meme .... most people a few months after its creation.

6. 'I created that meme!' said Anna, although it was anonymous.
   CLAIMED
   Anna .... that meme, despite it being anonymous.

Speak up

5 Work in pairs and discuss the questions.
1. Do you think it's right to use people's images in memes without their consent?
2. Look at the photo and write another meme caption for it.

SPEAKING

Power up

1 Work in pairs. What three top tips would you give another student preparing for a Speaking test?

2 Work in pairs. Take turns to ask and answer the questions.

Student A
1. Where are you from?
2. What do you do there?
3. If you could take a visitor to one part of your hometown, where would you take them? Why?

Student B
1. How long have you been studying English?
2. What do you enjoy the most about your studies?
3. How do you prefer to keep in touch with your classmates? Why?

3 e Work in pairs. Look at the three photos of people using traditional forms of communication. Take turns to compare two of the photos and discuss how easy or difficult it might be to communicate in these ways.

4 e When you have finished comparing the photos, answer the question below.

Why might these people have chosen this form of communication?

5 e Work in pairs and complete the task.

Here are some situations in which people need to communicate their ideas with others. Talk together about why it might be important for people to communicate their ideas clearly in these situations. You have about one minute to decide in which situation it's most important to communicate clearly.

- talking in the classroom
- negotiating with parents
- talking online
- speaking with friends
- giving presentations at work

Why might it be important for people to communicate their ideas clearly in these situations?

6 e Work in pairs and discuss the questions.
1. What are the main differences between spoken and written communication?
2. Some people think it's more important to listen than to talk. Do you agree? Why/Why not?
3. Do you think we communicate more or less effectively as a result of technology? Why?
4. Who do you think should be responsible for teaching young people to communicate clearly? Why?
5. Do you think countries do enough to communicate with other nations? Why/Why not?
6. Do you think good communication skills are rewarded financially? How?

Did you know it's estimated that you've probably spent 700–800 hours studying English to get to this point?

10 Speak to me

WRITING

Power up

1 Work in pairs and discuss the questions.

1 Is it common for people your age to do work experience? Why/Why not? How could it benefit you?
2 Which of these skills do you think you have? Which do you need to develop?

---
ability to work under pressure   communication skills
decision-making skills   leadership skills
problem-solving skills   self-motivation
time manage ment skills

---

3 Have you ever been to a talent show or seen one on TV? Did you enjoy it? Why/Why not?
4 Have you ever been to a summer festival? Did you enjoy it? Why/Why not?

2 Work in pairs. Discuss how difficult it is to plan a talent show or summer festival. Then work with another pair and complete the table with at least two ideas in each box. Think about location, people, facilities, etc.

	What can make it successful?	What can make it unsuccessful?
talent show	The acts are brilliant.	The acts are boring.
summer festival	There's a variety of things to do.	It rains.

Plan on

3 Read the tasks and identify the key points you have to write about in each one.

1 You want to spend your summer doing work experience at a company that produces an online newspaper. You decide to write to the recruitment manager at the company and explain why you would like to do work experience there and how your skills will benefit the company.

Write your **letter** in **220–260** words.

2 Your school recently held a talent show to showcase the work that students have been doing in after school clubs. The principal has asked you, as a student representative, to write a report explaining the extent to which the talent show was successful and making recommendations for next year.

Write your **report** in **220–260** words.

3 You see the following advertisement on a student website.

Summer event

All over the country there are some wonderful events that take place every summer: fairs, outdoor film festivals, firework displays, etc. As a travel company, we'd like to feature some of these on our website so we're looking for reviews of a summer event you've been to.

Write and tell us the reasons why you think people would enjoy the event and why they might not. We'll publish the best reviews on our website.

Write your **review** in **220–260** words.

4 Look at the tasks in Ex 3 again. In which one should you include:
1 an eye-catching introduction?
2 a greeting?
3 a purpose for writing?
4 information about things that work(ed) well and less well?
5 reasons and examples to support your opinion?
6 suggestions for improvement?

5 Match these words with task 1, 2 or 3 in Ex 3. Some words may be suitable for more than one task. Then think of at least three more advanced words or phrases you could use for each task.

acts   competent   computer literate
disorganised   flexible   lack of sanitary facilities
laid-back atmosphere   overcrowded   performer
talented   training   wide variety

6 Read the language box and complete it with the text genres from Ex 3.

explore language

set phrases

Learn useful sets of phrases to help you produce more authentic texts in different genres.

1 ....: The aims of this ... are to .../ I would suggest that in future ...

2 ....: Have you ever ... ?/Would you love to ... ?

3 ....: I am writing to put my name forward for possible ... opportunities./Yours faithfully, ...

7 Are these phrases suitable for a Letter (L), Report (RT) or Review (RW)? Write *All* for phrases that are suitable for all three.
1 Dear Sir/Madam, ...
2 Most people I interviewed suggested that ...   .
3 I look forward to hearing from you in due course.   ....
4 By contrast, ...
5 In short, ...
6 At the start of the event ...   .
7 I hope that you find my request attractive.   ....
8 Despite the fact that ...   .
9 As preparation for this report, I ...   .
10 By the end, ...
11 All in all, ...
12 In my view, ...
13 I would suggest ...   .
14 Not only did they ..., they also ...   .
15 What's the first thing that comes to mind when ... ?   ....

8 Look at the tasks in Ex 3 again and decide which one you are going to complete. Then work in pairs and explain your decision to your partner. Think about:
- which topic you have most to write about and would most enjoy writing about.
- which text genre you feel most comfortable with.
- the kind of language you'd need to produce and how comfortable you feel with this.

Write on

9 Write a paragraph plan for your letter, report or review.

10 e Write your letter, report or review in 220–260 words. Remember to:
- make sure you answer the task well.
- produce a well-organised text with connected ideas.
- write well-organised paragraphs with clear topics.
- use a range of language with as few mistakes as possible.

Improve it

11 Work in pairs and read each other's writing. Does your partner's writing meet the criteria in the list in Ex 10? Why/Why not? Say two things you like about it and one thing that could be improved.

12 Edit your writing, taking your partner's feedback into account. Then read it and check it meets the criteria in Ex 10.

Some strange festivals include a mud festival in South Korea and even baby jumping in Spain.

GRAMMAR FILE

GRAMMAR FILE UNIT 1

REFERENCE

present tenses and time expressions

We use different time expressions with different tenses. Some go at the beginning of a sentence and some at the end. Others go between the subject and the main verb or after the verb *be*. It is useful to notice the typical position of each time expression.

present simple

We use the present simple to talk about habits, repeated actions and things that are true with:

expressions of frequency (e.g. *every other day, once in a while, from time to time*).
Every so often he comes round for dinner.
adverbs of frequency (e.g. *regularly, frequently, occasionally, rarely, often*).
He **frequently** forgets to do his homework.

present continuous

We use the present continuous to talk about actions happening now or around now, temporary situations and changing situations with:

expressions describing now or around now (e.g. *at the moment, right now, this year, nowadays*).
He's **currently** taking a drama course.
Note: We can also use these time expressions with the present simple with state verbs (e.g. *have, think, believe, feel, see*).
expressions describing temporary actions (e.g. *currently, for the time being*).
My tablet's broken, so I'm using my dad's **for the time being**.
adverbs of frequency to describe annoying habits (e.g. *always, continually, constantly*).
She's **always** taking my stuff without asking!
expressions describing changing situations (e.g. *all the time, these days, nowadays*).
She's getting better at dancing **all the time**.

present perfect simple and continuous

We use the present perfect simple to talk about states that started in the past and continue now, recently finished actions or past actions with a present result. We use the present perfect continuous for an action or a series of actions that started in the past and continue now. It stresses the action rather than the result.

We use both tenses with:

unfinished time expressions (e.g. *for, since, this morning, in the last two days, over the past few years, all day*).
I've been calling you **all day**. (focus on action)
time expressions for recent time (e.g. *recently, lately, in recent weeks*).
I've read three books **in the last week**. (focus on result)
yet, **already**, **just**, **ever**, **never** (present perfect simple only)
Just, ever and *never* go in the middle position.
The manager has **just** chosen the team.

phrasal verbs

Phrasal verbs are made up of a verb and a particle – a preposition or adverb. Grammatically speaking, there are four types of phrasal verb.

type 1: inseparable, intransitive

The verb and particle cannot be separated and no object is needed.

Don't slouch in the chair like that. **Sit up**!
I auditioned for the lead role in the school play but **missed out**.

type 2: separable, transitive

The verb and particle can be separated and an object is needed. The object can go between the verb and particle or come after it. When a pronoun is used, it must come in the middle.

If you do a hobby well, it can **open opportunities up/open up opportunities** in other areas.
A lack of motivation can **hold you back** from achieving more.

type 3: inseparable, transitive

The verb and particle cannot be separated. An object is needed and it comes after the particle.

Ben **took to** diving immediately.
I **came by** an interesting article the other day.

type 4: three-part

There are two particles after the verb. These are inseparable and an object is usually needed.

A few students **drop out of** school each year.
You won't **get away with** cheating.

Note: Some phrasal verbs can be type 1 as well as type 2, 3 or 4. This is because they have different meanings and don't always need an object.

I watched the traffic until it was safe to **pull out**.
Because of injury, he's **pulled out of** the competition.

PRACTICE

present tenses and time expressions

1 Choose the correct verbs to complete the sentences.
1. A teenager from New Delhi **is / has been** collecting pencils for the last ten years.
2. So far, he **collects / has collected** over 14,000 of them from forty different countries.
3. He **spends / has spent** hours online looking for new pencils over the past few years.
4. Once in a while, family members **help / are helping** him to buy more expensive items.
5. He **is / has been** currently in the Indian Limca Book of Records.
6. All this week he **counts / has been counting** his pencils in the hope of getting the world record.

2 Complete the essay paragraph with the correct form of these verbs. Do you agree with the writer?

be   have   offer   read   study   tell

Currently, many universities ¹.................................. fewer places to students, making the application process more competitive. Schools ².................................. continually .... students to take up a hobby to make their application appear more attractive. However, showing a real interest in your chosen subject frequently ³.................................. a greater effect. If you can demonstrate that you ⁴.................................. about this subject over the past few years with genuine enthusiasm, the interviewers will be impressed. An applicant who ⁵.................................. the subject in school over just a few months with no out-of-class reading will come across less well. This is why reading articles on your chosen subject from time to time ⁶.................................. an excellent idea.

3 Add one of these time expressions to the correct place in each sentence.

all day   continually   currently
for the past few years   this week   yet

1. Cara's been at her desk, staring at a university application form.
2. She wants to study games design.
3. She's been at the top of her computer class.
4. Her parents complain that she's staring at a computer screen.
5. She's been researching various universities.
6. She hasn't decided which university to apply for but has to decide soon.

phrasal verbs

4 Choose the correct words to complete the sentences. Sometimes both are possible.
1. He's really **bounced back / bounced him back** since his injury.
2. I take **after my dad / my dad after** when it comes to languages.
3. Don't **give it in / give in** after one failure. Keep going!
4. I tried writing the essay but ran up **against a few problems / a few problems against**.
5. I was silly to pass **a chance like that up / up a chance like that**.
6. It can be hard **for you to fit in / to fit you in** when you start a new school.
7. She couldn't believe it when she walked **away with first prize / with first prize away**.
8. Everyone starts **a new hobby off / off a new hobby** with enthusiasm but it doesn't always last.

5 Look at the phrasal verbs in Ex 4. Which type is each one: 1, 2, 3 or 4?

6 Complete the advice with the phrasal verbs in brackets. Decide which order the words should come in. Do you agree with the advice?

How to meet a challenge

1. If you .... (mess up / something), start again. That's how you learn.
2. When you .... (run up against / a problem), don't panic. Think logically.
3. Learn to .... (come up with / solutions) to problems quickly.
4. Don't let obstacles .... (hold back / you). Find a way to get round them.
5. Make sure you have the support you need to .... (see through / you) a difficult challenge.
6. Never .... (pass up / the opportunity) to get advice from others.
7. If things don't go your way, try to .... (bounce back) as fast as possible.
8. Never .... (give in). Keep going!

GRAMMAR FILE UNIT 2

REFERENCE

cleft sentences for emphasis

We can emphasise one part of a sentence using a *wh-* clause and a form of *be*. Look at the words added to the sentences below.

[He doesn't appreciate] [how hard new concepts can be.]
What [he doesn't appreciate] **is** [how hard new concepts can be.]

I don't understand the reason he's saying this.
What I don't understand **is** the reason he's saying this.

We use a *wh-* clause and a form of *be* before the object in a sentence.

[He wants] [a new motorbike.]
What [he wants] **is** [a new motorbike.]

We use a *wh-* clause and a form of *about … is* for emphasis.

[I love the photos] on [that website.]
What [I love] **about** [that website] **is** [the photos].

inversion for emphasis

We can put some negative adverbial phrases at the beginning of a sentence for emphasis. Examples of adverbials you can use in this way are: *nowhere, at no time, not once, never, in no way*.

He **didn't** mention that anything was wrong **at any time**.
At no time did he mention that anything was wrong.

When we do this, we invert the subject and verb. Look at the highlighted subject + verb construction.

I have never seen him so angry before.

Never have I seen him so angry before.
Notice how the form of the verb changes.

He **didn't apologise** even once!
Not once did he apologise!

He **isn't** right in **any way**.
In **no way is he** right.

relative clauses – *whatever, whenever,* etc.

We can use *however, whoever,* etc. to give the meaning 'it doesn't matter how, who, etc.' or 'it doesn't make any difference'.

However hard I try, I just can't seem to make him understand.
(I can't make him understand!)

Whatever you may think, I'm not going to help him!
(I'm not going to help him! I know you think I should!)

special uses of *which* or *whom*

We can use *which* or *whom* in certain expressions in relative clauses, e.g. *some of which, many of whom, as a result of which, without whose*.

I have a lot of friends. You already know **some of them**.
I have a lot of friends, **some of whom** you already know.
There are a lot of special interest groups in my town. **Many of them** welcome under-eighteens.
There are a lot of special interest groups in my town, **many of which** welcome under eighteens.
Last night's storm caused considerable damage, **as a result of which** many services have been delayed today.
I would like to thank all of the volunteers, **without whose** support we could never have held this sport competition today.

writing – language of recommendation

After *suggest*, we can use a *that* clause or an *-ing* form.
I suggest **that you ask** John.
I would never suggest **trying** to do this alone.

In very formal sentences, you can omit *that*.
I suggest **you ask** Mr Davies for help.

After *recommend*, we can use a *that* clause, an *-ing* form, *sb for sth* or *sth to sb*.
I recommend **that you ask** a professional.
He recommended **trying** the new hot chocolate drink.
I would definitely recommend **John for the role** of sports captain.
I wouldn't recommend **that software to you**.

PRACTICE

cleft sentences for emphasis

1 Write the words in bold in the correct order to complete the conversation.

A: John's having trouble at school with his Chinese classes.

B: Really? Well that's not surprising. ¹**why he chose / what / can't understand / is / such a difficult language / I / to study.**

....

A: I don't know. I mean, ²**most people / is / the amount of effort / needed to learn / don't appreciate / any new language / what.**

....

B: Yes, but Chinese has such a difficult written system. And ³**when / he / is work in international trade / really wants to do / what / he's older.**

....

A: Well, I guess ⁴**what / put more hours / is / in / he needs / to do.**

....

cleft sentences and inversion for emphasis

2 Complete the second sentence so that it has a similar meaning to the first sentence using the word given. Do not change the word given. Use between three and six words.

1 He wouldn't admit in any way that he was responsible for the confusion.
   NO
   In .... that he was responsible for the confusion.

2 He never said that he wanted to stop playing football.
   TIME
   At .... that he wanted to stop playing football.

3 In the singing competition, the organisers didn't say that they had already decided on the winner.
   WHAT
   In the singing competition, ... was that they'd already decided on the winner.

4 I only realised I'd lost my purse when I arrived home.
   ARRIVED
   Not until I .... that I'd lost my purse.

5 I made a big mistake and I felt really bad.
   HAD
   Never .... bad about a mistake.

relative clauses

3 Complete the sentences with *whatever, however, whenever, whoever* or *wherever*.

1 .... I say, she still thinks I'm lying!
2 I feel really sad .... I see that film.
3 .... hard I try, it just never seems to be enough.
4 .... you work with, I'm sure they'll help you a lot.
5 .... you go, I'll always be here for you.

4 Join the sentences using relative clauses.

1 The town has a lot of art galleries. Many of them can be visited for free.
   ....

2 There were a lot of people outside the stadium. Some of them were without tickets.
   ....

3 The city had several shopping centres. None of them were open before 10 a.m.
   ....

4 The main road was closed. The result was that the traffic in the village was very heavy.
   ....

5 The team managed to rescue a lot of the sports equipment from the fire. Much of it was unusable.
   ....

5 Match the conversations (1–5) with the meanings and functions (A–E). Use the phrases in bold to help you.

1 **A:** Do you think I should wear the blue shoes or the black shoes with this?
   B: Whatever!

2 **A:** Have you seen Steph lately?
   B: Yeah, I saw her two weeks ago, **or whenever it was**, and she looked fine!

3 **A:** What do you do at the weekends?
   B: I go to the mountains **whenever I can**.

4 **A:** You know this is quite a demanding exam.
   B: I know, but I'll do **whatever I can** to pass.

5 **A: Whatever were you thinking**, telling him about last night's party?
   B: I have no idea!

A anything
B dismissively, with impatience
C criticism, surprise
D at any time, every time
E I don't exactly know when

GRAMMAR FILE UNIT 3

REFERENCE

the passive

The passive is formed with the verb *be* in the correct tense and the past participle.

present simple	am/is/are + past participle	He's **influenced** by her.
present continuous	am/is/are being + past participle	He's **being influenced** by her.
present perfect	has/have been + past participle	He's **been influenced** by her.
past simple	was/were + past participle	He **was influenced** by her.
past continuous	was/were being + past participle	He **was being influenced** by her.
past perfect simple	had been + past participle	He'd **been influenced** by her.
going to	am/is/are going to be + past participle	He's **going to be influenced** by her.
will	will be + past participle	He'll **be influenced** by her.
modal verbs	may/could/should (etc.) be + past participle	He **may be influenced** by her.
infinitive	like/want/need (etc.) to be + past participle	He **likes to be influenced** by her.

We use the passive form in three key situations:

when the subject is unknown or unimportant
We use the passive when we don't know who/what did the action. This is particularly common in the news. We also use it when we feel the subject is unimportant and we want to focus on the action or person/thing that the action happened to. In this situation, the subject is usually clear from the context (e.g. *by people, by the police*.)
Two paintings **were stolen** from a gallery in Amsterdam yesterday.
I'd say my character **has been** heavily **influenced** by my parents.
Robert **was asked** to do his homework again (by the teacher).

to avoid responsibility and blame
We use the passive when we want to avoid taking responsibility for something ourselves or when we want to be diplomatic and not mention who did the action.
The toast'**s burnt**.
I don't think my exam **was marked** correctly.

for text cohesion
In a text, we often want to have the same subject in two or more clauses/sentences to create consistency and cohesion. In order to do this, we often use the passive.
Maria **was told** to go to the head teacher's room where she **was told off** for talking in class.
Television **was invented** in a number of places. In the US, it **was developed** by Farnsworth while in the UK, it **was created** by Logie Baird.

We may also want to start a clause/sentence with an idea (i.e. the subject) mentioned in a previous sentence (i.e. the object).
Learning a new language can present a lot of challenges. These **can be overcome** by setting goals.
To cure my colds, I always ate grandma's soup. It **was made** with chicken, which apparently helps.

reporting verbs and the passive

We use the passive with reporting verbs (e.g. *say, believe, think*) to report what people say, believe, think, etc. without the need to state who. These structures are used in more formal texts and situations, mostly to state a generalised viewpoint. The passive is generally used with the following reporting verbs: *believe, claim, consider, estimate, expect, feel, hope, know, prove, say, show, think, understand*.

We use the following two structures when the reporting verb refers to an action in the same time period. The reporting verb can be in either the present or past tense.

***it* + passive reporting verb + *that* clause**
It is often **said that** carrots help you see in the dark but it's not really true.
It was once **believed that** the Earth was flat.

subject + passive reporting verb + (*not*) *to*-infinitive
Carrots **are said to help** you see in the dark but it's not really true.
The Earth **was** once **thought to be** flat.

We can use the following structure when the reporting verb refers back to a past action. The reporting verb can be in either the present or past tense.

subject + passive verb + (*not*) *to have* + past participle
Christopher Columbus **is** often **believed to have been** Spanish.
The fairies in the famous 1917 photos **were proven not to have existed**.

PRACTICE

the passive

1 Complete the sentences with the correct passive form of the verbs in brackets.

> **According to research, friendships can influence you in interesting ways.**
>
> 1 Your self-control .... (can / increase) if you have strong-minded friends.
> 2 Financial risk-taking .... (decrease) when you have more friends.
> 3 In one study, stress levels .... (raise) when participants had too many online friends.
> 4 According to another study, over the last few years your lifespan .... (affect) by the number of friends you have.
> 5 Your choices next week .... (probably / influence) by your friends.
> 6 Your character in ten years' time .... (shape) by your friends.

2 Choose the correct active or passive form in the article. Sometimes both are possible but one is more appropriate.

> **Strong-willed friends can increase your self-control**
>
> It's important to recognise how much we are influenced by our friends. For example, if they choose to eat unhealthily, ¹**they tempt us / we are tempted** to do the same. If they decide to go out and exercise every day, ²**they will encourage us / we will be encouraged** to do the same. This influence ³**causes us / is caused** to seek out particular friends at particular times in our lives. According to a study which ⁴**published / was published** in 2013, when we lack self-control, ⁵**it motivates us / we are motivated** to spend time with friends who are self-disciplined. So, when ⁶**you next need encouragement / encouragement is next needed** to reach a goal, you should befriend people who have the willpower to help ⁷**you do that / that be done**.

3 Complete the sentences with the correct active or passive form of the verbs in brackets. Sometimes both are possible but one is more appropriate. Choose an appropriate subject and tense.

1 Social media friends may not be good for you. .... (link) to an increase in anxiety about offending people.
2 When people see perfect photos their friends put online, ... (may / negatively / affect) by them.
3 Researchers followed 1,500 adults over ten years. At the end of the study, ... (discover) that the adults with more friends had outlived the others by twenty-two percent.
4 Having friends positively affects blood pressure, heart rate and cholesterol. .... (all / lower) and the risk of disease is reduced.
5 Research has shown that when people lack social interaction, ... (take) bigger risks with money.
6 You are also more likely to take financial risks if .... (reject) recently.

reporting verbs and the passive

4 Complete the sentences with the correct form of the verbs in brackets.

1 Social media .... (say / change) the world.
2 It .... (think / have) many positive effects.
3 It .... (also / know / cause) some issues in the past.
4 Users .... (believe / focus) too much on what others are doing.
5 Such actions .... (think / result) in feelings of envy.
6 Using social media .... (estimate / occupy) millions of hours of our time yesterday.

5 Make passive sentences from the prompts.

1 the birth order of siblings / say / influence / us as children

2 it / now / think / parents' expectations / be / the cause

3 it / believe / most parents / assign / a role to their children according to their birth order

4 middle children / generally / think / be / the negotiators

5 for centuries, older children / expect / take / the role of leader

GRAMMAR FILE UNIT 4

REFERENCE

participle clauses

We use a participle clause to join two clauses using fewer words. It can also make sentences more interesting. We can form participle clauses with the present or past participle.

active forms	long form	participle clause
past	which showed a road trip	showing a road trip
present	that is popular among visitors	being popular among visitors
future	who will need extra help	needing extra help

passive forms	long form	participle clause
past	which were modified to include …	modified to include
present	that is based on coffee	based on coffee
future	who will be introduced later	introduced later

shortening relative clauses

We can use participle clauses to shorten or *reduce* relative clauses.

We use a present participle where the main verb is active. The tense does not matter.

Gideon Jacobs decided to post a series of photos ~~which~~ supposedly **show**~~ed~~ a road trip.
Gideon Jacobs decided to post a series of photos supposedly **show**ing a road trip.
The people ~~who~~ **visit** the fake beaches felt happy.
The people **visit**ing the fake beaches felt happy.

We use the past participle where the main verb is passive. The tense does not matter.

The photographs ~~which were~~ **modified** to include Gat's image became an internet sensation.
The photographs **modified** to include Gat's image became an internet sensation.

Joining two clauses

We can also use participle clauses to join two clauses. The subject of both clauses *must* be the same. We use a present participle when the main verb is active and a past participle when the verb is passive. The tense does not matter.

~~Because he~~ **felt** an affinity with Gat's dreams, he felt inspired to pay for a real trip.
Feeling an affinity with Gat's dreams, he felt inspired to pay for a real **trip**.
~~Riedler~~ **talk**~~ed~~ to the subjects of his photos and soon realised that the sentimentality was not fake.
Talking to the subjects of his photos, Riedler soon realised that **the** sentimentality was not fake.
~~Because it was~~ **based** on a lie, the claim was soon dropped.
Based on a lie, the claim was soon dropped.

The participle can come at the beginning or between the clauses.

Knowing the truth would hurt, I kept silent.
I kept silent, **knowing** the truth would hurt.

prepositions with *-ed* forms

We use *-ed* forms in past participle clauses, passive forms or as adjectives. They are often followed by a preposition.

in participle clauses

Equipped with a new computer, Joao started on his essay.
Referred to as the best on the market, the new VR headset went on sale.

in passive verbs

The device has been **fitted with** a new function.
The headset was **made by** a start-up company.

as adjectives

We were all **confused by** how real the VR experience was.
None of us were **dissatisfied with** the experience.

PRACTICE

1 Choose the correct participle to complete the sentences.

1. Tourism **influenced / influencing** by the surrounding natural resources often flourishes.
2. Many countries boast historical sites **dated / dating** back hundreds of years.
3. Swimming was the favourite holiday activities in a survey **based / basing** on British tourism habits.
4. People see many sites from the top of the London Eye, **included / including** the River Thames.
5. Many people head to warmer climates, **attracted / attracting** by the promise of hot dry weather.
6. People look more closely at tourist sites, often **gazed / gazing** for hours.
7. Improvements in public transport **brought / bringing** about by tourism benefit everyone.
8. Local wildlife often benefits from tours **organised / organising** around safari activities.

2 Match the first half of each sentence (1–6) with the second half (A–F).

1. In 1700, people travelled to study plants
2. The new species transported back to Europe
3. In 1800, people travelling for health reasons
4. Most travellers in the early days were rich,
5. People often stayed in private homes
6. The introduction of hotels attracted visitors

A. adapted to the native climate.
B. arriving in ever increasing numbers.
C. made up the majority of international travellers.
D. had to be kept indoors.
E. having inherited their wealth from their families.
F. offering accommodation for the night.

3 Change one of the clauses in each sentence into a participle clause.

1. Around a billion people who arrive in a foreign country annually travel for tourism purposes.
2. Because it brings in almost a trillion US dollars, tourism is a globally important industry.
3. The fastest growth has been Asian tourism, which has almost doubled in the last twenty years.
4. Europe still has the most visitors and it attracts around 500 million a year.
5. Technology will reduce flying times, which could cut the flight from LA to Sydney to two hours.
6. Hotels which have been rated as seven-star will become more common.
7. Because it has a negative effect on the environment, air travel will need new forms of fuel.
8. Eco-tours are replacing package holidays and are currently increasing in popularity.

4 Complete the sentences with prepositions.

1. 27 September is recognised .... World Tourism Day.
2. Mass tourism was first adopted .... wealthy Europeans in the seventeenth century.
3. Problems related .... tourism include pollution.
4. Tourism is suspected .... increasing rubbish in the sea.
5. Many tourist sites are protected .... local organisations.
6. These organisations are dedicated .... preserving sites for future generations.
7. They don't want the sites to be reduced .... rocks and stones.
8. Limiting visitors combined .... maintenance helps to protect tourist sites.

5 Complete the blog with these -*ed* forms and prepositions.

armed   combined   delighted   disappointed   identified
persuaded   puzzled   replaced

Don't believe everything you read

¹.................... excellent online reviews of the four-star White Sands holiday resort, my parents decided to book a suite there for our annual family holiday. It was expensive but it looked amazing, so we were all absolutely ².................... their choice. Unfortunately, when we got there, we were really ³.................... what we found. The four-star hotel with a luxury pool had been ⁴.................... a three-star motel with a paddling pool. ⁵.................... the stark difference, I did some research online to try and solve the mystery and discovered that the reviews had been fake.

It seems that fake reviews are common these days but ⁶.................... the right information, you can avoid them. According to research, you can tell a fake review by the language used. Key features have been ⁷.................... the regular use of *I*, *we*, *really*, *very* and superlative adjectives ⁸.................... lots of exclamation marks. Apparently, by spotting these, you can identify a fake review correctly ninety percent of the time.

GRAMMAR FILE UNIT 5

REFERENCE

modal verbs in the past

To use a modal verb in the past, we use modal verb + *have* + past participle.

You **must have felt** so cold!

We can also use the continuous form of the verb to show that the action was ongoing or was interrupted. We use modal verb + *have* + *been* + *-ing*.

It **could have been raining** at the time. I don't really remember.

We can use modal verbs in the past to speculate or make deductions about the past (*may/might have, couldn't/couldn't have, can't have, must/had to have*).

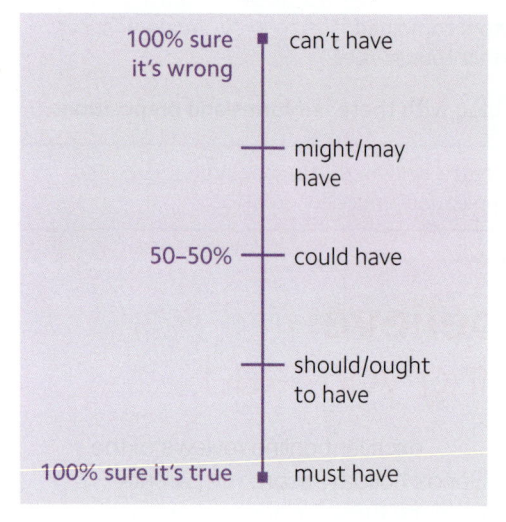

```
100% sure it's wrong    ─ can't have

                        ─ might/may have

50–50%                  ─ could have

                        ─ should/ought to have

100% sure it's true     ─ must have
```

He **must have been** terrified! (I'm sure he was terrified.)
You **can't have been** serious! (I'm sure you were NOT serious).

To express certainty in the past, we change the infinitive NOT the modal.

		modal	infinitive	
present	You	must	be	frozen!
past	You	must	have been	frozen!

We can use modals in the past:

to speculate or make deductions about the past (*may/might have, couldn't/couldn't have, can't have, must/had to have*).

It **must have been** there! (I'm sure it was there.)
It **had to have hurt** when he fell like that!
You **couldn't have known** about it! (There was no way that you knew about it.)
He **can't have told** the whole truth! (I'm sure he didn't tell you the whole truth).

to criticise or express regret about the past (*shouldn't have*).

You really **should have told** me! (You did the wrong thing not telling me.)
I **should have been** famous! (I regret not being famous now.)

to talk about things that were and weren't necessary (*needn't have, didn't need to*).

We use *needn't have* + past participle for something that we did but later realised wasn't necessary.

I **needn't have washed** this cup. I'm just going to throw it away. (I washed the cup unnecessarily.)

We use *didn't need to* + infinitive for a thing that we didn't do because we realised it was unnecessary.

I **didn't need to travel** to London in the end. (I didn't go.)

We can also use the continuous form of the verb to show that the action was ongoing or continuous. We use modal verb + *have* + *been* + *-ing* form.

		modal	infinitive
finished action	The rain	might	have stopped
continuous action	It	must	have been raining in the night

The man **could have been wearing** a suit. I don't really remember.

emphasising comparatives and superlatives

We can emphasise comparatives but need to take care with the words we use.

-er and more comparatives

We use *far, a great deal* (formal) and *way* (informal) to emphasise a comparative.

It was **far more expensive** than I was expecting.
It was **a great deal less interesting**.

as … as comparatives

We use *just, nowhere near, nothing like, half* and *twice* to emphasise *as … as* comparatives.

The second film was **nowhere near as good as** the first.
My essay was **twice as long as** the word limivtt.

superlatives

We use *by far* to emphasise a superlative.

It was **by far the best** film I've ever seen.

We use *just, nowhere near, nothing like, half* and *twice* to emphasise *as … as* comparatives.

The second film was **nowhere near as good as** the first.
My essay was **twice as long as** the word limit.

quantities

We can also use these phrases to compare quantities.

There were **far more people** than I expected.
There were **nowhere near as many people** as last year.
I bought **twice as much food** as we needed.

Note: Do NOT say ~~twice/half more~~ food.
Say *twice/half as much* food.

There were only **half as many people** in the meeting today as there were last week.

PRACTICE
modal verbs in the past

1 Match the first half of each fun fact (1–6) with the second half (A–F).

1 Disney's first Mickey Mouse film was animated by just one man.
2 Vincent Van Gogh spent most of his life dealing in other people's art.
3 King John of England was illiterate.
4 The story of Hamlet existed in Scandinavia years before Shakespeare was born.
5 Thomas Edison filed over 1,000 patents for his inventions.
6 American independence was finally granted on 3 September 1783.

A He couldn't have signed the *Magna Carta* himself.
B His technicians should have got the credit for most of those, though.
C His might not have been the original version, but it was the best!
D It might not have been a problem that his paintings never sold.
E They shouldn't have chosen 4 July to celebrate.
F It must have taken him ages!

2 What is the function of each modal verb in Ex 1?

A ....
B ....
C ....
D ....
E ....
F ....

3 Complete the sentences with *didn't need to* or *needn't have* and the correct form of the verbs in brackets.

1 I had got some money out of the cashpoint earlier, so I .... (get / more).
2 I spent half an hour polishing my mum's car, then it started raining. I .... (do / it).
3 Oh, flowers! How kind! You .... (do / that).
4 The match was cancelled, so we .... (play / today).
5 I got this game for my birthday, so I .... (buy / myself).
6 I found my dog asleep in the cupboard upstairs. I .... (be / so worried).
7 My university interview tomorrow's been cancelled, so I .... (spend) all day today preparing.
8 I've got all weekend to do my homework, so I .... (do) it last night.

emphasising comparatives and superlatives

4 Choose the correct words to complete the sentences.

1 That was **nowhere near / by far / way** the best day ever!
2 There were **far / nothing like / twice** more people at the event this year.
3 It was **a great deal / nowhere near / by far** as cold as I expected.
4 This game was twice **as / more / the most** expensive in the shop as it was online.
5 There was **a great deal less / fewer / half** interest in the first option.

5 Complete the sentences with the correct comparative or superlative form of the adjective.

1 Email is nowhere near .... (old) the '@' symbol.
2 The pyramids are twice .... (big) any other building from that time.
3 Stonehenge is by far .... (ancient) building in England.
4 The pyramids in Mexico were just .... (tall) the ones in Egypt.
5 The Santa Maria de Loreto is by far .... (fine) wooden structure still in existence.

6 Complete the sentences with the correct comparative or superlative form of these adjectives.

by far   far   half   nowhere near   twice

1 What a disaster! Only .... as many people as we invited came.
2 Halo 4 was .... as good as Halo 3.
3 If I keep saving, I'll have .... as much money by the end of the month.
4 Well, that whole experience was .... better than I expected.
5 You're just the best sister .... !

GRAMMAR FILE UNIT 6

REFERENCE

past and present narrative tenses

We generally use past narrative tenses when we talk about things that happened in the past such as stories and anecdotes. We use these past narrative tenses:

past simple	completed actions in the past, in chronological order
	'Watch your step,' he **said** as he **marched** towards the building.
past continuous	actions in progress in the past up to another past action
	We **were walking up** the stairs when we **came across** some interesting architecture.
	giving background information
	When we **arrived at** the hotel, some people **were taking** photos.
	two actions in progress happening at the same time
	As we **were climbing** into the building, another group **was climbing** out.
past perfect simple	completed past actions that happened before a second past action
	The owners **had neglected** the building for years before it was knocked down.
past perfect continuous	past actions in progress up to the time another past action happened
	We were exhausted because we**'d been walking** round an old theatre all morning.

We use present narrative tenses when we want to tell a story or an anecdote about a past event but we want to make it sound more immediate and therefore engaging to the listener. We use these present narrative tenses:

present simple	completed actions in chronological order
	So, the man **walks up** to me and **asks** to borrow my phone.
present continuous	actions in progress up to the time of another action
	We**'re wandering** around the building when the owner turns up.
	giving background information
	The sun**'s coming up** behind the building and **shining** a strange light on it.
	two actions in progress at the same time
	I**'m taking** photos while the other group members **are just looking** around.
present perfect simple	completed past actions that happened before a second past action
	I realise I can't take any more photos as my phone**'s run out of** memory.
present perfect continuous	past actions in progress up to the time another past action happened
	We**'ve been wandering** around the building for hours when I realise it's dark outside.

We often use present narrative tenses when we describe the plot of a film, book, play, etc., tell a joke or give a commentary.

The book tells the story of a man who **redevelops** a hotel and then **discovers** a ghost **is haunting** it.
A horse **walks** into a bar. The barman **says**, 'Why the long face?'
He**'s running** down the left wing with the ball. Smith **tries** to tackle him but Jones **gets** past and **scores**.

phrasal verbs

Transitive phrasal verbs need an object. Intransitive phrasal verbs do not.

I'd never **put someone down** because of the clothes they wear. (transitive)
I don't want to **stand out**, so I try to **blend in** when I'm in a crowd. (intransitive)

Some phrasal verbs have the same meaning when they are transitive and intransitive.

If it breaks, just **stick it together** with glue. (transitive)
The stamps had got wet and **stuck together**. (intransitive)

Some phrasal verbs have related intransitive and transitive forms with the same meaning.

We **jumped onto** the bus when it arrived. (transitive)
The bus arrived so we **jumped on**. (intransitive)

Some phrasal verbs have different meanings when they are transitive and intransitive.

The tree was getting too big, so we **cut it down**. (transitive – cut through the main part of a tree)
I was eating too much chocolate, so I decided to **cut down**. (intransitive – reduce the amount)

You can use a dictionary to find out whether you need an object or not. Good dictionaries will say whether the verb is intransitive or transitive for each meaning.

PRACTICE

past and present narrative tenses

1 Choose the correct forms to complete the stories.

A I once ¹**found / had found** £200 in a plastic bag in the street. I ²**looked / was looking** around but couldn't see who ³**dropped / had dropped** it, so I took it to the nearest police station. After a month, a policeman called me to say no one ⁴**collected / had collected** it and I could have it. Lucky me!

B Last week I ⁵**cycled / was cycling** down a one-way street when this car ⁶**came / was coming** out of nowhere and nearly hit me. The driver ⁷**got / was getting** out the car and screamed at me but it was him who'd ⁸**travelled / been travelling** in the wrong direction.

C So, right, I ⁹**run / 'm running** down the stairs to try and catch the last train when suddenly, I ¹⁰**slip / 've slipped** and slide all the way down the stairs. Everyone ¹¹**stops / is stopping** and stares at me. Not only that, by the time I get up, I ¹²**miss / 've missed** the train.

2 Complete the blog with the correct past or present form of the verbs in the brackets.

My favourite childhood story was *The Enchanting Wood* by Enid Blyton. Growing up in an urban area meant I ¹............................ (not get) to wander through woods very often, so one where trees apparently ²............................ (whisper) to each other ³............................ (grip) me from start to finish. In the middle of the wood is the Magic Faraway Tree, a tree that ⁴............................ (stretch) so high into the sky you don't know that there's a different land there every week. As a child, I desperately ⁵............................ (want) to visit 'The Land of Take-What-you-Want' for obvious reasons but I ⁶............................ (also / fascinate) by 'The Land of Birthdays' and 'The Land of Goodies'.

The story ⁷............................ (follow) three siblings who ⁸............................ (recently / move) to the area and a range of magical characters who ⁹............................ (make) their home in the tree, including Moon-Face and Mr Watzisname. No one ¹⁰............................ (know) Mr Watizname's real name until a later book in the series, when it ¹¹............................ (turn out) to be twelve syllables long. I was proud I could say it but only after I ¹²............................ (spend) hours memorising it syllable by syllable!

3 Make a joke from the prompts. Use present narrative tenses and add any other words necessary. Add other information to make it more interesting if you like.

Local office manager / need / staff. Put / sign in window / say 'Help wanted'. Dog / wander up / to window / examine / advertisement. Go inside / look at receptionist / whine. Receptionist / call / office manager. Dog / indicate / with head / seen / advertisement. Office manager / surprise. Say / 'I can't employ you.' Point to / sign / 'Must be able to type'. Dog / head over / computer / type a page quickly. Office manager / shock. 'You / intelligent but sorry / can't employ you. Must / be bilingual.' Dog / look / man / say 'Meow'.

4 Translate a joke you know from your language into English using present narrative tenses. Is it still funny?

phrasal verbs

5 Match the first half of each sentence (1–6) with the second half (A–F).

1 I used to be badly-behaved but I've since turned
2 Several students have pulled
3 I expected the exam to be tricky but it turned
4 It was a really bumpy flight but we came
5 She was so ill we didn't know if she'd pull
6 Oh no, the bin's tipped

A out to be pretty easy.
B through at one stage.
C through it in one piece.
D out of the school play.
E over again.
F over a new leaf.

6 Complete the phrasal verbs in the text with a particle. Add an object if necessary.

I had a plan to keep fit by running around the neighbourhood every morning before school. I'd get up at six and start ¹............................ by running up and down the stairs a couple of times. I'd then go ²............................ for a 5K run. The problem was that it tired ³............................ for the rest of the day. I tried to go out for a run after school but it was hard to keep ⁴............................ with all my homework. In the end, I decided I was running too often and so cut ⁵............................ . Now I run just every other evening.

These days my best friend joins me. One day, I saw him walk out into a busy road. I shouted ⁶............................ and he fortunately stopped. Cars beeped and I could see he was scared so I went over and checked ⁷............................ . He was OK I carried on running but he followed me home. Have you guessed it yet? He was a dog. My parents let him stay and when it turned ⁸............................ he was a stray, I got to keep him for good.

# GRAMMAR FILE UNIT 7

REFERENCE

subject-verb agreement

Some nouns look singular but are followed by a plural verb or vice versa. Some words can be followed by both a singular or plural verb.

nouns that are followed by a singular verb

society
subjects (mathematics, politics)
titles of books (X-Men is …)
names of stores (Starbucks is …)
games (dominoes, darts)
series, species
Dominoes is still very popular with young children.
Mathematics is my strongest subject.

nouns that are followed by a plural verb

media, criteria, phenomena
the police
adjectives used with *the* to express a whole group (*the Chinese, the disabled, the elderly, the rich*)
The police are looking or an eighty-year-old woman, believed to be dangerous.
I think **the media are** responsible for a lot of the negativity in the world.

nouns that can be followed by a singular or plural verb

audience
class
company
data
department
government
group
staff
team
places that are plural (*crossroads, headquarters, the United States*)
The **audience was** a bit tough this evening.
The **audience were** a bit tough this evening.
Note: A lot of the words in this category refer to groups of people.

complex noun phrases

In a complex noun phrases, the verb agrees with the main subject (often the first noun).
Finding a healthy balance between your usual mess and that urgency to clean, **is** optimal.
Things like controlling impulsiveness, seeing things from other people's views and understanding consequences all **take** time to be learnt.

nouns that refer to quantity

In noun phrases expressing quantity, the verb agrees with the main noun.
percentages: Around **twenty percent** of the **water is** / Around **twenty percent** of the **people are** …
fractions: **two thirds** of the **air is** / **two thirds** of the **members are** …
the majority: **the majority** of the work is / **the majority** of the **students are** …

countable and uncountable quantifiers

Different quantifiers are followed by different kinds of noun.

quantifiers that are followed by singular countable nouns

each
every
neither
the whole
Neither option sounds very good to me.

quantifiers that are followed by plural countable nouns

a couple of
countless, several
both
none of
all the
upwards of (100)
The marathon normally attracts **upwards of 10,000 spectators**.

quantifiers that are followed by uncountable nouns

bags of
a great deal of
We've got **bags of time** before the match starts.

quantifiers that are followed by uncountable nouns or plural countable nouns

no end of
tons of
heaps of
an awful lot of
There are **an awful lot of problems** to fix.

PRACTICE

subject-verb agreement

1 Choose the correct verb forms to complete the sentences.
1. Hamleys **is** / **are** the biggest toy shop in the world.
2. Physics **is** / **are** one of the three main science subjects.
3. The police **helps** / **help** to solve crimes.
4. The Japanese **eats** / **eat** a very healthy diet.
5. Any international TV series **has** / **have** a big budget.
6. The main foundations for success **is** / **are** hard work and luck.

2 Choose the best ending (A or B) for each sentence. Sometimes both are possible.
1. Two thirds of the money in sport
   A goes to funding coaching.
   B go to paying the players.
2. Millions of people play darts,
   A which are a cheap hobby.
   B which has a top prize of thousands.
3. The audience at most performances
   A was made up of friends and family.
   B were generally pleased with the show.
4. A lot of companies store data
   A which contains sensitive personal information.
   B which need to be protected carefully.
5. The main headquarters of the company
   A is based in Paris.
   B have over 100 employees.
6. The majority of employees
   A has their own office.
   B have a base in the capital city.

3 Identify the main subject in each sentence. Then complete the fun facts with the correct form of the verbs in brackets.

countable and uncountable nouns

4 Complete the story with quantifiers.

That's all!

Max went out to buy a new race horse. He went to see a lot of different horses but **¹**........................ of them were what he was looking for. **²**........................ the ones he saw were either too small or too slow. Finally, the last horse he looked at was perfect. It had strong legs and was eager to go, and **³**........................ these qualities were the ones that he needed. He asked the owner if he could take the horse out for a run, to see how fast it could go. The owner agreed, but warned Max that there were **⁴**........................ things about this particular horse that were a little unusual. 'His trainer was a bit of a joker,' he explained. 'To get the horse to stop, you have to say, "That's all!" and to make it go, you need to say, "Thank goodness."'

Max nodded his head and set off. The horse was a dream. It was running down a dirt track, as fast as the wind, but when Max looked ahead, he could see a cliff edge. He tried shouting 'Stop!' and 'Whoa!' but **⁵**........................ word worked. He couldn't remember what to say. **⁶**........................ attempt brought him more dangerously to the edge. Just as they were getting to the last few metres, he remembered the word. 'That's all!' he shouted, and the horse finally stopped, just in time. Max breathed a sigh of relief.

'Oh,' said Max, wiping his brow, 'Thank goodness!'

Fun facts about sport

1. The number of people involved in sports at a local level usually .... (go up) after the Olympics.
2. The 'half-time kettle effect' in the UK .... (be) when there's a power surge during a break in the football and everyone in the audience .... (put) the kettle on to make tea!
3. The officially recognised state sport in Maryland, USA, ... (be) jousting.
4. The fastest red card in the history of football matches .... (be) after two seconds. Player Lee Todd, one of the UK premier league players, ... (be) sent off for swearing about the noise of the whistle.
5. The basketball courts at the top of the Supreme Court in the US .... (have) the nickname 'the highest court in the land'.
6. The auction of Wladimir Klitschko's gold medal for children in need .... (be) successful. But despite paying over a million dollars, the new owner .... (be) such a fan, he returned it to Klitschko immediately.

GRAMMAR FILE UNIT 8

REFERENCE

the future

on the verge of/on the point of + -ing	something that will happen very soon
	Is technology **on the verge of changing** the way we watch films forever?
	TV is **on the point of becoming** more culturally important than film.
be to + infinitive	something that will definitely happen or an official arrangement
	The company **is to rerelease** its bestselling film in high definition.
be set to/ be due to + infinitive	something that is expected to happen
	The cinema **is set to close down** after falling ticket sales.
	The film **is due to be** released on 4 October.

We use the future continuous for an action in progress at a specific future time. It is formed with: subject + *will be* + *-ing* Modal verbs can also be used instead of *will*.

By the time I'm thirty, no one **will be watching** TV as a family any more.
In the near future, people **might be sitting** in a cinema with a virtual reality headset on.

We also use the future continuous for something that will happen as a matter of course.

I**'ll be getting** the bus to school again tomorrow, so I'll download a film to watch.
We're going on holiday next week. I**'ll be taking** a load of e-books with me to read as usual.

We use the future perfect for an action that will be complete by a future time. It is formed with: subject + *will have* + past participle. Modal verbs can also be used instead of *will*.

By the time I'm middle-aged, technology companies **will have developed** new forms of entertainment.

conditional sentences

basic conditional forms

There are four basic types of conditionals. Each one is made up of an *if* clause and a main clause. These clauses can be switched round. When the *if* clause goes first, the two clauses are separated by a comma. When the main clause is first, there is no comma.

The **zero conditional** (*if* + present simple, subject + present simple) describes a general truth.

If you **get** a good night's sleep, you **feel** more awake the next day.

The **first conditional** (*If* + present simple, subject + *will* + infinitive) describes a possible future action and its likely result.

You**'ll have** a good story **if** you **write** those ideas down.

We can use *as long as*, *providing/provided that* and *on condition that* with the first conditional to express the need for one action to happen before another action can happen.

As long as you revise well, you'll be fine in the exam.
We'll do a good job **provided that** we work hard.
I'll let you stay out later **on condition that** you do all your homework first.

The **second conditional** (*if* + past simple, subject + *would/might/could* + infinitive) describes a hypothetical or unlikely situation and its likely result.

I**'d try** and write a novel **if** I **could write** better.

The **third conditional** (*if* + past perfect, subject + *would have* + past participle) describes a hypothetical action or situation in the past and its likely result.

If I'd paid more attention at school, I **could have learnt** to write better.

We can use *supposing (that)*, *imagine (if/that)* and *what if* with the second and third conditionals to ask the listener to imagine a past or present situation.

Supposing we**'d put** our heads together, we **would have come up** with something brilliant.
Imagine if we **were** famous writers, people **would take** photos of us wherever we went.
What if we **had tried** to write something together? That **might have worked**.

other conditional forms

It is possible to mix conditionals so that, for example, we describe a past hypothetical situation and a hypothetical result in the present.

If you **hadn't done** that, we **wouldn't be** in trouble now.
They**'d be** the champions right now if they**'d scored** that last goal.

Sometimes a conditional sentence is hidden because *if* and the subject are omitted in the *if* clause. However, it has the same meaning.

Do that again and I'll get really angry! (If you do that again, I'll get really angry!)
Watch this video and you'll love it! (If you watch this video, you'll love it!)

PRACTICE

the future

1 Read the predictions about film-making in 2030. Complete them with the correct future perfect or continuous form of the verbs in brackets.

1 Many of the films showing in 2030 .... (receive) crowdfunding.
2 Ordinary people .... (collaborate) on new film ideas online as a matter of course.
3 VR manufacturers .... (create) a headset that is used by every cinema goer.
4 Technology companies .... (make) new advances all the time.
5 Camera technology .... (improve) so much films will look stunning.
6 As part of the norm, film makers .... (use) robots as stunt doubles.
7 Some 2030 films .... (make) because their scripts were voted on by film fans.
8 By 2030, a few film scripts .... (write) by artificial intelligence.

2 Choose the correct future forms to complete the extracts from news stories.

1 Film-makers are **due to** / **on the verge of** withdrawing their film from general release after complaints about its content.

2 The latest sci-fi film premiere, which was **due to** / **on the point of** take place tonight, has been postponed.

3 A director **is to** / **will have** change the end of his film after film-goers gave it a big thumbs down.

4 The world's most famous actor says he's **set to** / **on the point of** quitting the business.

5 A new romcom is **on the verge** / **set to** earn millions after critics give it five stars.

6 The latest sci-fi blockbuster will **be losing** / **have lost** millions before it even hits the cinemas.

7 The young actress is **set to** / **on the verge of** making a surprise announcement, according to a source.

3 Complete the news stories with the correct form of these verbs.

announce   cancel   enjoy   make   release   take off

1 Large numbers of downloads suggest that a new games craze is set to .... this week.

2 This time next year, gamers .... the sequel to last year's bestselling game.

3 A developer is to .... additional content for their game that they had planned to release.

4 A games developer is on the point of .... that she will soon produce a new game app.

5 The latest FIFA game is due to .... this week.

conditional sentences

4 Match the first half of each sentence (1–8) with the second half (A–H).

1 Supposing I hadn't bothered with that film, I
2 You can have a TV in your room on
3 Gaming is such a great hobby. Imagine
4 I'm auditioning for a part in a film. What
5 I can play the piano quite well provided
6 I have a good voice as
7 Supposing we'd won Battle of the Bands, we
8 I'd have enjoyed that film,

A condition that you don't have it on all night.
B if I mess it up?
C long as the notes aren't too high.
D could have done something else instead.
E if I weren't so tired.
F would have been on national TV.
G if I could do it for a job.
H that I have the music in front of me.

5 Use the prompts to write conditional sentences. Make any other changes necessary.

1 you / can have the part / play / condition that / you learn / lines / by next week
2 the play / go ahead / long as / all / cast / fit and healthy
3 supposing / I / memorise / these lines earlier, I / not / worried about forgetting them right now
4 what if / I / panic / on stage / and forget my lines?
5 imagine / no one / come / watch us. it / be / so embarrassing

GRAMMAR FILE UNIT 9

REFERENCE

verb + -ing form or infinitive

pattern	verbs	example
+ to-infinitive	arrange, attempt, claim, consent, deserve, hesitate, intend, neglect, prove, refuse, swear, threaten, vow	My brother **vowed to win** the competition the following year.
+ -ing	cease, delay, deny, involve, postpone, quit, resent, risk	If you don't leave now, you **risk missing** the bus.
+ object + to-infinitive	assign, convince, expect, force, forbid, oblige, persuade, tempt	The General **assigned the soldier to protect** the president.
+ object + -ing	catch, discover, leave, resent	He really **resented me changing** class.
+ (object is optional) + -ing	detest, envisage, imagine, miss, recall, regret, resent	We **envisage** (the company) **cutting** down on carbon emissions.

Some verbs are followed by both an -ing form or a to-infinitive with no change in meaning.
bear: I can't **bear to see/seeing** him like this.
begin: He **began talking**./He **began to fall**.
dread: I **dread seeing** him again./I **dread to think**!
propose: How do you **propose to deal** with him?/ **propose finishing** early.
start: He **started talking**./He **started to talk**.

Some verbs are followed by an -ing form or a to-infinitive with a change in meaning.
forget: I'll never **forget meeting** him.
Don't **forget to call** me. (= You need to do this.)
mean: Having a dog **means taking** responsibility for it. (= involves)
I didn't **mean to hurt** you.
need: This room **needs cleaning**. (= Someone should clean it.)
I **need to talk** to you.
regret: I don't **regret going** to university.
We **regret to inform** you … (formal)
remember: I can **remember putting** my purse into my bag.
Please **remember to feed** the cat.
require: This **requires signing**. (= Someone needs to sign it.)
You **are required to attend** the meeting.
stop: I **stopped eating** meat last year.
I **stopped to take** a photo.
try: I **tried talking** to him, but he wouldn't listen. (= I did it.)
He **tried to escape**. (= He wasn't successful.)

Sense verbs (*feel, hear, notice, observe, overhear, see, smell, taste* and *watch*) are followed by an -ing form or a to-infinitive with a slight change in meaning.
I **heard her singing.** (= in progress)
I **heard her sing** last night. (= completed)

reporting verbs

Most reporting verbs can be followed by either a *that* clause or a verb pattern (*to*-infinitive, -*ing* form, preposition + -*ing* form).
I **recommend that you read** page 29.
I **recommend reading** page 29.

pattern	verbs	example
+ -ing	admit, advise, deny, mention, recommend, suggest	He **denied taking** the money.
+ to-infinitive	advise, agree, beg, claim, convince, encourage, forbid, instruct, invite, offer, order, persuade, promise, propose, refuse, threaten, urge, warn	My parents **forbade me to talk** to him again!
+ preposition + -ing	admit to, advise against, apologize for, complain about, confess to, insist on, remind of	She **confessed to stealing** the money.
+ *that* clause	acknowledge, announce, assure, confirm, declare, demand, explain, inform, notify, reassure, recognise, report	The police **confirmed that they weren't** looking for a suspect.

PRACTICE

1 Match the first half of each sentence (1–6) with the second half (A–F).

1 New international agreements oblige
2 The mayor swore
3 Few countries can postpone
4 A lot of people resent
5 Campaigners hope to encourage
6 The new legal changes will postpone

A looking for alternative forms of energy any longer.
B people to change.
C governments to reduce the amount of CO_2 that they produce.
D opening the new recycling plant.
E environmentalists telling them to change their lifestyle.
F to do more to clean up the city.

2 Complete the essay paragraph with the correct form of these verbs.

attempt   consent   forbid   involve
observe   resent   risk   tempt

In the past, conservation work ¹............................ foreign professors travelling to distant lands to study wild animals. They had to find someone local to ²............................ to show them where the animals could be found. Many locals ³............................ having to stop hunting their local wildlife. Often the law ⁴............................ people to harm animals that were stealing their livestock or they ⁵............................ being attacked as populations of wild animals became less and less afraid. Many universities have ⁶............................ to change this by training and employing people locally, not as guides, but as the experts themselves. Once the people were given financial security and incentives to look after the animals, they were no longer ⁷............................ to kill them. The people living alongside the animals were able to ⁸............................ the animals behaving naturally, and collect quality information.

3 Make sentence from the prompts.

1 A don't forget go / bank
    ....
  B I'll never forget / meet / him last year
    ....

2 A the flight usually / require / book / well in advance
    ....
  B this ticket require / you / travel / specific days
    ....

3 A I / really / try / tell / him / truth, but it was impossible!
    ....
  B why don't you try / write / him / email / and see how he responds?
    ....

4 A this car / need / clean / immediately!
    ....
  B my sister / really / need / replace / school bag
    ....

5 A I'm so sorry! I / never / mean / hurt you!
    ....
  B taking the bus / mean / have / a long walk / either end
    ....

4 Choose the correct verb forms to complete the sentences.

1 My friend encouraged me **recycle / to recycle / recycling** more.
2 The school insisted on **reduce / to reduce / reducing** waste.
3 The government claims **offer / to offer / offering** help with heating costs.
4 We should forbid companies **use / to use / using** excess packaging by law.
5 The school recommends **switching / switch / to switch** to solar power.
6 Our teachers advised us **walk / to walk / walking** to school more often.

EXTEND VOCABULARY

Unit 1

idioms
be a piece of cake
be over the moon
break the ice
cross your mind
lose track of smth
take smth on board
the final straw
turn a blind eye to smth

adverb collocations
carefully selected (adv + -ed form)
closely associated (adv + -ed form)
easily understood (adv + -ed form)
equally important (adv + adj)
fully aware (adv + adj)
greatly increase (adv + v)
immediately obvious (adv + adj)
increasingly aware (adv + adj)
largely responsible (adv + adj)
newly acquired (adv + -ed form)
particularly effective (adv + adj)
relatively minor (adv + adj)
significantly reduce (adv + v)
substantially different (adv + adj)
widely available (adv + adj)

Unit 2

noun suffixes

-ance
allowance
assistance
attendance
circumstance
clearance
distance
disturbance
dominance
elegance
guidance
ignorance
maintenance
significance
substance
tolerance
relevance

-ure
agriculture
expenditure
failure
leisure
literature
measure
miniature
mixture
procedure
signature
structure
venture

-al
approval
capital
criminal
individual
journal
material
official
potential
principal
professional
proposal
survival

Unit 3

media collocations
broadcast a news bulletin (v + n)
censor a news story (v + n)
controversial news story (adj + n)
dig up a story/scandal (v + n)
expose the truth (v + n)
full disclosure (adj + n)
give a press conference (v + n)
go to press (v + n)
in the spotlight (prep + n)
issue a press release (v + n)
leak a story (v + n)
off the record (prep + n)
subscribe to a newspaper (v + n)
up-to-date/up-to-the-minute news (adj + n)
work as a freelance reporter (v + n)

Unit 4

prepositions with -ed forms
astonished by
delighted by
determined to
disappointed by/with
extended to
focused on
frustrated by/with
horrified by
involved in
(un)qualified for
(un)related to
restricted to
shaped by
suspected of
used for

prefixes

dis-
disconnect (v)
dishonest (adj)
disorder (n)
dislike (v)
dismiss (v)
disorganisation (n)

mis-
misinterpret (v)
misplace (v)
misread (v)
mistakenly (adv)
mistrust (v)
misuse (v)

pre-
preconception (n)
prejudge (v)
preorder (v)
prepaid (adj)
prepay (v)
preschool (adj)

re-
redevelop (v)
redo (v)
reheat (v)
repay (v)
reorganise (v)
reuse (v)

over-
overachieve (v)
overdevelop (v)
overwork (v)
overflow (v)
overpay (v)
overuse (v)

under-
underachieve (v)
undercooked (adj)
underdevelop (v)
underestimate (v)
underpay (v)
underuse (v)

verb + noun collocations
discuss the implications
get insight
give an impression
have an implication
leave an impression
lose contact with
make contact with
make a threat
receive a threat
show insight

Unit 5

phrasal verbs of attitude and opinion
come across (as very pleasant)
Come off it!
do away with (a need for smth)
fall for (an idea)
(smth bad) gets to (me)
identify with (sb)
keep back (information)
stand by (what you say)
take to (a new sport)

adjectives and dependent prepositions
attached to
annoyed with/about/at
anxious about

dissatisfied with
doubtful about
fond of
jealous of
mad about
safe from
typical of
successful at

Unit 6
phrasal verbs
build up
calm down
clear up
give up
keep back
keep on
open up
set off
set out
shout out
sit up
stand by
start off
take off
throw up

adjective suffixes
-able
favourable
considerable
desirable
memorable
noticeable
predictable
remarkable
unsuitable

-ible
flexible
incredible
invisible
irresponsible
visible

-al
accidental
artificial
beneficial
controversial
emotional

ethical
functional
identical
intellectual
official

-ful
cheerful
disgraceful
doubtful
dreadful
graceful
hateful
shameful
truthful

-less
breathless
hopeless
limitless
meaningless
painless
pointless
priceless
useless

-ic
artistic
athletic
atmospheric
characteristic
dramatic
optimistic
magnetic
strategic

-ive
competitive
decisive
(in)effective
objective
offensive
reflective
selective
supportive

-ly/-y
curly
hilly
hourly
oily
smelly
timely
unfriendly
wobbly

Unit 7
phrasal verbs of food and drink
boil over
drink to (sb, good health)
seal in (the juices)
wait on (sb)
weight out (the flour)

similar words
all together (*phr*) / altogether (*adj*)
aloud (*adj*) / allowed (*adj*)
bare (*adj*) / bear (*n*)
brake (*n and v*) / break (*n and v*)
cue (*n*) / queue (*n*)
disinterested (*adj*) / uninterested (*adj*)
draw (*n*) / drawer (*n*)
pole (*n*) / poll (*n*)
principal (*n*) / principle (*n*)
stationary (*adj*) / stationery (*n*)

Unit 8
prepositional phrases
at any rate
(happen) at random
(do smth) at short notice
by any chance
(be) in a temper
(be) in the right
(be) in the spotlight
(be) off the hook
(be) off the record
off the top of your head
(watch) on demand
(be) on general release
(be put) on hold
(be) out of place
(be) out of step (with)
(be) out of this world

negative prefixes
disadvantaged (*adj*)
discomfort (*n*)
discourage (*v*)
disgraceful (*adj*)
disrespectful (*adj*)
illegally (*adv*)
illegitimate (*adj*)
illiterate (*adj*)
immature (*adj*)
immoral (*adj*)
impatient (*adj*)
impossible (*adj*)
improper (*adj*)
incorrectly (*adv*)
indirectly (*adv*)
inexperienced (*adj*)
informally (*adv*)
intentionally (*adv*)
irrational (*adj*)
irregular (*adj*)
irrelevant (*adj*)
irresponsible (*adj*)
mishear (*v*)
mislead (*v*)
misuse (*v*)
unbearable (*adj*)
unforgettable (*adj*)
unintelligible (*adj*)
unpredictable (*adj*)
unrelated (*adj*)

Unit 9
adjective + noun collocations
black hole
chemical fertiliser
chemical pesticide
crude oil
diverse ecosystem
environmental catastrophe
harmful fumes
high altitude
large colony
man-made reservoir
mineral deposit
natural decay
natural diversity
natural force
natural gas
natural predator
natural shelter
natural surroundings
safe haven
unwanted pest
widespread drought

EXAM FILE: SPEAKING

Part 1: Interview (2 minutes)

Task overview
In Speaking Part 1, the examiner will ask you and your partner some personal questions about your life, your experiences, your interests, your plans, etc. Answer the questions and listen to your partner's answers.

Example task
Note: This part begins with similar questions to these:
- Where are you from?
- What do you do here/there?
- How long have you been studying English?
- What do you enjoy most about learning English?
- What do you love doing in your free time?
- Do you like cooking? Why/Why not?
- What motivates you to study hard?
- If you could go on a dream holiday, where would it be? Why?
- What plans do you have for your future studies?
- Are you the kind of person who loves to win?
- If you could only use one website for a year, what would it be?

Exam help
- Listen carefully to the question. If you don't hear it or don't understand it, ask the examiner to repeat it.
- Expand your answers so you have more opportunity to demonstrate a wider variety of language use.
- Don't prepare answers. Listen carefully to the question and make sure you answer the exact question the examiner asks you.
- Smile, speak up and sound enthusiastic. Nerves can sometimes make you sound quiet and uninterested.

---

useful language

talking about likes and preferences

I spend most of my free time watching football.

What I love doing is running.

I prefer eating **to** cooking but I can cook to a degree.

I'm (not) really into going to the gym these days.

I'm quite keen on creative things like making origami.

I can't stand doing anything in the kitchen.

If I had to choose one, I guess I'd pick YouTube.

talking about plans, dreams and ambitions

What I really want to do is study languages at university.

I'm hoping to go on an exchange programme for a year.

I'm planning on running a marathon next year.

My main goal is to get a degree.

If I had the opportunity, **I'd** sail around the Caribbean.

Provided that I could take my best friend, I'd go mountain biking in France.

giving reasons

That's the reason why I want to study medicine.

The main reason I like skateboarding **is that** I get to hang out with friends outdoors.

I won't look anymore **because/as/since** I seem to burn everything I touch.

The reasons for this are that my older siblings fight over everything and they usually beat me, so I prefer not to compete.

Part 2: Individual long turn (4 minutes)

Task overview
In Speaking Part 2, the examiner will show you three pictures and ask you to compare two of them while answering two questions. You will speak for about one minute. You should explain what's similar and different about the pictures and speculate about the two questions. Your partner is then asked a question about your pictures before being given their own to talk about. After your partner has talked about those pictures, the examiner will ask you a question about them.

Example task

Candidate A: The pictures show people doing activities with their family. Compare two of the pictures and say why people have chosen to do these activities and how the activities might be beneficial to the family members.

Candidate B: Which activity do you think is the most fun? Why?

Exam help
- You'll be able to read the questions above the pictures, so you don't have to memorise them.
- Talk about just two of the pictures, not all three.
- Don't describe the pictures. You must compare the two pictures you choose.
- Use the language of speculation, comparison and contrast to demonstrate advanced language.
- Try to organise your ideas so the examiner can follow them easily. You are given credit for good organisation.
- Listen carefully to your partner when they are talking about their pictures so you can refer to what they said when you answer the follow-up question, but don't interrupt them.

useful language
speculating
They look as if/though …

I guess that X may/might/could have wanted to …

Both X and Y must have …

X might have …

They can't have had …

I'm pretty sure that …

It's possible/likely that …

X is probably enjoying …

comparing and contrasting
In both images, the people have …

X has … **while/whereas** Y doesn't.

Both pictures show people who …

X has to … **In contrast,** Y doesn't …

X is …. **This is similar to/the same as/different to** Y.

On the other hand, Y is the riskiest/most pleasant/etc.

describing an opinion or feeling
In my view, X and Y have … for the same reason.

For me, X has the biggest risk/is the most demanding etc.

I'd say that X is the safest/most helpful/ etc. of all of these …

As far as I can tell, both X and Y …

What strikes me the most is how (brave/happy) these people must be to do this.

Both photos make me feel nervous/smile/etc. because …

SPEAKING FILE

Part 3: Collaborative task (4 minutes)

Task overview
In Speaking Part 3, the examiner will give you a question with five prompts in a diagram. You must discuss the question and the prompts with your partner for around two minutes. After two minutes, the examiner will ask you a second question which will require you to discuss the prompts further for a minute and make a decision.

Example task

- birth of a new baby
- getting a degree
- getting married
- retiring
- getting a new job

How important is it for people to celebrate these things?

Follow-up question: Which of these things do you think is most important for everyone to celebrate?

Exam help
- Make sure you listen to what your partner says and respond to it.
- Interact with your partner naturally so that you both get an opportunity to speak.
- Give reasons for your opinions.
- Try to speak about each prompt but don't worry if you don't get to all of them.
- Use a wide range of language. Paraphrase if you can't think of a word.
- Keep speaking until the examiner stops you.
- When the examiner asks you to discuss the second question, don't make a decision too quickly. Speak about some of the prompts before you decide. Don't worry if you don't come to a conclusion or can't agree – you won't lose marks if this happens.

---

useful language

giving and asking for an opinion

As far as I'm concerned, marriage should be celebrated the most.

Personally, I don't think it's important to celebrate retirement.

In my view, after forty years of work, everyone deserves a retirement party.

I'd say that a new job is cause for celebration but less so than a new baby.

It seems to me that we should celebrate whatever we can!

Would you agree with that?

What's your view?

What do you think?

Which one would you say should be celebrated the most?

giving an opinion tentatively

I guess people celebrate the birth of a child because it changes their family.

I suppose after years of hard work, people should congratulate you on your degree.

giving reasons and examples

The main reason is that celebrations are the only time families get together.

The key thing is that traditions adapt as generations change.

This is due to the fact that young and older people have different interests.

We'll lose some traditions **since/because/as** young people aren't interested in them.

To give an example, my grandparents went to May Day festivals but we don't do anything special.

To illustrate my point, last year the only time my extended family were together was at a wedding.

Part 4: Discussion (5 minutes)

Task overview
In Speaking Part 4, the examiner will ask you and your partner some questions based on the topic in Part 3. These questions will focus on opinions, so you will have to agree or disagree with each other. The examiner will listen as you and your partner speak and may ask some follow-up questions to encourage each of you to say more.

Example task
How important are celebrations for family life?

Some people say that some celebrations have become too commercial. Do you agree? Why/Why not?

Do young people celebrate differently to their grandparents? How?

Do you think that it's important for countries to enjoy public holidays? Why/Why not?

What are some reasons for preserving cultural traditions like holiday celebrations?

Would you say that the original meaning of some celebrations has got lost? Why/Why not?

Exam help
- Make sure you listen to what your partner says and respond to it.
- Interact naturally with your partner so that you both get an opportunity to speak.
- Extend your answers by giving reasons and examples, agreeing or disagreeing with your partner or expanding his/her answers.
- Don't ignore your partner, but use the time when they are talking to listen and prepare what you want to say next.

---

useful language

agreeing

Yes, you're right.

I agree with that.

That's a good point.

disagreeing politely

I know what you mean, but deciding to spend your life with someone is a big decision.

That's a good point, but I don't think a new job is so significant.

managing a discussion

Let's start with having a new baby.

Shall we move onto a new job?

What do you mean (by that)?

Getting back to what we were saying before, marriage shows commitment.

Sorry, can I say something?

clarifying a point

What I mean by that is we don't celebrate it.

What do you mean?

coming to a conclusion

So, which one do you think should be celebrated the most?

So, we've decided on marriage, is that right?

EXAM FILE: WRITING

Essay

Example task

Your class has watched a studio discussion about ways that people can be persuaded to recycle more. You have made the notes below:

- using the media
- education in schools
- financial penalties

Some opinions expressed in the discussion:

'TV channels can make documentaries about the effects of not recycling that everyone can watch.'

'Schools can educate young people on the importance of recycling.'

'The government can introduce fines for people who don't recycle.'

Write an essay for your teacher discussing **two** of the ways for persuading people to recycle in your notes. You should **explain which way would be more effective, giving reasons** in support of your answer.

You may, if you wish, make use of the opinions expressed in the discussion, but you should use your own words as far as possible. Write your essay in **220–260** words.

Example answer

Recycling has become important in recent decades as we gain a greater understanding of our impact on the environment. However, not everyone understands how important recycling is and as a result, they do not recycle consistently. This essay will suggest two key ways that these people might be persuaded to recycle more: education in schools and introducing fixed penalties for non-recycling.

The first method, through schools, means providing lessons for children about recycling. The reason for this is that education opens people's minds and such lessons will hopefully encourage young people to get into the habit of recycling from an early age. They may also teach their parents to do so. Once children start recycling, the habit will continue into adulthood and they will teach their own children to recycle.

The second method of fixed fines provides a punishment for people who do not recycle. While this sounds negative, punishment can often be a deterrent for undesirable behaviour. If people think they may lose money if they do not recycle, it might influence their decision to recycle or not. As a result, more people will recycle their waste.

In conclusion, both education and fines are likely to have a positive impact on the numbers of people recycling. In my view, education in schools is the one which will have the greatest impact. This is because research shows education has changed people's behaviour for the better in many areas of life and it is therefore very likely to be effective in the area of recycling too.

In your introduction, introduce the topic and state the two ideas you'll talk about.

In your main paragraphs, introduce the main idea, give reasons and/or examples, and say the effect of this or why it's important.

Link ideas with linking words and phrases.

In your conclusion, summarise the main points so that they logically lead to an idea or suggestion for the future.

Exam help

- Start with an introduction and end with a conclusion.
- Focus on one idea in each main body paragraph. Only talk about two ideas – no more.
- You can use your own reasons and examples to develop the two ideas given in the question or use the ideas in the notes. If you use the latter, paraphrase them.
- Use a formal academic tone, which means more formal vocabulary and no contractions.
- Write between 220 and 260 words. Make sure that everything you write is relevant and avoid repetition.

useful language

introduction

This essay will suggest two key ways/factors/reasons/etc.

There are two key ways/factors/reasons etc.

Two potential ways/factors/reasons are …

introducing ideas

One option/approach is to …

A second option is to …

The first idea is to …

Another potential idea is to …

making a point

Above all, …

It is worth bearing in mind that …

giving reasons

One reason for this is that …

This is due to (the fact that) …

because/since/as …

explaining the effect of something

… lead to/result in …

As a result, …

As a consequence, …/Consequently, …

linking ideas

However, …/On the other hand, …/Although …/ Despite the fact that …, While …

In addition, …/Furthermore, …/Moreover, …/ Besides …,/Alternatively, …

This underlines the fact that …/ What it has shown us is that …/ In view of this …,

writing a conclusion

To sum up, …/To conclude, …/In conclusion, …

Report

Example task

You are a member of the student committee at the school where you study. Last year the school invested in a sports programme which included buying new sports equipment and providing after-school sports clubs. The aim was to encourage more students to take up sport outside school hours.

The principal has asked you to write a report explaining which aims the investment in sports has managed to meet, describing any problems that have occurred and making recommendations as to whether funding is continued next year or not.

Write your report in **220–260** words.

Example answer

Introduction
The aims of this report are to state whether the money invested in sports at Canford School has achieved its goal and to recommend whether the school should continue to invest in the sports programme in the forthcoming year. In order to prepare for this report, students participating in the programme and a cross-section of other students were interviewed.

[State the aim(s) of the report and how the data was collected.]

Benefits of the programme
There is no doubt that the sports programme has created more sports opportunities for students. There is now a hockey club, a judo club and a climbing club for both male and female students, all of which are well attended. Students were positive about their experiences stating:
- the coaching is excellent.
- the equipment is of good quality.
- the wide variety of sports on offer is motivating.

[You can use bullet points or numbers to list points, but only use a small number.]

Issues
Unfortunately, the majority of students who have joined the new clubs were already involved in other sports clubs previously, choosing to leave an existing club to try out a new one. However, the majority of the new sports equipment was purchased in the later part of the school year, and so more people may participate in future.

[Give each section a sub-heading.]

Conclusion and recommendations
In general, the sports programme has achieved its goal as more students are doing sports after school. For this reason we would recommend that the school continue to invest in the programme next year. However we would like to recommend that the school promotes the clubs more heavily in order to attract even more students, especially female students, to the programme for next year.

[Make recommendations based on the information previously presented.]

Exam help

- A report is designed to evaluate something objectively using research, draw conclusions, and recommend a course of action based on the objective evaluation.
- Start with an introduction and end with a conclusion.
- Make sure your sub-headings relate to the question.
- Use a formal or semi-formal style.
- Write a balanced view of positives and negatives, drawing on results from a survey, interview or similar kind of research process.
- Link your ideas so that the reader can follow your points easily (see page 166 for a list of linking language).
- Write between 220 and 260 words. You'll be penalised for writing irrelevant information, repeating points or not writing enough points.

useful language

introduction

The aims of this report are to …

In order to prepare for/create this report, … were interviewed.

… were asked to complete a questionnaire.

reporting on data collection

Many/Most people I interviewed …

The (vast) majority of people felt that …

A minority suggested that …

introducing a bulleted/numbered list

The main reasons for this are: …

… for the following reasons: …

The key strengths mentioned were: …

The main problems given were: …

giving a balance of opinions

Unfortunately, the majority …

While many felt …, there were several …

That is not to suggest that …

making recommendations

We would suggest …

We could think about …

I would recommend (+ -ing form) …

We should …

WRITING FILE

Letter/Email

Example task
You have received an email from an English friend.

> ...
> I'm so worried about performing in the school play next month. I have the leading role and I'm just so nervous. I don't know what to do! It involves some singing as well as dancing.
> I'd like your advice, please. What would you do if you were me?
> Best wishes,
> Kim

Write your email in reply.
Write your email in **220–260** words.

Example answer

Hi Kim,

I was so glad to get your email. It's feels like it's been ages since we last spoke, and I've missed your funny emails and jokes!

Firstly, huge congratulations on getting the leading role in the school play! I know that there's always a load of competition, and you'll have got the part through hard work and talent. I'm thrilled that the director has recognised just how gifted you are!

I understand that you get nervous but, you know, everybody does. You're really not alone! I think the main thing is to rehearse the songs and dance moves so many times that it just becomes second nature. The more you practise, the more confident you'll be. Besides, who doesn't feel better after singing and dancing around the house all day?

Whenever I have something challenging, I'm always imagining the worst, and I'm sure you do that, too. I read somewhere that professional performers always sit down and think through everything they're going to do in incredible detail. It helps to balance out the fears! Mind you, perhaps you could also think about what you'll do, just in case the worst happens! I'm sure there's nothing a smile can't fix.

Anyway, I really can't wait to hear how it all goes, and I'd love to come and support you. Can you perhaps send me the link to get tickets for the show? It'll help to have a friendly face in the audience, too, I bet!

All the best — and I know you'll nail it!
Chris

- Whether it's an email or a letter, start with *Hi* or *Dear ...* and finish with an appropriate ending, e.g. *Best wishes, ...* . You don't need to write an address.
- Use language appropriate to the purpose of writing, e.g. to reassure, congratulate, etc.
- Use appropriate linkers to join your ideas together.
- Finish your letter/email with a reference to future contact.

Exam help
- Letters/Emails can be both formal and informal in the exam. Use language that is neutral or appropriate to your target reader.
- Respect the conventions of starting and ending letters and emails.
- Group ideas into paragraphs.
- Link your ideas with either neutral linking words or formal/informal linking words depending on the task.
- Make sure you include all the relevant information in your letter/email.
- Write between 220 and 260 words.

useful language

greetings

informal
Long time no see! How are you?
Getting your email really cheered me up!

formal
Many thanks for your letter dated ...
I am writing with regard to ...

explaining the purpose

informal
I'm writing to tell you all about ...
I have something exciting to tell you.

formal
I would like to complain/apply for ...
I am writing on behalf of ... to ...

using linkers

informal
Besides, ...   Anyway, ...   Mind you, ...

formal
An additional consideration might be ...
Not only ... but also ...

finishing your letter/email

informal
You really must give me all the juicy details when we next meet!
I can't wait to catch up/get an update/see how it goes!

formal
I look forward to hearing from you at your earliest convenience.
Thank you in advance for your help in this matter.

Review

Example task

The food section of our website is looking for reviews of a fast food restaurant or café in your area. Write a review evaluating the restaurant or café and say whether you would or wouldn't recommend it to others and why.

Write your review in **220–260** words.

Example answer

Drink, eat and play a game

Would you love to drink coffee, eat cake and play board games? Then the Old Time Café is the place for you. It's situated in the north of the city and offers customers the chance to play old-fashioned board games while enjoying a snack. It offers a vast range of coffee, from regular to more unusual beans. There's also a range of tasty, homemade cakes.

It's a relaxed café, conveniently located in the centre of town, so you can get there by public transport. It has simple decoration, and comfortable chairs to sit and have a drink in an unhurried atmosphere, but what makes it truly special and unique is the fact there are literally a hundred different board games to play. You can play the kinds of games you played as a child or the ones that your parents played. It might sound boring but it's actually a lot of fun.

The only problem with this cafe is that you have to leave your mobile phones at the door. My friends and I all found this difficult at first. We were all desperate to know what we were missing out on but we soon forgot about it and concentrated on the games. After all, we weren't missing out anything at all. It was our friends that weren't with us who were missing out.

All in all, this is a fascinating café and I'd certainly recommend it, providing, of course, that you're someone who's happy to leave social media alone for an hour.

Annotations:
- Start with a question or a statement that grabs the reader's attention.
- Briefly describe what you're being asked to review.
- Use a variety of language, e.g. adjectives, to bring the description alive for the reader.
- End with a summary of your review.

useful language

describing strengths

It's absolutely hilarious/totally thrilling/really gripping/incredibly tasty/truly astonishing/really inspiring.

It'll have you on the edge of your seats/wishing for more/coming back for a second helping.

I was thoroughly convinced/definitely signed up for more/with them all the way.

describing weakness

It's absolutely rubbish/totally frustrating/really disappointing/incredibly frustrating/so gloomy/a bit of a letdown.

It wasn't exactly Oscar-worthy/five-star dining/Shakespeare's best works.

You'd be better off giving … else a try/be hard pushed to find a worse …, to be honest.

giving an opinion

From my point of view, …

I'd say that …

What I loved/hated about it was …

What I found frustrating was …

making recommendations

I'd certainly/definitely/really/strongly recommend it.

Despite the fact that …, I'd still recommend it.

All in all, …

Make sure you don't miss it.

You should definitely give it a go.

Exam help

- Include a title.
- Read the question carefully and decide what style you should use. Is it a less formal, more journalistic review, e.g. for a website? Or is it something more formal?
- Make the review as engaging as possible, e.g. pose questions, make it funny.
- Start by describing what you're reviewing but make sure you don't give away the ending to a film or book you're writing about.
- Divide your review into paragraphs and make sure each paragraph has a clear purpose.
- Try to use a range of more advanced language to show that you have a broad vocabulary.
- End your review with a clear recommendation and a reason.
- Write between 220 and 260 words.

WRITING FILE

Proposal

Example task
You attend a school that has no drama club but you feel it should have one. You decide to write to the school principal, giving reasons why a drama club would benefit your school.

In your proposal, you should explain what would be needed in order to run the club and outline the basic costs involved.

Write your proposal in **220–260** words.

Example answer

> Proposal for a school drama club
>
> Introduction
> It is my view, and that of many of my classmates, that a drama club would complement the existing clubs offered after school. The purpose of this proposal is to outline two key reasons why such a club would be beneficial and to provide details of what would be needed in order to run it successfully.
>
> Reasons for a drama club
> Drama gives everyone the opportunity to be creative and express themselves. In a busy school curriculum, there can be little space for these important skills. A drama club can offer this, and provide essential light relief from the pressures of studying.
>
> In addition, drama clearly brings people together, collaborating to put on plays and performances. They have to take direction, as well as learn how to communicate clearly with others. These helpful skills can prepare young people for university studies and work in the future.
>
> Cost and facilities
> To create an effective club, we would need a large room and a teacher with an interest in drama to lead the group. While we will need a small budget of around £100 per year for props, the majority of these can be provided by the students themselves or their parents.
>
> Conclusions and recommendations
> We highly recommend that the school start a drama club at the beginning of next term. Mr James has volunteered to run the group and over twenty students are keen to join already. With a budget of £35 each term, we believe the drama club can be a great success and an asset to the school.

Annotations:
- State the purpose of your proposal in the introduction.
- Divide your proposal into sections with a heading for each.
- Link sentences with words such as *these*, *this* and *such*.
- Finish with a clear conclusion and recommendation.

Exam help
- A proposal is designed to describe a need and persuade the reader of a particular course of action with regards to that need.
- Give your proposal a relevant title.
- Divide your proposal into sections that are based on the question.
- Use formal or neutral language throughout. To decide on the most appropriate style, consider who the reader is.
- Make sure your views are to the point and clearly explained.
- Link your ideas to ensure that your points are clear and persuasive.
- Write between 220 and 260 words.

useful language

introduction

The purpose of this proposal is to …

After carrying out a survey of students, …

There was widespread agreement that …

It is the view of many (friends/classmates/colleagues) that …

being persuasive

This is necessary for …

These … are vital for …

These are beneficial because …

making recommendations

It is our recommendation that …

We (strongly) suggest that …

It is our belief that …

Implementation of these proposals would result in …

ACTIVITY FILE

Unit 1, Writing, page 17, Ex 9

Your class has watched an online debate about ways to reduce the amount of time children spend looking at a screen. You have made the notes below:

> Ideas for reducing time children spend online:
> - school intervention
> - rules set by parents at home
> - government guidelines
>
> Some opinions expressed in the debate:
>
> 'I didn't use a computer when I was at school so six-year-olds shouldn't use them either.'
>
> 'Parents need to enforce stricter rules at home about the use of technology.'
>
> 'Governments should ban children's TV for more than a short time to stop kids watching it.'

Write an essay for your teacher discussing **two** of the ideas in your notes. You should **explain which way is more effective** in reducing screen time for children, **giving reasons** in support of your answer.

Write your essay in **220–260** words.

Unit 2, Listening, page 26, Ex 1

The top four smells are: lime, grapefruit, orange and peppermint.

Unit 3, Vocabulary, page 39, Ex 2

Over 18 points
You love a good news story but your tendency to believe everything you read may mean you get taken in by fake stories.

13–17 points
You don't believe everything you read but you're still sometimes attracted by exciting stories that may or may not be true.

8–12 points
You're a discerning reader, making sure you don't just believe everything you read. But does this take all the fun out of it?

Unit 3, Speaking, page 43, Ex 8

newspapers — magazines — vlogs — films — television

How far do these forms of media influence people?

Which form of media has the greatest influence on most people?

page 14: Jumpman

ACTIVITY FILE

Unit 3, Writing, page 45, Ex 9

Your class has listened to a radio discussion about ways to encourage more young people to study science subjects at university. You have made the notes below:

> How can more young people be encouraged to study science subjects at university?
> - role models
> - parental influence
> - government grants
>
> Some opinions expressed in the discussion:
>
> 'Schools need to employ more female science teachers to be role models for young girls.'
>
> 'Parents should try to get all their children interested in science at a young age by taking them to science museums.'
>
> 'The government should give financial grants to young people who choose to study sciences at university.'

Write an essay for your teacher discussing **two** of the ideas in your notes. You should **explain which way is more effective** in encouraging more girls to study science subjects at university, **giving reasons** in support of your answer.

Write your essay in **220–260** words.

Unit 4, Reading, page 50, Ex 2

page 17: a screensaver!

Unit 4, Writing, page 59, Ex 7

Study exchange!

The Academics Abroad Programme (AAP) is offering a prize of a six-month study exchange in an English-speaking country of your choice. Winners will attend local language classes and live with a local family. Write and tell us which country you'd like to visit and why, how the experience will benefit you in future and why we should choose you as the most deserving winner. The most persuasive letter will win the prize.

Unit 4, Writing, page 59, Ex 8

1. Each of you should write a sentence or two giving two reasons why you should win the prize. Use linkers of addition to join them. Use your imagination and try to sound better than everyone else!

    I believe you should select me because …

2. Collect all the sentences from your group and swap them with another group.
3. Read the other group's sentences and decide which entrant should win the prize.
4. Tell the other group who won the prize. Find out which member of your group they decided should win the prize.

Unit 5, Reading, page 64, Ex 2

A Did you know that if you find yourself stuck in a dull conversation, mentioning that you have a pet frog has been proven to liven things up?

B Lost your wallet? Statistically, it's more likely to be returned to you if you put a baby photo in the front.

C Putting a potted plant on your desk should increase your creativity by fifteen percent.

Unit 5, Reading, page 64, Ex 11

The Teen's Guide to World Domination – School and relationships are just not as simple as they were when your parents were young, and teens have to respond to difficult situations almost daily. This book offers sound advice on dealing with the seven topics that have teens freaking out.

The Laugh Out Loud Joke Book – With over 300 jokes, you'll never wonder what to say when the conversation goes dry again.

Dating for Under a Dollar – Filled with inexpensive ideas to help you get the most of social opportunities without spending a fortune.

Unit 5, Grammar, page 66, Ex 9

John knew that the box labelled 'Apples and oranges' was incorrect and only contained one type of fruit. He took an orange from that box, so he knew that it must have been the 'Oranges' box. That left him with two boxes: one labelled 'Apples' and one labelled 'Oranges'. He knew the label saying 'Apples' had to be wrong, so the only label left for that box was 'Apples and oranges'. The final box had to be 'Apples'.

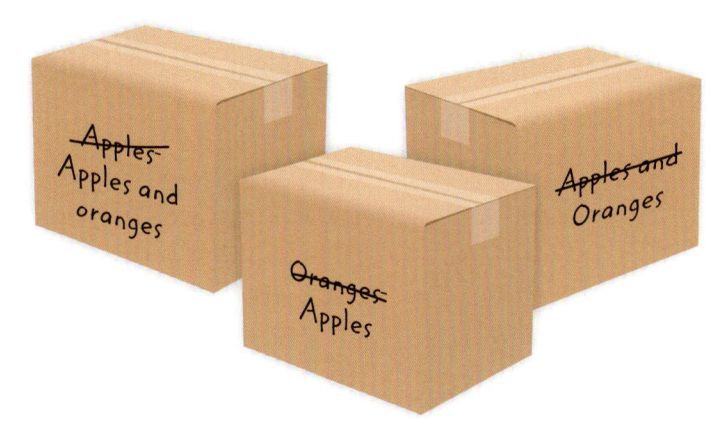

Unit 5, Speaking, page 71, Ex 8

`Letterbox` – A social network to connect local people who want to work together. Start a running club or help an elderly person with their shopping or gardening.

ACTIVITY FILE

Unit 5, Writing, page 73, Ex 9

You have attended a talk on ways to encourage people to help each other. You have made the notes below:

> What are effective ways of encouraging people to help each other?
> - online support groups
> - open public buildings
> - stronger links between schools and the community
>
> Some opinions expressed in the talk:
>
> 'Now when I have a problem, I just go online to see if anyone else has any advice.'
>
> 'Sports centres and community centres are great places to hold charity events, like music nights.'
>
> 'I feel better about helping others when we do it as a class project.'

Write an essay for your teacher discussing **two** of the ways in which people can be encouraged to help each other more. You should **explain which way is more important, giving reasons** in support of your answer.

You may, if you wish, make use of the opinions expressed in the talk, but you should use your own words as far as possible.

Write your essay in **220–260** words.

Unit 7, Grammar, page 94, Ex 4

Breakdown of the cost of a Premier League football shirt			
Retailer	£18.13	Club fee	£2.97
Sportswear firm	£12.76	Marketing	£1.39
VAT (tax)	£8.24	Distribution	£1.17
Manufacturing and shipping	£4.79	**TOTAL**	**£49.45**

Unit 7, Writing, page 101, Ex 7

There are plans to turn a football and sports field in your town into additional car parking space, as it is currently underused as a sports facility. You feel that the field should be kept for sports. You decide to send a proposal to the town council explaining why you think the field should be used for sports rather than a car park, suggesting what can be done to encourage more people to use the facility and explaining how this would benefit the town.

Write your proposal in **220–260** words.

Unit 8, Grammar, page 108, Ex 6

1 Read your article and check your predictions from Exercise 5. Do NOT read the other articles!
2 Note down the future phrases and forms used in the article.
3 Note down up to twelve key words or phrases to help you summarise the article without reading it.
4 Use those key words and the future phrases and forms to summarise the article for the other students in your group.

Student A

China is set to become the biggest movie market in the world over the next two years after huge growth in the number of people going to the cinema there. Despite Hollywood dominating movie viewing for decades, the Chinese film market is due to overtake the USA market thanks to falling cinema ticket sales in the US. An industry insider predicts that US film companies will soon be chasing the high demand in China and this will affect the types of movies made in Hollywood.

Student B

Entertainment and reality are on the verge of merging as virtual reality blurs the lines between the two. Experts say in the near future we'll be enjoying entertainment as if we're part of the action and not just on a screen. They suggest we're on the point of being able to invite the latest boy band to perform in our living room – something that'll excite fans everywhere. Having said that, some experts argue that this will only happen after the cost of VR headsets has come down.

Student C

Radio is to get up close and personal with new technology that will allow listeners to have a completely personalised experience. According to an expert, in a few years' time you'll no longer need to spend time scrolling through your playlist to find the right song – your personal DJ will do it for you. Machine assistants will soon have developed the ability to recommend the perfect song according to where you are, the time of day it is and your previous personal preferences. Once that happens, you're set to get your own soundtrack through life.

Unit 8, Writing, page 115, Ex 9

Your class has listened to a radio discussion about ways to encourage young people to read more stories. You have made the notes below:

Ideas for encouraging young people to read more stories:
- length of story
- theme and topic
- mode of delivery

Some opinions expressed in the discussion:

'Short stories or stories divided into episodes can grab your attention without taking up too much of your time.'

'It's important to address the kinds of things young people are interested in.'

'Reading a story online gives you the chance to interact with others readers and comment.'

Write an essay for your teacher discussing **two** of the ideas in your notes. You should **explain which way is more effective** in encouraging more young adults to read more stories, **giving reasons** in support of your answer.

Write your essay in **220–260** words.

SPEAKING TASKS

Unit 2, Speaking, page 29, Ex 7

Student A
The photos show people communicating ideas in different ways. Compare two of the photos and say why the people might have chosen to communicate in this way, and how they might be feeling.

Student B
Listen to Student A. Then answer this question: Which type of communication do you think is the most challenging?

Unit 5 Speaking, page 71, Ex 7

Work in pairs. Take turns to compare two of the photos.

When you finish, ask your partner these questions.
- Why do you think people choose to help others around them?
- Which method of working together in the community would be most effective?

Unit 7, Speaking, page 99, Ex 9

Work in pairs. The photos below show alternative ways of getting exercise. Take turns to compare two of the photos. When you have finished, the student listening should answer one of the questions below.

1 Why do you think the people have chosen to exercise in these ways?
2 How enjoyable do you think the exercise might be?

Unit 9, Speaking, page 127, Ex 8

Work in pairs. The photos below show people working outside. Take turns to compare two of the photos. When you have finished, the student listening should answer the question below.

Which job do you think is more important to the community? Why?

AUDIOSCRIPTS

1.1 and 1.2

Speaker 1: I guess I'm quite crafty. I quite enjoy bits of sewing and things like that. I know that when my friends have gotten married, which is, you know, from time to time, I would make them something for their wedding – a traditional Victorian sampler or something. And, actually, as we speak, I am wearing a scarf that I knitted myself. A little festive number, so I'm quite proud of my knitting skills at the moment.

Speaker 2: For several years now – I've been doing pottery. That's making things of clay, as you may know, and then firing them. And I'm still trying to explore different techniques, different materials. There's an infinite number of choices in pottery, actually.

Speaker 3: So, since I was twelve I've been doing acting. So I do … mainly from a film background in Australia, which is lots of fun. I also did a theatre tour when I was fifteen around Europe, which was really cool. It was the story of Ned Kelly.

Speaker 4: Well, I've been into football for quite a long time and so I used to play and now I am a football coach. So I'm still coaching. I coach a team at home in Manchester and then I recently started coaching a girls' team here in London as well since I've moved here.

Speaker 5: I have done cheerleading for the past six years and I'm actually a cheerleading coach at the moment, so I've stopped competing and I'm coaching it now. So it's a combination of acrobatic stunting, gymnastics, dance jumps.

Speaker 6: I've always done a lot of dance, and currently I'm doing some Brazilian dance. I used to belly dance for a long time. But over the past few years, I've put it a bit on the back burner, but it's nice to be getting back to it now. Now that my children are a little older and I can leave them for a bit.

Speaker 7: I've been writing my whole life, so it's my main hobby. I started when I was a kid, writing small stories and I still do now. And I've a bit of a blog, writing about London and the city.

Speaker 8: I've been doing cooking for a very long time cos I'm a human being and as human beings, we have to sustain ourselves by eating. I cook every day, and recently I've been doing a lot more baking. I've been inspired by the *Great British Bake Off* and so far I've made a piñata cake, cake pops, and yesterday I made a Christmas cake.

1.3 and 1.4
M = Max   K = Katy

M: I'm just saying that school isn't always the best thing for helping you to accomplish your goals.

K: So what are you suggesting instead then?

M: Well, I think you can learn more from pursuing your interests outside of school. Joining clubs – that kind of thing.

K: So you're saying that everything we learn in school is a waste of time. Are you serious? How can you get on in life without having an education?

M: Yeah, of course you need qualifications and so school's important for that. But it's not only knowledge that helps you flourish; you need skills too. Apparently, these days most employers say the key skills are communication skills, creativity, team work, digital skills and so on. Those are the kinds of things you learn from recreational activities, aren't they?

K: I don't know. Give me an example.

M: Well, loads of sports require team work and the ability to communicate well. Any arty activity encourages you to be creative.

K: Hmm, I guess.

M: And hobbies present new challenges, which push us to achieve and give us confidence. If you underperform or something goes wrong, you learn to get over it and start again. And there are always other people to help you overcome those setbacks – friends, team mates, people online and so on.

K: Woah, you've thought about this a lot! I still think you can do all that at school, sorry. You do team sports at school, and there are art lessons and technology lessons. We do group work all the time.

M: Yes, but art lessons tend to cover a fairly narrow range of art. You don't do things like, er, origami or … or … design and making your own clothes. Schools can't cater for everyone's interests or talents, so lots of students have to do out of school activities to fulfil their potential.

K: Well, OK, I see what you mean, but you can't focus solely on what you do outside of school. That's like focusing only on school. I think the key thing is not to let homework occupy all your time but do other things too, so you learn from both school and the things you love doing outside of school.

1.5 and 1.6
N = Narrator   B = Boy   G = Girl   M = Man   W = Woman

1

N: You hear two teammates talking about playing American football.

B: Welcome back to the team! I'm glad your campaign worked. It was dumb not to let you play just cos you're a girl.

G: I know. You soon forgot I was a girl once I'd knocked you down! I accept I'm not the best player in the team and it wasn't really about letting me be part of a winning team, even though you probably have a sneaking suspicion I could make a difference. It was about the people making the rules treating me in the same way they always tell us to treat each other – with respect, and that wasn't happening in team selection.

B: So is the campaign over now?

G: Not really, though I'm not sure where to take it from here. They've compromised and let me play, but not other girls.

B: You should keep fighting then. I reckon you have a few options. You'll obviously continue your internet petition, but it might not get much further than it already has. You could try to get on TV to highlight the issue there, one of those popular daytime chat shows or something – they'd love a story like this. A demonstration near city hall could work, but you'd need a lot of people and if you couldn't get them then no one would notice. I guess it's a tricky one, but it's important to get it right.

G: Sure, thanks. Something to think about, anyway.

2

N: You hear two friends discussing opportunities for Olympic athletes.

W: I'm reading this article on sportspeople who overcame big challenges before competing in the Olympics. There's a javelin thrower who had to teach himself to throw via YouTube videos and a runner who grew up in a boiling hot refugee camp with no gym or running shoes!

M: Well, I have to say that's pretty heroic – to put so much effort into overcoming obstacles like that. In fact it just goes to show, that you don't need to have the best of everything to be competitive on the world stage.

W: You'd think so, wouldn't you? But both of them were sent off to train with excellent facilities and expertise once their talent had been spotted. Their efforts should be celebrated, but I wonder whether they'd have got to the Olympics without that kind of funding.

M: Good question!

W: I bet there are loads of naturally talented people who end up not fulfilling their potential, just because they're not seen by the right people at the right time. It makes you question whether it's a level playing field at all, and it must be particularly bad in some of the poorer regions of the world too. I wonder just how fair big global sporting events really are. It's not that these people aren't gifted though, and hopefully things will change.

3

N: You hear two friends talking about some research into sports and child development.

M: This research says that kids who develop early tend to get picked out as promising sports stars and those who develop late are ignored.

W: OK, well, there's nothing too shocking there when you think of our competitive school sports system. What happens when those early developers fail to live up to expectations?

M: Well, nothing really. Apparently, the child and everyone else believes they're talented, so they get the best coaches and train really hard. Ultimately, they achieve success while the late developers believe they're no good at an early age, so just give in.

W: Hmm, that's tough. Nothing will change though. Not enough people in education are aware there's an issue. Does it give any suggestions on dealing with it?

M: Not really. You know, when I think about me and sports at middle school, I was so uncoordinated. I was glad to give it up. Maybe I could have been an athlete if I'd worked at it like those sporty kids – but I'll never know now. Still, according to this research, early developers tend to focus solely on their sports and improve less in other areas, but I concentrated on my studies and did well there, so I can't complain.

1.7 and 1.8

1 The main assumption people make about gaming is that it's for kids and that you'll grow out of it by the time you hit your twenties. But it's not true! It's relatively unknown but the average gamer is actually in their early thirties and there are supposedly more gamers over the age of thirty than under the age of eighteen, so it's not just a young person's pastime at all. You have to remember that kids were playing the first computer games in the eighties and many of those people are still playing now – in their forties. *They* didn't grow out of it!

2 Games are generally considered to be a waste of time by people who don't play them. But why? What makes them different to watching a film or listening to music? Those things are much more passive than being immersed in a game where you're actually doing something active. It's frustrating cos gaming is really popular, so how could so many people be getting it wrong? No matter how many people play it, it's still looked down on.

3 A misconception I often hear is that games are for lazy people who have no intelligence. You know, the kind of image of a teenager who plays games all day instead of studying and then flunks out of college. Just think about the intelligent people involved in the gaming industry. Most of them love games, which is why they make them. Lots of games push you to use your brain and I've learnt loads of interesting things about the world through them too, stuff I've then read up on later to learn more. So games have greatly increased my intelligence and I haven't even started on the *skills* you learn through gaming yet.

4 If you asked people to describe a gamer, I reckon they'd describe a boy every time. Yes, fewer girls play than boys, that's true, but plenty of girls like it too. I have female friends who spend hours playing puzzle apps and yet they still insist they're not gamers. They are! It's a misconception that consistently annoys me. Girls like gaming too!

1.9 and 1.10

Ela: I'd probably go to Cairo.

Ben: We tend to spend time outside. We like to experience enjoyment by participating in team sports such as football or rugby as competition has always been a key aspect of our friendship.

Rei: One where I can spend all day just chilling out at home with my friends, playing a few games, listening to music – that kind of thing. Doing stuff outdoors isn't really my thing. I prefer hanging out with a small group of friends and having a laugh with them.

Martin: I'm not that great, to be honest, but it depends on the activities. I can do my homework with music on, for example, but I'm rubbish at doing things when I'm talking. For example, when I'm out chatting with my mates, we end up going in the wrong direction because I just can't concentrate on directions at the same time.

1.11 and 1.12

1 I couldn't write any Chinese at all when I started learning the language. I had to learn [beep].

2 If you really love sport, adventure and the outdoors, then mountain biking is something you should [beep].

3 Hmm, I can run long distances pretty fast. I won our local junior marathon last year. I guess that's my biggest [beep].

4 When people work really hard at something, it's amazing what they can [beep].

5 My sister really annoys me sometimes. I think she does it on purpose, so I try hard not to get angry and to [beep].

6 I live at a boarding school during the week but I go home at weekends because it's not too far away. This is great for me because I spend time with friends and family. I think I get [beep].

1.13

I've loved painting all my life and so this year I'm trying to turn what is essentially my hobby into a job. I've painted over ten paintings in recent weeks in an attempt to create a collection that I can sell. Every now and then, to see how attractive people think my paintings are, I take them to the local arts market where I try to sell them. I've sold around ten so far, which I feel really positive about. People like them! I'd like to spend more time selling them but for the time being, I'm concentrating on producing as many as I can to sell on my stall. I've been working hard, and my productivity has improved over the last few weeks. As well as having my stall, I also have a website where people can buy them online. Several times a week, I check to see how many visitors I've had to my site so I can gauge how popular my work is. Three people are looking at it as we speak, which is exciting!

2.1 and 2.2

Researchers have been asking some very interesting questions about the brain recently. The invention of brain-scanning techniques has revolutionised our understanding. Never before have we had such rich information available. For years scientists prided themselves on observing the world without any emotion. Nowhere was this better illustrated than in characters from popular culture, such as Sherlock Holmes, whose powers of observation were second to none. But we now know that seeing is not necessarily believing. What happens is that information is filtered through our senses and then through different sections of the brain, and that may not be very reliable. It's possible, and actually quite common, to look directly at something, and not understand what we see. You would think that something as obvious as a gorilla would show up anywhere. What we now know is that gorillas can be hidden almost anywhere.

2.3 and 2.4

We believe that we're able to separate our senses, and see, hear, and taste clearly. And on the surface of it, this is often true. However, those sensations we get from the world around us aren't always translated into neutral thoughts. Put very simply, our brains get in the way. A very good illustration of this is an experiment with cherry-flavoured drinks. We've come to expect cherry drinks to be red in colour. When scientists altered a cherry flavoured drink to be orange in colour, testers had the impression that it was orange-flavoured. In fact, our perception of food and our expectations are so strong that anything unexpected can make us feel ill. Participants in an experiment were enjoying a meal of steak and chips in a restaurant. What they didn't know was that researchers had played with the lighting in the restaurant so that the dish looked its normal colour. When the lights were lifted, they saw that the steak was in fact blue, and the chips were green. Before that, they had no concept of what the real colour was. Many refused to continue eating, and some even reported feeling ill. This experiment gives us a clear insight into how much our brain filters information coming from the senses.

2.5 and 2.6

For me, it has to be the smell of bread baking in the oven. My mum baked every week on Wednesdays and there would be warm out-of-the-oven bread and homemade jam greeting me when I got off the school bus. It was the best thing ever, and I used to munch it while struggling with my homework in my room in the evening. Even now when I walk past a baker's, whenever I notice that scent, it smells like comfort and security all mixed in together. It's like I'm running off that bus again! I'd love to be back in that situation now. Whatever the future brings, I know it'll be fine.

2.7

1 For me it has to be the smell of bread baking in the oven. My mum baked every week on Wednesdays and there would be warm out-of-the-oven bread and homemade jam greeting me when I got off the school bus. It was the best thing ever, and I used to munch it while struggling with my homework in my room in the evening. Even now when I walk past a bakers, whenever I notice that scent, it smells like comfort and security all mixed in together. It's like I'm running off that bus again! I'd love to be back in that situation now. Whatever the future brings, I know it'll be fine.

2 There's one scent that makes me stop whatever I'm doing and take a few moments. It makes me think I should ignore the pressing matters of my life and take time to just let my mind wander, remember how everything has a solution. That scent is the smell of a little purple flower. I grew up in Kerala in India and there was a tree that overhung a tiled pool in front of the temple. Sometimes I had to hang around outside waiting for my brother, and I used to enjoy watching those little flowers drop into the water. It was so relaxing smelling the trees

AUDIOSCRIPTS

and watching them float around against the bright white tiles, making patterns. My school days were so happy.

3 If I think of nostalgic smells, for me it's the smell of roller coasters, when you get to the last part of the line and you're inside and nearly on the ride. I have to admit, it's a kind of cool feeling, mixed with the oily smell of the rails. It was a relief that the wait was nearly over. It's not so much associated with a particular memory. But when I think back to the thrill and goose bumps of that moment, it helps me to keep other things in perspective – to stop showing off for others or worrying about their opinion, and focus on myself. It's so easy to get hooked up on ambition and work.

4 My first paid work, while I was still at school, was in an old distribution warehouse. It was hard going because I had to make sure packages went out fast and I was all new to it. There were a number of smells around the building, but there's one combination that just grabs my attention and takes me straight back there – the smell of cardboard and car engines. It was an unmistakeable combination. Even now, I can't ignore it. Now I've got a real career, I remember just how far I've come in life and how much further I may still have to go.

5 There were lots of smells around me growing up, some of which still make me feel emotional even now. The scent of slightly boggy woodland in springtime is my favourite. I don't get to smell it that often, now I live and work in the city, but when it does come my way, it just stops me right there in my tracks. The childhood memories of exploring the land around my grandparents' home come flooding back. We felt we were unbeatable and up for anything. That scent just gives me the same feeling of confidence we had back then and helps me to feel able to deal with things. They were happy times.

2.8 and 2.9

Well, I was looking for something for a biology project, and I heard about this incredible new piece of research on elephants. The researchers were working with elephants who lived alongside two different African tribes, Kamba and Massai. Whenever the elephants saw someone from the Kamba tribe, they were relaxed. The Kamba are quite friendly towards elephants. Their neighbours, the Massai, however, have a much more aggressive history towards the animals around them, sometimes attacking elephants, as a result of which, relations with them have suffered. Whenever an elephant detected a Massai, it would run away. The researchers know that these animals have a highly evolved sense of smell, and the Massai and Kamba have quite distinct diets, which would give them a different odour. Others suggested they could recognise the distinctive red colour that Massai wore, but the elephants even ran away from a car that had carried a Massai member in the last few days. Whatever the reason, it is the first time that animals appear to be able to classify another species into quite specific subclasses of culture. It's the kind of thing we thought only humans could do.

2.10

1 I get fed up when people try and set rules for using your phone. I mean, they don't tell you how to behave at any other time, so why should I care what they think?

2 All my friends upload photos of their lives, and I sometimes feel a bit left out, so when I go anywhere, I'm always worried about getting the right kind of photo. It sometimes means I don't enjoy the event so much.

3 You know, when everyone's worried about how they're going to look in the photos, they spoil it for everyone. I'm just as happy to do without phones.

4 I don't know how I feel about videoing my friends. I guess if something really funny's happening, you want to share that moment, but sometimes I just want to live the moment.

2.11

OK. So, in this photo there are a lot of people at a big event. I think it's a race, or perhaps at a film when they show it for the first time, and all the actors and stars come and walk down the red carpet. There's a kind of fence that you put for this sort of event in front of the crowd. In the second photo there's a girl in class. She's wearing a green and blue T-shirt and she's sitting next to a boy wearing a checked shirt. The girl has a phone hidden under the desk and she's looking at that and not paying attention to the teacher.

2.12 and 2.13

OK, so, obviously, the thing that links these photos is people using their mobile phones when they probably shouldn't. I suppose at a big public event, it's probably understandable that people would want to use their phones to take photos to share with friends later. But in the first picture, everyone in the crowd is watching the event through their phones, and not really 'in the moment', I think you'd say. There's an old lady in the crowd, and she looks as if she's enjoying it because she seems to be giving it her full attention. It could be that she's just from a different generation. In the other photo, there's another young guy and I guess he's out on a date, but either he doesn't like the girl and so he's ignoring her or it could be that he's not very smart because he looks like he's been spending the entire time checking his phone. She's just as bad, though, to be honest. I guess they won't be seeing each other again any time soon. At least in the first photo, no one's got a real problem with the phones. I think that the two photos show how using mobiles has become a kind of automatic habit these days, and we're not really paying attention to what's around us.

2.14 and 2.15

1 My brother thinks his trainers smell alright, but I think they're [beep]! I can smell them from the bottom of the stairs – they're so bad!

2 I don't think you can ever go by first impressions. I think appearances can be really [beep] and you need to take time to get to know someone before you start making judgements.

3 I don't read a newspaper or watch the television news any more. There was a time when they gave people valuable [beep] into what was happening in the world, but that's just not true anymore. They all tell you what they want you to hear.

4 My sister was cooking a chocolate cake and there were some [beep] smells coming from the oven. I couldn't wait to try it!

5 The dog ate one of my shoes while I was out one day. It had holes in it by the time he finished, and it was covered in slobber. I think it was [beep] that I wasn't going to be able to wear that shoe again!

2.16

A: OK, so the plans for the festival are going well. We just have to get approval from the local council. Did you get the results of the survey?

B: Yes, it's all looking very positive. I mean, whatever you do, there'll always be some local opposition, but there seems to be a lot of support for the general idea of a festival. At no time did any of the locals in the village say that they were against the festival taking place. They were all in favour.

A: Great. What I don't understand is why the local council want us to hold the festival inside. What did the people you spoke to say about holding it outside?

B: That got a lot of support, to be honest. I think we might be able to persuade the council to change their minds. In no way is it possible to tell whether they have reached a final decision about holding it inside.

A: And how many did you speak to in the end?

B: We interviewed around twenty people, many of whom said that they would definitely come along and support the festival.

A: That's brilliant! So, I think we're ready to take out proposal for the biggest water fight festival back to the council. It's going to be absolutely brilliant!

3.1 and 3.2

P = Paula   B = Benjamin

P: So, today we're talking about those fake news stories that seem to do the rounds on social media. No matter how obviously fake they are, they still go viral. I'm joined by media professor Benjamin Thompson.

B: Hello, Paula.

P: Hello. So Benjamin, why do these stories even exist?

B: Well, some fake news stories are simply an example of humour – they're supposed to be making fun of real news stories – a kind of satire. But others want to publicise their website. They create those stories to get visitors to their website because advertising there makes them money. They use sensational headlines to make this a more attractive option.

P: Oh, like 'You'll never guess what this lady did next' type headlines?

B: Exactly.

P: So, why is it so hard to make these news stories disappear from social media?

B: You've asked a good question. I mean, experts tend to blame the readers but before we start doing that, we need to understand why readers believe and share the stories. There are a few key reasons, actually. The first one is that people simply don't read the stories. They read the headline, think it sounds interesting and then share it with all their friends without actually going any deeper than that.

P: Really? That's surprising but actually, I've probably done it myself.

B: If people read the article in full, they might realise it's fake and expose the lie. Er, another reason people believe these stories is that people don't look at the source of the story. The source can often tell you if it's a legitimate story or not very quickly. Something from the BBC, for example, is clearly going to be a lot more reliable than something written by a blogger you've never heard of before.

P: That's true. Anyone can publish something online now and claim it's correct.

B: Exactly. Another problem is that fake stories often have related content that are legitimate stories. If someone sees a sensational headline to a fake story, clicks on it and sees links to legitimate stories from legitimate sources on the same page, they immediately assume the fake story is legitimate too.

P: Right, I think I fall for that trick too.

B: I expect we all do. Confirmation bias also has a role to play in fake news stories.

P: What's confirmation bias?

B: Well, people like to confirm their existing ideas and opinions. So if they read something that does this, they tend to believe it without trying to critically analyse it.

P: Oh I see. 'It says what I already think, so it must be true.'

B: That's right. Let's say there's a high-profile person you've never liked. If you read an article exposing some kind of scandal that person has been involved in, it'll confirm your existing beliefs that they're bad. We don't really want to read things that go against what we already know or think, so you don't want to read an article saying that this public figure contributed money to a good cause.

P: I guess you're right. I've never actually thought of that before.

B: The final reason is that when something goes viral, social media users see it over and over again. This gives readers the sense that it's legitimate. People tend to think that groups of people can't all be wrong, so their assessment of the story as being true must be correct. It provides some kind of objective reality and yet, as we've just discussed, there are lots of reasons why groups are incorrect about stories being real.

P: Very interesting. OK, so the next question then is how we can deal with this issue and help people to be more critical of what they read.

3.3

1. I always think I know more than other people. So, if someone corrects me, I don't take it on board until I've double checked it elsewhere. It's a terrible habit, really.
2. I look up information online all the time but hardly any of it sticks in my mind. I guess I don't try hard enough to memorise it.
3. Why do we have to do this test? The teacher didn't say so. I'm beginning to think there's some kind of hidden agenda.
4. If you saw someone using their mobile to look up information in an exam, would you tell the teacher or turn a blind eye?
5. The grades on my report card were all wrong, so I went straight to the school office to set the record straight.

3.4

I = Interviewer   P = Paul   S = Sally

I: With me today is Sally Cahill, expert on false beliefs, and Paul Roberts, professor of political science. So, Paul, let's start with you. You developed a website on false beliefs. Why did you do that?

P: Well, false beliefs are facts that people think are true but actually aren't. For example, it was once falsely claimed that former president Obama didn't have a US birth certificate and as a result, his mother is still thought by some to have given birth to him outside the country despite his birth certificate saying otherwise. While I was at university, one political campaign caused so much misinformation to go round that I launched my website to try to set the record straight. I didn't really get anywhere though because once false information is believed to be true, it sticks in people's minds. That's what my new book's about.

I: Sally, what do we know about false beliefs or misinformation?

S: There's a little research on it but most of it has been done in artificial conditions rather than in the real world, which might be less effective. One good study suggests that our brain views different kinds of misinformation in two ways. If the truth is no threat to us, then we're happy to be corrected and take the correction on board. But if the truth poses a threat to us in some way, we turn a blind eye to it and hold onto the false belief, even if we're told the information's wrong soon after we hear it.

I: *Well, that's interesting. So it's about how willing we are to accept the correction. Have there been any studies on it?*

S: There was one done in Australia, where the participants heard details of a crime or heroic event. They were given some wrong information which was quickly corrected. However, some participants still tried to give that incorrect information when reporting it later, despite giving the other facts correctly. Researchers concluded that it was the people's values that determined whether they did this, not their personality or any hidden political agenda.

I: So, how should misinformation be corrected?

S: People need to concentrate on getting people to understand how their values can affect how they take in information. Clearly, the more willing they are to accept different people and ways of life, the more able they are to recognise false beliefs.

P: You know, apparently, if you recall a time you felt good about yourself, it actually makes you more open-minded and therefore able to report information accurately. Of course, it's unrealistic for people to go round thinking about something positive before they read information but it's an interesting idea and one we must focus on. Simply correcting information is definitely not the answer and the theory suggests we should probably also avoid appealing to political ideas that reflect who we are.

I: So how exactly would this work in practice? Do you have any examples?

P: Well, there's the interesting case of raw milk. It's said that there are health benefits to drinking raw milk by some raw milk lovers but health experts say it's three times more likely to cause medical problems if handled incorrectly. Now, if I were those experts, I wouldn't try to present the correct facts. I'd emphasise that we've drunk pasteurised milk for decades and it's not been harmful to us or our children at all. That way we avoid any reference to self-identity.

I: Sally, is there anything else you think can help to stop false beliefs?

S: Yes. It's much harder to do when leading public figures without any expertise send out false messages. What you need is all the people with the right knowledge to agree on what the right information is. When this happens, the correct messages spread broadly without interference. However, this can be tricky now that social media makes it easy for anyone to be heard, knowledgeable or not. Members of different political parties, for example, like to have their say but they don't always have the facts and rarely agree.

3.5

1. Mount Everest is understood to be the highest mountain in the world but in fact, it's only the highest mountain above sea level. Mount Kea in Hawaii is actually the highest mountain in the world when you count the part of it that's underwater.
2. It's often believed that body heat mostly disappears through the head, which is why our parents told us we had to wear a hat in winter. But we lose as much heat per square centimetre from our heads as any other part of our body.
3. Elvis Presley is understood to have had naturally black hair but in fact, he was born with blond hair, which turned brown as he got older. He dyed it black.
4. Blood without oxygen is known to be red and this is a true fact. It's bright red when it passes through the heart and becomes darker as it moves further away. However, because our veins look blue, there's a false belief that our blood is actually blue when it's deoxgygenated. This isn't true and is simply a trick of the light.
5. The Great Wall of China is believed to be the only man-made object visible from space but this is a false belief. There are many man-made objects that can be seen from space and in fact, the Great Wall of China is one of the most difficult to see because it isn't very high.

AUDIOSCRIPTS

6 People are considered to have more than five senses. We talk about sight, sound, taste, smell and touch but there are other senses too. For example, nociception is the ability to sense pain and propioception is the ability to connect two parts of the body without visual confirmation – for example, the ability to touch your nose when you have your eyes closed. Poking yourself in the eye is an example of a propioception fail.

7 Albert Einstein is believed to have done badly at school but in fact, he was successful and his grades were good. When he was seven, his mother wrote that he received good grades and was again top of the class.

8 Water is reported to drain in different directions on each side of the equator. You can even pay people at the equator to demonstrate this using a bucket on one side and another bucket on the other. The fact is, the direction the water drains really depends on the shape of the bucket – or sink or bath – and the angle at which the water enters. Those buckets at the equator are specially made to attract tourists.

3.6 and 3.7

E = Examiner   A = Anja   H = Hisham

E: How influential are these people on a child's development?

A: OK, let's start by talking about parents.

H: OK, well, I think they're extremely influential. It … It's your parents that you look up to when you're little and so, whether you like it or not, they influence your character. Our parents make us who we are to a large degree. Would you agree with that?

A: Yeah, absolutely. Also, they teach us about what's right and wrong and these values are massively important because they continue with us into adulthood.

H: That's very true. OK, shall we move on to the next one – teachers?

A: Yeah, I think teachers have a great influence on us intellectually. Not that parents don't, but the purpose of school is to open our minds to new things, new ways of thinking. When I was at primary school, I had this lovely teacher who got me interested in science. I'm hoping to become a vet one day because I'm really interested in biology and animals and, well …

H: That's great! Good for you! Er, getting back to what you were saying, teachers certainly can inspire children to think in new ways. Like parents, I also think they help to shape our character because we spend so much time with them.

A: Yeah, they're definitely very influential. Er, I'm trying to think how much our neighbours influence us though. Do you have any ideas?

H: Well, er, I think they teach children how to act with adults. We have to have good manners and show respect when they come to our house or we go to theirs.

A: I know what you mean but I think it depends on how well you know your neighbours. I don't know mine, so I'm not sure they've had much of an influence on me. What about friends?

H: Friends influence our actions more than anything, I'd say.

A: What do you mean exactly?

H: Well, we try new activities because our friends are doing them, so they push us to do different things. Of course, that sometimes means they encourage us to do things we shouldn't do because we want to impress them or whatever.

A: Yeah, peer pressure can be a negative influence, can't it?

E: Thank you. Which of these people do you think have the biggest influence on children?

A: Hmm, good question. What do you think?

H: Er, I'd say parents because they raise you as a child and teach you about morals. You learn language from them. You basically learn to be you.

A: Yeah, that's true, though I think you spend a lot of time with friends over the years and some people are closer to them than they are to their parents.

H: Yeah, and teachers are also there with you during the most important time in your childhood but I still feel their influence has less of an impact because you change friends and teachers over time.

A: That's a good point. Celebrities can influence you to a degree. When I was young, I was really obsessed with this boy band. I had all their posters up on the wall and my friends and I talked about them all the time. All I wanted to do was meet them but, of course, that was impossible …

H: Sorry, can I say something? Celebrities might cause a few obsessions! And influence our tastes in music and our clothes, but they don't stick around for the whole of your childhood, do they? And neighbours come and go too. As you said, we might not even know them.

A: So, we've decided on parents. They have the biggest influence, right?

H: Yeah, I think so. With friends a close second.

3.8 and 3.9

1 My dad pays me for cleaning his car but not at a very high [beep]!
2 I love performing on stage – singing, dancing, acting – everything! If I was offered a part in a musical on Broadway, I'd jump at the [beep].
3 I remember faces really well but I can never remember names. For some reason, they just don't [beep].
4 Ben fell asleep in class again today but Mr Smith either didn't notice or he turned a [beep].
5 Why does everyone love Brendan so much? They think he's hilarious and follow him around everywhere. I really don't understand his [beep].
6 I really enjoyed the festival on Saturday. The music was great and there was loads to do. All in all, it was a really fun [beep].
7 My grandparents can't see why social media is so important these days. They just don't understand the [beep].
8 Are you sure this is the best way to do this experiment? I'm not sure it's a very effective [beep].

4.1

Dharavi is a neighbourhood like no other. Located in the city of Mumbai in India, it's home to almost a million people. It's hard to estimate exact numbers because there are so many arriving from poor rural areas daily. It's also an economically active area, bringing in up to a billion US dollars a year. The pottery and textile workers continue a tradition passed down over more than a century. And more recently, jobs have appeared in the recycling industry, employing around a quarter of a million people. Despite the size of the economy, Dharavi is a slum, with high levels of poverty, and so it has many problems caused mostly by poor housing and overcrowding. Average annual incomes are only a thousand dollars a year per person. And there are other problems too. The neighbourhood floods regularly, and although it's supplied by fresh water, gas and electricity, thefts of these basic resources are common. Diseases are also a major concern. But, against the odds, Dharavi has become a popular tourist destination visited by travel groups from all over the world. The slum sits on what is now an expensive patch of land in central Mumbai. Many in the local government want to move the residents and sell off the land to developers. With these threats to its existence, it's not surprising that this rare community is attracting global interest before it disappears forever.

4.3 and 4.4

Midnight in the deserted streets of Mumbai, and Krishna Pujari was just about to clock off from work. He was working nights to support his studies at university, and was dead on his feet. But a group of young British backpackers had just come into the restaurant, and Krishna was the only one there who could speak English. Their meeting should have started and ended there, but it turned out to be significant for Krishna and for one of the travellers, Chris Way. Chris and his friends were keen to stay away from the touristy parts of the city. When they bumped into Krishna again at a cricket match the following day, both their lives changed forever. In the following weeks Chris completely threw himself into life in Mumbai and soon took the decision to extend his trip. Over the next couple of years, the two became close friends.

One day, Chris came to Krishna with a plan. He wanted to start a travel company showing people around Mumbai, but he wasn't interested in the standard attractions of the city. Chris wanted to take people into the slums of Dharavi. Krishna was appalled at the suggestion. In school, Krishna had learnt that Dharavi was one of the dirtiest places in the world. It was not a place where tourists would be able to soak up the culture. But Chris was determined. He'd seen slum tourism work in other parts of the world and felt certain that there were more people like him, who'd be interested in seeing more than the standard attractions offered on a package holiday.

Eventually, Krishna gave in and agreed to accompany him one afternoon. It was a part of the city he hadn't even visited before. Expecting the visit would change Chris' mind, Krishna was shocked by what they found as they wandered around the slum. There were stalls selling crafts and a thriving business area, and the people were friendly and welcoming. After that one visit, Krishna didn't need to think twice. Together, they set up Reality Tours and today they take around eighteen thousand visitors into the slums each year.

4.5–4.7

Hi, I'm Marisa and I'm here to talk to you about virtual reality. Did you know that it's been used in manufacturing for ages but only recently gained mainstream interest? In its current form, it's most closely associated with gaming but I don't doubt that there are other uses that will become more commonplace in future. So, that's why I decided to go on a virtual reality adventure – an adventure I want to share with you today.

To help me decide where to go, I tried an atlas, then a map but only really found success when I used a popular app that allows you to virtually walk down streets all over the world. Eventually, I decided to go on a balloon ride across the Serengeti National Park.

Let me tell you this, I won't forget the experience in a hurry. A couple of friends who'd tried something similar told me they were scared by the experience and I'd read an article which described it as surreal, but for me the whole thing was spectacular and I recommend you all try it.

When the balloon took off, I truly felt as if I were leaving the ground and flying high into the sky. I'd expected to see dry, dusty land, not the fertile land in front of me. It was certainly different to the scenery I'm used to in the real world, which I'd say is mostly hilly.

I looked at the picturesque view. The horizon was sparkling so much I actually had to squint. I could make out something below us. At first, I thought it was bushes but then realised it was a huge herd of wildebeest. It must have been the season for migration, which is sometime in late May or early June, just before the summer.

I've heard experts say that for virtual reality to really work and feel like the real world, you need to be able to touch things. But even without that, my brain tricked me into thinking I was really on that balloon ride. I even tried to lean on the basket at one point and almost fell over!

So, all in all, the experience had a big effect on me. There was one negative issue that came up though. The media has reported that users can get dizzy when wearing the headsets. I was fine with that but I was really tired when I'd finished. Fortunately, I didn't get the eye pain some doctors predict.

So, there's a lot of talk about whether VR will benefit the tourist industry in future. What I think it will do is result in more effective decision-making. Before booking a trip, travellers will be able to virtually explore resorts and hotels. Of course, virtual reality will also present opportunities to people who can't fly. This is an exciting prospect and I'm looking forward to seeing where it takes us, both in the real and virtual sense! So now, any questions?

4.8 and 4.9

You reach the peak of Mont Blanc. Stunned by the amazing view, you remind yourself you're not actually on a mountain top but in your bedroom. Next stop: the world's longest roller coaster ride. Virtual reality (VR) has been identified as a technology that will play a significant role in our lives. But can VR experiences ever fully replace real-life ones? Could it get to the point where, thrilled with the exciting virtual experiences we have, we become unhappy with the real world?

4.10 and 4.11

A misunderstanding has lost a couple over a thousand pounds after they booked flights for their holiday out of the wrong Birmingham. Expecting a dream trip to Las Vegas, the couple turned up at the busy Birmingham Airport in the UK, only to find that they were booked on a flight leaving from Birmingham, Alabama, over six thousand kilometres away. The airline company said they were sympathetic with the couple's situation, but there was no point trying to get them onto another flight that day, as all flights to the States were fully booked. Returning home in disbelief, the couple have vowed to spend the next few months saving money for new flights and have rearranged their hotel booking for next year. A spokesperson for a travel company said they cannot overstate enough how important it is for customers to preview bookings online before clicking on that final 'Purchase' button, as most people underestimate the number of things that can go wrong if they don't.

4.12

H = Hayley   M = Mark

H: Well, I don't know about you, but personally, I think that the local government should build more cycle paths. If they did that, then more parents would feel better about letting their children cycle to school. The main reason for this is that at the moment kids have to cycle on the roads and because a lot of people drive pretty fast through the city without paying much attention to the speed limit, it puts cyclists' lives in danger. To give an example, where I live there are at least one or two accidents involving cyclists every month. Cycle paths would mean children could get from home to school and back more easily and, above all, more safely, without having to worry about cars. What do you think?

M: You've made a really good point, but in my town there are already cycle paths, so this isn't the main issue. Parents find it easier to drive their kids to school, but this just results in more congestion on the roads and is frustrating for everyone. Schools could ban cars from parking near the school. They could also organise cycle trains. This is where an adult cycles through the town and picks up school kids on their bikes as they pass their house. The kids all cycle behind each other creating a kind of train. More parents would be persuaded to let their children cycle because it'd be easier and safer. So schools need to do more to encourage kids to use the cycle paths.

4.13 and 4.14

1 The film was a comedy and it was absolutely [beep]!
2 The village was so beautiful and [beep] it looked perfect!
3 We picked the blueberries from the [beep] and ate them immediately.
4 You need to be honest and show [beep] for people to trust you.
5 When animals live in a large group, we call it a [beep].
6 When you try really hard, you put in a lot of [beep].

4.15 and 4.16

1 My worst holiday experience was when I went camping with my mum and dad. I was starving, and so Mum offered me a sandwich, but, bursting to go to the loo, I decided to put the sandwich down for a minute. When I came back, it was covered in ants!

2 The school holidays were finally there and I couldn't wait for our beach and amusement park holiday. On the first day, I twisted my ankle hiking. The next day I cut my foot swimming near some rocks. The following day, I was on the roller coaster when it broke down. We stayed stuck at the top for ages!

3 I guess it's not really a holiday, but I spent last summer working the vacation, cutting the grass in the neighbours' houses down our street. In one of the houses, I always forgot they watered the grass with a sprinkler system. Just as I started, the thing went off, spraying water everywhere, all over me! The worst thing was it ruined my phone.

4 Well, we were on holiday in this really nice villa, with our own swimming pool and everything. Mum had won the holiday in a raffle! We got there in the afternoon, tired but happy but, entering my bedroom, I saw this huge lizard thing! I couldn't relax and sleep properly for the rest of the week!

5.1 and 5.2

So, there's this field of psychology that I work in called mob psychology, or crowd psychology. Around the time cities started expanding, people noticed that we behave differently when we're in crowds than when we're alone. For example, a higher number of people who grow up in a bad neighbourhood turn to criminal activity. Some people started to think that the people around young children in those neighbourhoods had to have played some role in that criminal behaviour. They realised that those children might have seen a lot of crime around them and thought it was normal. That can't have been good for them, and wouldn't have happened if they'd been in a better neighbourhood.

More recent studies have looked at how people behave in a crisis. It seems that when there's a crowd around, people are less likely to help. People will walk past another person obviously in distress, or people who could have easily intervened in a situation just walk on by. You might think that you would behave differently, but there's an easy way to understand this in your everyday life. Imagine you'd ordered a pizza and heard the doorbell ring. Now if you'd known you were the only one in the house, you'd have gone straight to the door, opened it and paid the delivery guy. You could have ignored it, but you knew no one else was

AUDIOSCRIPTS

around to pay the guy, so you did it. Imagine that same situation with around five people in the house. The doorbell rang, but you ignored it. Why? You might have been thinking that someone else must have opened the door already and left them to take action. This is mob psychology, or the bystander effect. There's a confusion of responsibilities that wouldn't have happened if you'd been on your own.

5.4 and 5.5

1 I was working in a shop and this guy came in and tried to buy a microwave with a million dollar note. I mean, I was sure he was just fooling around because they don't make anything bigger than a hundred dollar note. I thought, he must have been having me on, but he insisted on being given, like, a hundred thousand dollars in change. In the end, we had to call the police.

2 OK, so I was working at a late night take-away and it was getting quieter, when we got this phone call. The guy on the other end of the phone wanted to know how much money we had in the register. He wanted to know if it was worth robbing us. I mean, like he wasn't going to settle for just a small amount. It made me so mad! I decided to stand up to the guy, but the manager called the police, and they were waiting for him when he arrived. He said he hadn't done anything, but he had all the equipment to come and rob the place.

3 My uncle was running a restaurant, and these two guys came in and threatened him if he didn't give them free food and all the money in the till. Anyway, they weren't exactly jumping at the chance to carry out their threat, so my uncle calmly told them he was busy, to hang back a bit and then come back in an hour's time, when he'd have more money in the till. They did, and the police were waiting there to arrest the two men.

4 I really hate vandalism – it's such a pointless crime, and vandalism gets to me every time. There was a children's campsite near my home and one night it got vandalised, but the person who did it was stupid enough to leave their name on the wall. At first, the police thought someone was winding them up, but when they tracked down the guy that had done it, they found enough evidence at his house to convict him.

5.6

Hmm, the worst gift ever? I bought a hand-made journal for a friend. I'd decorated it and written a special message for her. I was so hurt when she gave it back as my gift on my birthday! I decided to get my own back, kept it and returned it to her again the following year. I guess when it comes to gift-giving, most people get it wrong at some point and now, instead of trying to come up with something that I think they'll like or find useful, I just give up and get them to tell me what they're after. Most people prefer that to the 'thoughtful' gift.

5.7

When it comes to giving gifts, just go for what someone likes, even if it means they end up with something almost identical year in, year out – I don't think it matters. My brother can't get enough of dodgy sci-fi comics, and if they're second-hand and wrapped up in brown paper, even better! By far the worst gift I ever got was a hat from my mum. I didn't want to hurt her feelings, so I made out that I loved it, and gave it to a charity shop later. She asked me later why she'd never seen me wear it!

5.8

1 Hmm, the worst gift ever? I bought hand-made journal for a friend. I'd decorated it and written a special message for her. I was so hurt when she gave it back as my gift on my birthday! I decided to get my own back, kept it and returned it to her again the following year. I guess when it comes to gift-giving, most people get it wrong at some point and now, instead of trying to come up with something that I think they'll like or find useful, I just give up and get them to tell me what they're after. Most people prefer that to the 'thoughtful' gift.

2 When it comes to giving gifts, just go for what someone likes, even if it means they end up with something almost identical year in, year out – I don't think it matters. My brother can't get enough of dodgy sci-fi comics, and if they're second-hand and wrapped up in brown paper, even better! By far the worst gift I ever got was a hat from my mum. I didn't want to hurt her feelings, so I made out that I loved it, and gave it to a charity shop later. She asked me later why she'd never seen me wear it!

3 My mum is the queen of giving gifts for the daughter she always wanted. I have a pierced nose, and short spikey hair, and when she gave me a girly pink outfit, she was hoping it'd change my mind about the way I dress. I refused to let it get to me though. Whatever it is you get, I think you have to make sure that you're not building expectations. If you ask me, you should keep the wrapping really plain, and save your money for the actual gift. And try not to push your own choices on the receiver. If all else fails, you can't say you didn't try.

4 To be a better gift-giver, you have to be realistic. How many people do you know who've never had a rubbish present? Whatever you get, make sure it's possible to return it to the shop if they don't like it – that means proving where you bought it. If you're going to ask what to get, you might as well just give money. Most people don't even try to work out what others would like. My grandmother once got me a CD for this singer that I hate. Only two weeks before, I'd told her I thought he was annoying, but at least it gave us a laugh. I passed the CD on to my sister.

5 Every year I got these thick woolly socks from my aunty. I was thirteen! I was never sure if she'd got me mixed up with someone else. Every year, I hoped she'd get something different. Thank heavens my mum never made me wear them! One year, the dog chewed the parcel and contents before I'd even unwrapped it. That's not to say that I don't appreciate functional things – I think they make the best gift. A friend got me a set of pens, and pens are always handy. They got used more than the one pen I had with my name on it. I was scared to use it.

5.10

Skiing experiences, rock climbing and adventure activities have become a normal part of children's birthday parties these days. Making a child's day perfect is far more challenging than it was in the past. So much so, that one mum decided that her son's birthday invite was part of a legal contract. She had organised a special treat for her son and when one of his friends, eleven-year-old Josh Wilton, failed to turn up as promised, the response he received was nowhere near as forgiving as he expected. Josh and his parents almost found themselves in court.

Josh had accepted the invite to attend a skiing party, but on the day his parents decided not to send him. A request for payment for the cost of the missed party was put into his school bag the following Monday. When Josh's mother refused to pay, the family were threatened with legal action. Lawyer Jim Smith said that this was by far the most extreme case that he has ever dealt with and stated that as far as he was aware, a birthday party acceptance couldn't be seen as a legal agreement. Still, it's a strong message to think twice before you next bail out on your friends!

5.11 and 5.12

I was walking to school one day, by a route I don't usually take, and I was appalled at the mess the park was in. The rubbish hadn't been cleared for ages and the play area was closed down. I was ashamed of my own neighbourhood for letting it get so bad, so I decided to do something about it. With the help of a teacher, I got together with a group of other students. They were all eager for a chance to help out in the neighbourhood. We cleared the rubbish and repainted. We had to find a qualified builder who was capable of fixing the play equipment because we might have made things worse. I thought it was a great result! Then one of my teachers was so impressed with the project that a month later I got a letter offering me a one-thousand-pound grant over the summer! It was with one condition: the money was subject to us carrying on with the project in another park! It just goes to show that contrary to popular belief, helping others really can help you too. And I was actually intent on doing it for the right reasons anyway.

5.13

S = Susie   E = Eric

S: Eric, I've heard your hometown has a really great community spirit. What kind of things do they do there?

E: Dunno, really. I guess we have celebrations in the town square for the big festivals.

S: I read that they did a lot of community work, like clearing up the parks together and growing vegetables in community gardens. I even heard they do a curry night, where they cook up a big pot of vegetable curry with the things they've grown.

E: Nice. Never been. You'd need to ask my mum.

S: Oh well, there must be something you've been involved in?

E: We had to do stuff with school. I had to sing in a … what's the word? Well, outside the shopping centre. Dunno why.

S: You? Singing in the choir?
E: Yeah. But I like it.
S: Well, I'd love to join you one day. Is there anything coming up soon?
E: Probably. Look online.

5.14

1. Unlike the other places, this one is very temporary. It's where they collect supplies when there's been a natural disaster and you just need to get food to the people affected quickly.
2. I'm not sure where they are. It could be a beach because there's a sea wall. It looks like someone must have left a load of rubbish behind, and the locals are clearing it up. Compared to the others, this is the kind of thing that would drive me nuts – out there clearing up some other guy's mess. It's a lot more unpleasant than the other two jobs, and they look freezing! I guess it's just as rewarding though, seeing the beach clear.
3. I think he must have asked people to … what's the word? It's when your friends and family pay you to do something really hard, like run a marathon. This must be the hardest activity, especially in those ridiculous costumes.

5.15 and 5.16

1. I was worried that my friend was being serious, but he was just [beep].
2. I tried to not to let her rudeness get to me, but it really started to [beep].
3. I love singing, so if the opportunity to go on stage comes up, I'd [beep] the chance.
4. You should push for the best. Don't just [beep] for the first thing they give you.

5.17 and 5.18

I hate going to parties. I don't mean birthday parties or chilling with a group of friends, but big, noisy parties. They're nowhere near as good as everyone expects them to be. People only do the big house party because movies make them out to be way more exciting than they ever are. It's just a bunch of people standing around in the same boring circle of friends that they already know. Be honest, most kids are just as likely to talk to someone new at a big party as they are sitting in the library or at home. It's not going to happen. They just talk about the same old garbage – if they can scream loud enough over the music. And these days you're twice as likely to end up with a bunch of strangers on the doorstep as before because most kids don't understand social media settings when they post about the party online. It's like a rule that at least one person will go overboard and end up doing something stupid. It's far more interesting staying at home and hanging out with friends. At least I talk to people there.

6.1 and 6.2

Speaker 1: OK, so we landed in Mexico City for the first time and when we got there, we were very tired travelling from Australia. And we got to a hotel room – and it was the middle of summer – and it had no fans, no air conditioning and the only window you could crack was fine, but then they were having a party downstairs till about 5 a.m. in the morning. So that was really great landing and not sleeping and then just sweating. So that wasn't too great, but Mexico City was very fun.

Speaker 2: OK, so I'm in the Hague in Holland, er, or the Netherlands … erm … and I'm on my bike, cycling along with my boyfriend and we're trying to get to the beach. And I'm looking it up on my maps and I think I've found the way … erm … and I, y'know, I've taken screenshots on my phone. Erm … but it turns out I've taken the wrong screenshots. So I'm cycling along … erm … and we're sort of going in a direction I think I can see the beach. We …we're end up at the beach … er … but it's the wrong beach and we've gone about three miles the wrong way.

Speaker 3: I think one of the best stories was when Jarrod, erm … went into a store to ask them for a spoon. And he was just doing hand actions cos he didn't know the Spanish word for spoon. And he just kept doing this … and then they had no idea. They, like, they were, like, 'Do you wanna go on a boat?' They were so confused, it was so embarrassing! We couldn't get a spoon to save our lives!

Speaker 4: And when I landed in Bangkok, I landed at about 11 o'clock at night. I thought I was going to land at 11 in the morning cos I was such a naive young traveller, and I walked behind the station and I was just mobbed by people. 'Give me your trade.' 'Come and stay in my backpacking place.' 'Come to my hotel.' 'Get in my rickshaw.' and things. And I genuinely didn't know what to do, so I got on a bus, thinking I was going on a bus in the right place. And it turned out to be a bus going nowhere near where I thought it was going to go. And then I kind of asked for help. I looked around the bus. All very nice people. Nobody spoke English. Apart from one person. Turned out to be a child about this tall – about eleven years old. And he was wearing a boy scout uniform. And I was in the scouts. Basically, he came up and said, 'Can I help you, sir?' You know, I was twenty-one. Nobody had called me 'sir' before!

Speaker 5: So, when I was travelling by myself in Milan, on my first night there I got food poisoning, and on the first day I was there by myself and I had to go and get my own medication, so I, food-poisoned, crawled to the pharmacy and the pharmacy person didn't speak any English, and I didn't speak any Italian, and I tried to, like, sign language that I had food poisoning and I felt really ill, and he couldn't understand and I tried to sit down on this beautiful chair and he yelled at me, and I'm not really sure why, and in the end I just, sort of, pretended to throw up on him and he gave me some pills and I walked away. And it was all good in the end, so that's OK!

6.3

Like many children growing up in rural India, four-year-old Saroo Brierley rarely had enough to eat and would often travel on trains to beg for scraps with his older brother. But one ill-fated trip changed his life forever. He'd stopped to have a nap at the station with his brother but when he woke up, he found he was alone. He saw a train in front of him with the door open, so he jumped on board, thinking his brother was on there too. But having looked everywhere, Saroo couldn't find him. He decided to stay on the train until it reached its destination – Kolkata, one thousand miles away. Alone and afraid, Saroo spent four weeks wandering the streets of the city. He tried to find his way back home but had nothing except the clothes he was wearing. It was a dangerous time. He almost drowned in the River Ganges and was almost abducted by a man who wanted to sell him as a slave.

Eventually, he was rescued from the streets and put in a juvenile home. But because he wasn't able to tell carers where he'd come from, he was soon transferred to an orphanage. There, he was adopted by an Australian couple who took him to live in Tasmania. He started a new life with a loving family and grew up to earn a degree and join his adoptive family's engineering firm.

However, while he was growing up, he never gave up hope of seeing his old home again. He knew it was an impossible dream without the name of his village, but he kept in his head images of the streets he used to wander and the faces of his family. He'd spend hours looking at maps for signs of the landmarks that he knew as a child and eventually he turned to Google Earth. Saroo remembered travelling for around fourteen hours in the train to Kolkata. Estimating the speed of the train to be about fifty miles per hour, he calculated that his hometown could be around a thousand miles from Kolkata. Saroo then drew a circle on a map with Kolkata at the centre.

But even after he spotted what he believed to be the town where he'd spent his earliest years, it took months for Saroo to organise a trip to test out his theory, and when he finally did reach his old home in the town, it was empty. It was then that he had another stroke of luck. As he was standing outside his old home, locals began to approach him and ask him his business. He told them his name, and the names of his mother and siblings. About ten minutes later, someone came and led him around the corner. There, there were three ladies. Saroo knew there was something familiar about one of them. It took him a few seconds but he eventually realised it was his mother, looking much shorter than she used to when he was four. They rushed towards each other. Saroo compared the emotion, tears and chemicals in his brain to nuclear fusion.

6.5 and 6.6

1
A: I think fashion designers decide what we wear. Whatever they create seems to end up in the shops and that's what most of us buy.
B: Actually, high street fashion is often different to catwalk fashion. I think designers have less impact than we think.

2
A: I guess I wear what my friends wear. If I see one of them in something really cool, then I'll go out and buy something similar myself.
B: Yeah, friends are certainly influential although I think social media has a greater impact on us these days.

AUDIOSCRIPTS

3

A: I think trends start locally. I mean, you see people on the street wearing something and then you want it.

B: Yeah, clearly, that's how trends spread. They start from normal people like us rather than fashion designers.

4

A: Fashion magazines are full of ads for designer clothes and accessories, so I suppose they decide what's trendy and what isn't.

B: Hmm, I agree that fashion magazines have an impact but not necessarily on people my age. I mean, none of my friends read them and we're all into fashion.

6.7

I = Interviewer   D = Danielle   R = Richard

I: Today we're talking about how fashion is created. I'm joined by fashion trend forecaster Danielle Mayer and fashion retailer Richard Bale. Now, Danielle, who or what decides exactly what new fashions are and how they're established?

D: This might surprise you but there's a group of experts around the world that spend all day every day tracking changes in areas including science, technology and the arts. They come together each year to present evidence about what's next. But this evidence only reflects what's going on globally so, in fashion terms, I know the most important influencers are actually ordinary young people on the streets – the ones who start trends in cities around the world. Such trends are what the experts report on and what those people in fashion, like designers, base their ideas on. It's not a fast process and can go on for two years or more, though that's fine.

I: Interesting. So if designers don't exactly create the trends, what's their ultimate aim, Richard?

R: Designers want to produce things that will be popular for the short period of time they're around and so they count on the information forecasters gather to identify their key themes. That's why designers often produce similar products made with similar materials – they've all used the same sources of information. In the end, designers want to sell things that will translate into sales and profit. That's their main goal. Of course, they like making things that look great and are well-made and environmentally-friendly as this helps them make a name for themselves. But the bottom line is they're a business.

I: Let's talk about the retail side of things now. What do you think makes a successful fashion retailer?

R: They need buyers to work out what clothes to order and which to turn down so their shops can meet demand. You know those folders that fashion houses create of their designs each year? Well, forecasters like Danielle provide something similar which is invaluable for top fashion stores – they create an easy-to-follow plan for the season ahead with mood images, print, colour and fabric recommendations. Until we have this, we can't talk to manufacturers about raw materials or colours.

I: So if we know what trends are before the start of fashion show season, what exactly do we learn from these shows?

R: Probably not as much as people think because their ideas are based on the forecasts of trend experts. What fashion shows mostly do is kick off the season and give shop buyers a clear roadmap as to what will be important to the customer because this is the time when ordinary people become aware of what's going to hit the shops.

D: It's hard to say exactly what the biggest sellers will be just from watching models on the catwalk but we definitely get a clearer sense of what people will want to buy in the near future – and, of course, they're fun!

I: Danielle, as a trend forecaster, how successful are you at forecasting the trends?

D: Well, once the season has come and gone, the team and I look back and reflect on whether we turned out to be right or not. We usually come through with the big trends. We have about a 99.9 percent success rate, I'd say. Having said that, I remember this one time when we said everyone would want to wear flared jumpsuits but people didn't take to them at all. I loved them myself. In a situation like that, you can't blame yourself and no one else in the industry does either. We all move on, which is good because otherwise the pressure of people relying on you would be too great.

I: Some people say social media has had a big impact on the fashion industry in recent years. What do you both think about that?

D: Well, it's much easier for anyone to have a voice in the fashion world because basically anyone with a camera can do it. What concerns me is that trends are spreading much faster now, so forecasters like me are having to change our research methods.

R: I think social media is just an extension of the streets, really. Yes, you can find a lot of stuff online but I think that just means there's something for everyone. And fashion designers can gather their own data too. Clearly, retailers like me are finding it hard to keep up. Trends come and go so fast that our jobs are changing quite rapidly, which we're all a bit nervous about.

6.8 and 6.9

In recent years, the Icelandic capital Reykjavik has become known for its trendy music scene and cool places to eat. Last night residents enjoyed a more unusual night time event when street lights were swapped for the Northern Lights. Despite having just a hundred and twenty-five thousand inhabitants, Reykjavik's light pollution means the Northern Lights are not usually noticeable from the city and residents have to travel some distance to see them. So, to make the Lights more accessible, officials opted to turn off street lights and asked residents to do the same. It was a chilly night, so the restless residents were thankful when the Lights were co-operative and put on an exceptional display for them. Officials said they are likely to repeat the event again, so book your plane tickets now. You can find photographic evidence of the stunning event on our website.

6.10

E = Examiner   A = Ali   M = Maria

E: Which two things have the biggest impact?

A: Well, they're all pretty important, aren't they? It's hard to choose. Er … I guess the least important is attractive buildings. We said before we didn't think that was important, didn't we?

M: Yes, it's nice but not key. I'd say open spaces are important. Without them, it's hard to escape from the craziness of city life.

A: That's true. And they're known to be good for your health. I think there's a lot of research that suggests that. Without them, you don't get to see anything of the natural world, which can have an impact on your physical and mental health.

M: Oh yes, and public transport's really important. Without that you can't get around the city, so people have to use cars. The roads get really congested then and everyone sits in traffic for hours on end.

A: You also need job opportunities. If people can't find work, they can't afford to live and then you get a lot of poverty with people getting sick. Without people paying taxes, it's hard to help those people.

M: Absolutely. I think that …

E: Thank you, you can stop now.

6.11

E = Examiner   A = Ali   M = Maria

E: Which two things are the most important?

A: Well, we said that attractive buildings aren't that important before, didn't we? So we can forget that one.

M: Yeah. We didn't talk about open spaces though. Actually, I think that a city needs them. Green areas help people to connect with nature.

A: I agree. You can relax there too, do recreational activities, that kind of thing. For me though, public transport is slightly more important. Without it, everyone would drive and there'd be so much congestion nothing would move.

M: Well, I agree to an extent. Public transport is useful but without jobs, people wouldn't have the money to pay for the transport or need to get around so much. So for me, job opportunities are far more important. If everyone's employed they can have a good standard of living, which is what you want from a successful city.

A: Yes, that's a good point. OK, so job opportunities is our first choice.

M: Are open spaces more important than public transport?

A: Well, open spaces are useless if the air's horribly polluted, so I think they're less important.

M: Good point. So, we think the two most important things are job opportunities and public transport.

E: Thank you.

6.12 and 6.13

1 In summer my neighbourhood's really exciting but in the winter the streets are empty from about 10 p.m. onwards. It's completely [beep].
2 I took a brilliant photo of all the skyscrapers across the water in Manhattan. They looked great against the really blue sky. What an amazing [beep]!
3 We can't live in our house at the moment as it's being redeveloped. There are workmen everywhere, smashing down walls and putting up new ones. It looks just like a [beep].
4 I live right next to a motorway which is always at a standstill because there's so much congestion. The noise from the drivers beeping their horns is [beep]!
5 My neighbourhood's had loads of money spent on it in recent years, so now it's quite upmarket, but for much of my childhood it was very [beep].
6 We used to live right in the city centre, where not many people lived, but now we've moved to a more residential area outside the centre, which is much more [beep].
7 Don't cross the road there. If you go round the corner, you'll find a pedestrian [beep].
8 You've never heard of the Eiffel Tower? I thought everyone knew it. It's [beep].

6.14

A couple of years ago, my parents and I were visiting my sister in Tokyo, where she was working. My parents had gone out for the day, leaving me with my sister. Unfortunately, while we were having lunch, I broke my tooth. My sister had to go to work but she pointed me in the direction of a dentist. I set off to try and find it. I was in a lot of pain and it felt as if I'd been walking for ages by the time I found the right place – or so I thought. Anyway, it was a kind of studio in the back garden of a house. I couldn't speak Japanese and I'd forgotten to get my sister to write me a note in Japanese, so I used lots of gestures to convey the fact I had tooth pain. He told me to lie down on this bed – not a typical dentist's chair. While I was lying there, I got a sense that something wasn't quite right. Suddenly, he leant over and produced this needle from the table next to him and started waving it near my ear. That's when I realised he wasn't a dentist at all but some kind of acupuncturist. I quickly got up, made my apologies and found my way home. The dentist – and relief from the pain – had to wait another day.

7.1

1 Well, the club take all the money, don't they? I mean, how much does it cost to actually make those shirts? The staff at the clubs are all overpaid! Ninety nine percent of the fans are fed up with it and want change.
2 Well, the government takes its share. Around twenty percent of the cost is always tax. Then I guess a number of people are involved in making the shirts, shipping them and selling them onto the customer.
3 The majority of the money goes to the shirt manufacturers, I think. The materials are quite expensive. The workmanship making them is better than most shirts, so I don't think many others take a cut.
4 I reckon the number of people making decent money is pretty small. Those shirts are controlled by big sportswear companies, not the clubs, so I reckon around a quarter of the money probably goes to the sportswear company. The media need to do more to get that message across. It's not the clubs exploiting their fans.

7.3 and 7.4

OK, so here's the thing. What should you do if you're completely knackered, but your project is due the next morning? Well, the most obvious thing is to reach for an energy drink – it's packed with six times as much caffeine as a cup of coffee, so that's got to wake you up, right? Well, it won't actually do you much good. As well as caffeine, it's full of sugar. One small can contains around thirteen teaspoons of the stuff. That'll give you a massive energy boost, but the benefits are very short-lived and that's no good. You'll just end up with an energy crash an hour or so later. If you really need to work through the night to get that project finished, have a cup of coffee and then take a nap for twenty minutes. The twenty minutes will be the time it takes for the caffeine to start working, and you'll wake up ready to do your best. Think about your posture – sitting straight increases oxygen levels. You could also go and work out for thirty minutes. You might think a workout is the last thing you want to do when you're really tired, but getting your heartbeat going is the best thing to make you feel more alert and ready to get up and go.

7.5 and 7.6

OK, so I've got this new product to review here today. We all know sports stars work with their brains as well as their bodies. Well, this latest product, the Halo Sport, is nothing like a positive thinking app that you listen to, which you might expect from a psychology tool. Looking at it, this wearable device could easily be passed off as just headphones, but it's actually much cleverer than that. It sends electric waves into your brain and will actually change the structure of your brain to make it work more efficiently. This makes it respond better to training so that, potentially, you become a better and more successful athlete. It's much more controversial than a baseball cap if you ask me.

The Halo Sport is a new device that can enhance all sorts of skills. It was initially based on technology developed by the military to improve combat skills, and has been trialled in the fields of gaming and mathematics – the latter with some success. None of those results can beat the performance in professional sports though, which is its main application today.

7.7

I'm a technology reviewer on the internet. When I first started making videos, I didn't even tell my friends or family about them. I always saw them as kind of a hobby and so I didn't feel the need to share them. But it quickly became obvious that I could turn this into a proper business by reviewing technology products for companies on my videos. So when all these consumer electronics started arriving at my home, I had to tell people. There's no such thing as overnight success in this business. I have to put a lot of hours into research, which is what fills up my days. Only after a week or so of that, do the technical skills of recording come into play. From there, it's a straightforward job, editing and uploading the video.

In addition to reviews, I make videos called *Over to you*, where I answer users' questions. I also have to do these things called 'explainers', a kind of how-to video. Given the chance though, I do other things called 'advanced projects', which always go viral. They involve creating things with my own equipment at a fraction of the price that my viewers would spend buying commercially produced videos.

I see my job as important because I'm helping people make the right choices, and telling them about products they didn't know existed. One of my most popular reviews was for the Halo Sport. This is a pair of headphones that make your brain more efficient. It was initially tested with the military, then got picked up by a team of wannabe engineers, who offered it commercially. People were so impressed by it that the company had to temporarily stop sales because of supply issues, like cosmetics companies with a new wonder product.

The Halo is a controversial product, though, and I felt it was also my job to get that across. Users get results with very little effort, and scientists are quite rightly concerned about the similarities between this product and untested drugs. We just don't know. The little data that's available is worrying and my viewers might want to think about that. I try to get this across in my videos.

When I make a video, I need to think about the audience and what they know. Gamers will have seen similar devices to the Halo Sport already, but for sports players, it's going to be brand new. Students often watch the videos too, but that's such a broad audience. When a new technology goes to a broader market, I have to find out what people are likely to know already so I don't annoy anyone.

I also have to think about who might be disadvantaged by the products too. The guys who own the Halo Sport have tested it out on students aiming to play professional sports and seen huge increases in the students' muscle strength. In other studies, though, people suffering from depression have seen their problems intensified.

That's been the main change in my job in the last year or so. There are new risks with some of these gadgets and they can catch on incredibly quickly. It's a whole new world. With devices like this one, the sales are often way ahead of any long-term studies into risks. I think a growing part of my role is to stress that above all, consumers should think about safety when considering whether to try innovative gadgets like these.

AUDIOSCRIPTS

7.8 and 7.9

A: Hi, I was told I could speak to you about the courses here at the Future Health Centre. I'm thinking of applying. Do you have a moment?

B: Sure, I'm just waiting for a friend. I've got bags of time. Fire away!

A: What do you think's the most exciting thing in future healthcare?

B: Well, there's always a great deal of research going on in healthcare. Obviously, most of that's looking at curing existing illnesses, but there are a number of projects which are looking at delivery of healthcare. In the past all of the researchers just assumed humans would deliver healthcare. Now we've got the technology giants getting involved, that's all changing. Every penny counts in healthcare and technology can really reduce costs of monitoring health or passing on advice. I think that's the most exciting area.

A: In what way?

B: Well, there are no end of computer algorithms out there at the moment that can already diagnose common illnesses more accurately than most doctors. Those are going to become more commonplace over time. And robots are already being built to replace some nursing tasks, like taking blood samples. Neither project is going to be without complication though, but all the projects at the moment are interesting.

A: OK, and what's it like to study at school …

7.10

Roberto: Hmm, well, the best time to exercise is probably in the morning. I walk my dog every morning before school. I also play football on a Saturday afternoon or in the lunch hour. They're good times. I don't choose those times. I play then because my friends are around. They're out of class at that time. I don't think anyone really chooses when to exercise. You exercise when you can.

Susanna: Erm, well, inevitably, like most people, I just exercise when I can. Whenever I plan to get up early, I end up sleeping through the alarm. That means that I usually end up using my lunch break to run around or, alternatively, staying on after school for sports clubs. While it may not be the best time for everyone, it works for me. Besides, it makes me feel more alert when I do eventually get home and start my homework.

7.11 and 7.12

1 The amount of energy that a food produces is measured in a unit called a [beep].
2 The substance in tea, coffee and some other drinks that makes you feel alert is called [beep].
3 The way you position your body when you are standing or sitting is your [beep].
4 An increase in the amount of energy that you have is an energy [beep]
5 A rapid decrease in the amount of energy that you have is an energy [beep].
6 The feel of your blood moving beneath your skin is known as your [beep].
7 When you are able to give all your attention to something, you are [beep].
8 One product that is marketed as able to produce higher levels of physical and mental ability is a [beep].

8.2 and 8.3

Speaker 1: I think that entertainment will look massively different. Like, there's some obvious things that will have changed. Like the resolution of things will have probably gone up – everyone will be watching 4K films instead of 1080phd films. And a lot more people will be using VR and augmented reality, so like holographics and things like that. But then there's probably changes that we haven't even thought of yet – like there's a lot of technology and research going into more immersive 3D audio now, so that things seem like you're actually outside, when you're in a movie. All the sounds are coming from the right directions towards your head. And it changes your entire experience quite a lot.

Speaker 2: Erm, I think it's all, it's all on a very personal level at the moment. Erm, everyone, everyone's got a tablet or a smartphone that they're playing on and I think we're just at the point of cutting out everyone in our … vicinity. I think we're just going to be so focused on what we're doing … Erm, I think what's set to happen is that the games industry will just go further and further. I know it's already massive and we're getting much more of this sort of virtual reality games coming through and I think that's due to become even bigger in the gaming world.

Speaker 3: I mean, I think in terms of graphics, the graphics are going to improve significantly. I mean, they do every year … erm, on things like games and stuff. I think there may be more improvements on sort of 3D kind of films and stuff…. Erm, at the moment I don't really see the appeal in it, but I think, I mean, there'll be improvements in that.

Speaker 4: Erm, the entertainment industry, I think, is on the verge of becoming less accessible. Erm, because of prices. It's becoming more expensive. Theatre prices going, film prices, music prices – it's all going up.

Speaker 5: Erm, I think in the future people will be experiencing entertainment a lot with … er, virtual reality and augmented reality. Just sort of with the, … er, I guess recent sort of advances with sort of wearable technologies, such as, you know, Google glasses and watches … I just think that there'll be an overlap of sort of real life versus … sort of animated life, and I think that line will get very blurred and it will become highly normal and very entertaining to be in your actual environment, and yet still be playing in a fantasy game.

Speaker 6: I think there'll be a really sort of rapid acceleration in the virtual reality sort of market. Cos it's already happening now and I think it will almost be a common sort of item for every home. I think everyone will be using it by the time we're thirty.

Speaker 7: I think the only thing that is going to have changed in entertainment is the mediums that we watch them on. I don't think that the stories that we enjoy or, you know, the types of things that keep us gripped are going to change. I think you can go back to ancient Greece and they were entertained by the exact same stories that we're entertained by now, so, yeah, I think, probably. Maybe it'll be holograms, but I think that might be it.

8.4

Girl: I've been asked to tell a funny story about my friend at her birthday party but I'm rubbish at stuff like that.

Boy: As long as you practise first, you'll be OK. Remember your voice is important. No one wants to hear a story told with a boring delivery. That doesn't mean that there have to be loads of different tones, though a monotonous one is pretty unappealing. The climax is obviously up there, especially if it comes as a real surprise, but it's no good if everyone's lost the plot. Probably the key thing is to capture everyone's interest right from the word go.

8.5

G = Girl   B = Boy   W = Woman   M = Man

1

G: I've been asked to tell a funny story about my friend at her birthday party but I'm rubbish at stuff like that.

B: As long as you practise first, you'll be OK. Remember your voice is important. No one wants to hear a story told with a boring delivery. That doesn't mean that there have to be loads of different tones, though a monotonous one is pretty unappealing. The climax is obviously up there, especially if it comes as a real surprise, but it's no good if everyone's lost the plot. Probably the key thing is to capture everyone's interest right from the word *go*.

G: You know, I went to a storytelling event last month. Supposing I'd paid more attention to the storytellers, I'd know what to do now.

B: Isn't storytelling for kids?

G: Oh, not necessarily. It's fun to be sitting in a group, listening to the same story and yet seeing something completely different in our minds. What makes the experience stand out is the focus on the rhythm of the language as opposed to just the meaning. It's something we miss out on when we read on our own. You know, I even cried at one point – but then I do that at home too.

2

B: The toughest thing about launching the paper is going to be getting people to read it. I think we can do that provided we bring people together and create a stronger school identity.

G: I'd say that's the result of getting readers rather than the method. Our focus should be on including articles for everyone, not just the people we hang out with.

B: I was thinking we need to include funny articles but maybe including varied stories is the way to go. There certainly are a lot of people from different backgrounds at our school, so we'll have lots of source material.

G: I love the idea of making people laugh but I think serious, worthy topics have their place too.

B: Fair enough. You know, at my old school the newspaper failed because the articles weren't very good.

G: How can we avoid the same fate?

B: Well, photos draw readers into an article, so we have to choose them carefully, but imagine if we overused them. They'd detract from the writing. Articles that feature personal stories about the lives of students can generate a lot of attention. But then again if they're written like academic essays, it puts readers off, so tone should be our main priority.

3

W: So, our attempt to appeal to young people has failed and we need to come up with a new strategy. Any ideas?

M: Well, we clearly can't rely on our company history any more. Talking about the company founder added an element of realism for our generation but teenagers obviously care more about what we stand for today. I think to appeal to them, we should've shown them what our brand means rather than tell them. What if we'd done something like that adventure clothing brand did recently? We might have been more successful.

W: What did they do?

M: They set up virtual pop-up shops in these beautiful locations around the world. Adventurous customers that travelled there were able to unlock a prize using their mobile's GPS.

W: So, it was the customers that had the adventure, then presumably shared their experience online. It's not difficult to see why it made an impact. It's a novel idea that should be celebrated but, of course, our brand's very different so I'd be very wary of doing something exactly the same. Having said that, if we did something as creative and relevant to us, it could really help youngsters get what we're about.

8.6 and 8.7

A: Well, I don't think it's acceptable to download any music you want although lots of people do it. I think we assume that if it's online, we can have it these days. But of course, imagine that everyone downloaded everything for free all the time. No one would make any money, so who'd want to make music anymore? Musicians don't just do it for the love of it, they do it to earn a living too so downloading anything you want isn't right at all.

B: You're right, it's unfair on the musicians who put all their time and effort into their songs. But then again, you get these large record labels that charge far more than they need to for a song and until that changes, people will just keep downloading stuff. Bringing the price down might make a difference as people would be able to afford to buy the music then. This could lead to more people paying for the songs. That's what needs to happen, really.

8.8 and 8.9

1 We're so lucky to live in this digital age. I mean, there's entertainment wherever you look. And now we have smartphones and tablets, it's right there [beep]. It's impossible to be bored.

2 I feel sorry for that director. Imagine spending nine months of your life and hundreds of millions of dollars making a film that no one wants to see. You put your whole life into it and then it's a complete [beep].

3 There's no way I'm performing that song on stage. I try hard to sing [beep] but somehow never manage it.

4 I love the idea of being a famous movie star. It sounds so romantic – you get to play glamorous parts in films, meet lots of good-looking people, go to lots of parties. But I expect that it's very different [beep]. Lots of people staring at you when you go anywhere, asking for selfies and so on.

5 I only really watch sci-fi or fantasy type films. I'm just not interested in any other [beep].

6 My cousin's in a band that's getting a lot of attention online. They're hoping to sign a contract with a [beep] soon.

7 I've got no idea what film I want to see tonight. I don't know much about any of them, to be honest, so I'm inclined to suggest we just pick one [beep] and hope it's good.

8 I saw this brilliant band play live last night. They had so much energy and the songs were really catchy. To be honest, it's probably the best [beep] I've ever been to.

8.10

According to some experts, machines are set to take over more jobs from humans. Already programmed to do manual tasks, the time will come when robots will be able to perform higher level tasks. In fact, some machines are on the verge of performing intellectual tasks already. By the middle of the century we may have created intelligent machines that make us redundant. This will mean that millions of people around the world will be looking for new forms of employment. One area where you'd think this situation is less likely to happen is in the music industry. After all, it's creative and surely a robot can't perform creative tasks? Well, scientists are already creating robots that make music. So, are musicians on the point of being replaced? I doubt it, but machines are due to have a bigger role in the production of music. We may not go and see our favourite robot band perform on stage, but we might listen to our favourite human band play music created or improved by artificial intelligence.

9.1 and 9.2

If, as environmentalists, we intend to move things forward, we need to consider very seriously how to make our message fresh and interesting. If we keep repeating the same things again and again, people will soon resent wasting their time listening to the same old complaints. Of course, we need to recycle more and we cannot risk harming important natural habitats any longer. But I increasingly overhear audiences saying that the environmental message has become a bit repetitive these days. We need to find ways to make people reconsider the environmentalist movement. We are, after all, facing massive problems.

And the message doesn't need to be boring. For example, do you know where the environmentalist movement all started? Scientists? Hippies in the 1960s? Actually, it was housewives in the late 1950s. They'd noticed soap suds pouring out of taps, caused by chemicals in the water supply. They obliged governments to take action, but once they went public with their complaints, their concerns over pollution quickly became just the tip of the iceberg.

And if you think we're the worst generation that ever lived, well, it depends on the criteria you use. Our ancestors permitted whole populations to destroy forests and saw fertile soil as an endless resource. In many parts of the countryside almost every tree had been chopped down for firewood. There are many things about environmentalism that we still need to talk about.

9.3 and 9.4

For a long time, the environment was something people talked about at home and in schools. Most of us will have learnt the three R's at school – *reduce*, *reuse* and *recycle*. We studied acid rain and its effects or learnt about the rainforests in geography, and we probably even visited a local conservation area to learn about the species that live there.

But actually working in the environmental field has completely changed in the last ten or fifteen years. With new international agreements on climate change, it's not something for school kids any more. When we talk about environmental work these days, we're talking major national and international economics. The push for sustainable development started with individual companies. Many of them can get tax breaks or gain market advantages from having a positive environmental record, and so we see more and more companies undergoing a green audit, where a record is kept of their impact on the environment, for good or for bad.

Governments are also encouraging better environmental practices. With laws limiting the amount any one company can pollute, emissions trading has become commonplace, particularly in Europe. Companies need a permit to produce emissions and if they want to go over that limit, they have to buy permits from others willing to sell them. A more specialised version of this is carbon trading. When the Kyoto Protocol, an international environmental agreement, put limits on how much carbon any one nation could produce, buying and selling rights to produce carbon took off at an international level.

So, for anyone still thinking that work in the environment is about wandering around on nature reserves, listening to the birds singing, think again. Many new skills are needed in this new global climate.

AUDIOSCRIPTS

9.5 and 9.6
To be honest, I wanted a cat that was a little more than a lazy ball of fur. My cat hates being alone so much that whenever I take a nap, she likes to bring her toy mouse and put it on my face. Then, when I wake up, she pretends that she's just chilling out, like [beep].

9.7
1 To be honest, I wanted a cat that was a little more than a lazy ball of fur. My cat hates being alone so much that whenever I take a nap, she likes to bring her toy mouse and put it on my face. Then, when I wake up, she pretends that she's just chilling out like I do, like nothing happened. It's such a laugh. I found her though a site that matches potential owners to abandoned pets. It was a friend's post online that put me onto it. Over a hundred animal shelters are connected to it, so I knew that they'd have a good chance of finding me a great match.

2 Me and my family chose Dream Pets to help find a dog because they take time to assess their animals' personalities, or rather traits – energy, focus, confidence and independence. Those ratings say which dog would best fit in with your lifestyle, and they get it right most times! I thought that demonstrated that it was run by people with the right priorities. My dog's full of energy, just like me, which is what I wanted. But he's so funny: after I put on different clothes, he barks anxiously at me because he thinks that I'm a different person! How? It's not like I'm trying to hide something!

3 My dog's crazy. He gets distracted so easily the slightest thing sets him off, and he's running around looking for the source. And I know that all dogs like to sniff each other, but mine tried to sniff a dog on a documentary. It cracked us up, until the dog nearly knocked the screen over. I got my dog from a special dog adoption agency. It cost more than a lot of other places, but I liked it. Being round the corner from my house, it was always a doddle to pop round for a chat during the application process.

4 I decided I wanted a dog from the rescue centre, but that wasn't without problems. A lot of pets need rehoming because of behavioural issues. Moving a pet into a new home can be tough, and they really helped to make that transition easier. I was keen that they provided a wealth of experience and tips to support me in the process. I love my dog to bits, but she's just such a coward! She's afraid of her own bark, and runs and hides between my legs every time, and is terrified of her reflection in the mirror! It shocked me at first. You'd think she'd get it by now.

5 My cat barely shows any interest in the toys I buy him, and rarely wants to be petted, but when my wife is around, the cat runs over to prove that his love is greater than hers. I'd love to know why! I got him from an animal shelter. I liked the fact that within a few days of giving the shelter my profile, I was having an email conversation with someone about which animal might be right for me, and when I could collect it. I found them really efficient in that way.

9.8
1 I found a chewed electric cable at the back of the TV and I think the hamster did it. Luckily, it wasn't plugged in at the time!

2 I'm really sorry. It was me that let the cat sit on the laptop. It looks like it's overheated now.

3 I love uploading cute animal photos. I put my dog in a pink ballerina costume, even though he's male. He looked so grumpy. He hated the fact that it slowed him down.

4 My rabbit loves digging tunnels, but I hate the mess, so I put wire fencing under the ground in my garden. Now the rabbit can't understand why it can't get very far.

5 My mum's friend came round and her stomach growled, and the dog growled back. My mum thought I should have stopped the dog – I think it was perfectly reasonable!

6 My dog kept stealing the cat's food. I eventually gave up trying to feed it tins of dog food and just gave it kitty fish chunks for its meals.

9.9 and 9.10
1 Well, the moon has always been a source of fascination for people throughout the centuries, and a lot of myths have built up around it. I guess the biggest one is that that the moon landings never happened – that this groundbreaking project was little more than some elaborate hoax. We have the technology now to prove that the videos and photos were, in fact, the real deal, and I don't think there's any truth to this myth.

2 A lot of farmers and gardeners insist that the lunar cycle has a direct impact on the natural development of plants. In fact, the word *honeymoon* comes from the time in the lunar cycle between planting and harvesting, when it was a good time to get married. Although the idea is still popular, there aren't really any university studies that prove this theory.

3 An earth day always seems to last exactly twenty-four hours, but it is actually slowing down by a tiny amount each year. The moon is a great big mass, right next to planet earth, and it's slowed the earth's rotation over the billions of years. Without the moon, the length of our days would be dramatically different. In fact, the moon has such a strong influence on the planet that without it, an earth day would last a mere six to eight hours.

4 A lot of myths and stories appeared in ancient cultures. One of the strongest was that when a full moon fell on a Sunday, it was considered a warning sign, but it was thought to have the opposite effect on a Monday. This is actually where the word comes from – Monday is the moon day. The reasons for this have been lost in time though.

5 Probably the strongest myth is around people's behaviour. From werewolves to being just a bit forgetful, for centuries it was believed that people develop aggressive behaviour around a full moon or are less likely to fall into a sound sleep. There is absolutely no scientific evidence of the latter and with modern street lights, few people's sleep is still affected by the increased level of light during a full moon.

9.11
There's a guy driving a taxi at night. He's unhappy. The other guy is working in a big nightclub, and he's a DJ. I think he probably loves his job. I think he probably likes his job because I can see that he's very good at it. All the people are looking at him and copying him.

9.12
Well, the first photo shows a man driving a taxi at night and, to be honest, he's not looking all that happy about it. Now, the second guy is a DJ, and he obviously likes his job much more. He's in a big nightclub and he's got the full attention of the audience. I mean, he should feel great about it because he's obviously good at it, but most people who work as DJs often have to have another job, and so I guess it can be exhausting trying to work two jobs. Maybe just like the first guy, he's having to concentrate a lot. I suppose neither of them get to spend their evenings with their mates or their families, which is what most people like to do.

9.13
Well, I see where you're coming from. Any kind of night work involves unsociable hours, and it can be hard to hold down a normal life. But I think being a DJ is different because you can invite your friends along to the nightclub, so you're not missing out. And think of all the people you meet. I think this is a better job!

9.14 and 9.15
1 I had a bad feeling about the situation, but I decided to ignore the [beep].
2 The professor was working on a completely new form of image recognition. The project was [beep].
3 There have been a lot of reports of a monster in the Scottish Lake, Loch Ness, but all of the photos so far have just been a big [beep].
4 I wanted to stay awake to watch the sun come up on the shortest day of the year, but I fell into a [beep].
5 The boy was suspended from school for two days because of his [beep].
6 A lack of social contact in the early years can have a negative effect on a child's [beep].

10.1
I've been an autograph hunter since I was a boy, seeing signatures as a link to my heroes. But like many, I was taken aback to see President Obama use twenty-two different pens to sign one document! I was unaware that passing such pens on as thank-you gifts was a historical tradition in the States, as the pens associated with important documents often take on an historical value of their own.

There are some people, though, who argue that in the modern era pens should be used for decoration only, not for signatures. I know a signature is a form of identification, but it has always been problematic because it's so easy to fake. I once had to give a hand scan when I took an exam to confirm my identity before sitting a test. The police have used face scans to distinguish individuals for many years. Pin numbers were introduced as a more secure way of identifying people, but as technology has moved on, dare I say, these will probably soon be outdated, too.

For the police and lawyers, traditional pen signatures have always posed the problem of what many lawyers call 'weak evidence'. Few tests can really prove the originality of handwritten signatures – they're easy to fake. But the key issue, really, is the problem of proving what's known as 'intention'. Signatures simply can't show whether the person really agreed to give their consent.

I read that the computer code to sign documents electronically has been around for many years. It existed long before the need appeared with online shopping. But people were reluctant to use computer signatures, especially for official documents. However, this changed in 2016, when legislation changed. In many countries, computer signing is now recognised as just as valid as traditional pen signatures, or what I like to call 'wet signatures'. The term 'digital signature' is already widely used to record a person's browsing history, and so I think 'electronic signature' is more likely to be adopted for this new official signing.

I'm a fan of the pen version, but I have to admit, I feel that the new online versions provide stronger security. This is because they're protected by passwords, which really offer guarantees. The signing process also automatically goes through a system of checks, and these use the same software that protects our online bank account numbers and credit card details. But I can't help feeling that we've lost the theatre that comes from pulling out a pen. No photographs will ever be taken of world leaders clicking a button, and this is something we've come to take for granted. No one will ever pause to admire a row of computer codes which is, essentially, what the modern signature is.

So, despite the changes, a handwritten autograph is still treasured when it appears on a book. The latest signing of a football contract for a top player still requires a pen to be produced in front of the world's press. And I feel that we're a very long way from persuading anyone to sign their wedding certificate with the click of a button. Such ceremonial processes have lasted generations and are likely to stay for some time.

10.2

I = Interviewer   J = Jenny   M = Mark

I: Today I'm talking to Jenny Davis, an expert on ancient Roman history, and Mark Strong, an historian. Jenny, you excavate ancient sites. Tell us, what's that like – is it dangerous?

J: Well, the bats flying around don't help. I'm not sure it's hazardous, but the rooms have to be dark to preserve what I've come here to see – ancient graffiti written on the walls. They would fade in the sunlight, so I have to work by torch, but it's well worth the effort. To be honest, the main issue is when the guards forget to let me out in the evening. And crumbling old stone columns really don't make the best back rest!

I: So Mark, you've studied ancient graffiti. Was that easy to do?

M: Well, we've always known that the ancient Romans liked to write on the outside of buildings. I'd read the work of scholars who've been cataloguing graffiti for years now. Their work showed huge promise. But, of course, over ninety percent of the graffiti vanished under the burning Mediterranean sun and we've needed new scientific techniques to help us to access much of it, which we now have.

I: So, Jenny, what have you learnt about graffiti in Roman times?

J: What we know is that in ancient Rome, graffiti wasn't a kind of vandalism, but more of a public conversation. One rather comical message expressed amazement that the walls hadn't fallen into ruins – there were so many comments up there. Graffiti was even found inside wealthy people's homes, so it wasn't a class thing. The walls are just full of greetings from friends, quotations from popular poems or clever political comments. The people of Pompeii, for example, tended to express far more goodwill than ill will, especially in their wishes for the whole town. It's quite distinct from the official declarations that survive. It's surprisingly supportive of the local government.

I: Mark, does graffiti have enough academic value to justify studying these writings?

M: I think so. We haven't really needed more about places like Pompeii as we already have many accounts of what happened, thanks to literature. Grafitti doesn't really contradict much of what we already believed. But both records are useful. The first will be more beautiful but the latter will be more sincere. And of course, it's about who did it. Major world leaders aren't given to scratching their names on a wall or confiding their reflections on the side of the public bath houses any more, but they do comment on social media feeds and I think all of these have historic value. Taken as a whole, they offer a fuller view of the official histories we know so well.

I: Jenny, have you found any similarities with modern graffiti?

J: One thing that struck me as familiar with modern graffiti is the number of declarations of love among the messages. And people weren't shy about offering their opinions on the way the town was run, which is also still the case today. We also saw lots of displays of cleverness in the comments and playful jokes, which can be a bit absent from this form of expression today. We were interested to see that the emperor Nero, was actually more popular than we tend to think. His popularity took a major dive after it became known that he'd kicked his pregnant wife though. Graffiti seemed to have served a similar function to the media, closely examining the private activities of those in power.

I: I understand there's now a whole international conference dedicated to graffiti?

M: Yes, we'll both be at next year's international conference. Last year's conference actually resulted in a book on the subject, which sold to a very broad audience. It certainly brought more attention to the need to preserve these alternative kinds of documentation. And they're getting busier too. Last year's conference drew so many participants that they ran out of space for everyone. You tend to only get people at these things if it's part of their professional life, as historians, so I think they do illustrate a change in the way researchers see these records.

J: Hmm. I think the success of the conferences is a sign of how the role of popular commentary is being revisited. There are a lot of different projects around the world to record these kinds of markings that became popular at various points in history. For many years they've been seen as trivial and were ignored. Now you see people including samples of graffiti in tours of popular tourist sites.

I: Well, thank you both!